JUST WAR, LASTING PEACE

JUST WAR, LASTING PEACE

What Christian Traditions Can Teach Us

John Kleiderer, Paula Minaert, and Mark Mossa, SJ

General Editor, Dolores R. Leckey

*A Project of the U.S. Jesuit Conference
and the Woodstock Theological Center*

ORBIS BOOKS

Maryknoll, New York 10545

Founded in 1970, Orbis Books endeavors to publish works that enlighten the mind, nourish the spirit, and challenge the conscience. The publishing arm of the Maryknoll Fathers and Brothers, Orbis seeks to explore the global dimensions of the Christian faith and mission, to invite dialogue with diverse cultures and religious traditions, and to serve the cause of reconciliation and peace. The books published reflect the views of their authors and do not represent the official position of the Maryknoll Society. To learn more about Maryknoll and Orbis Books, please visit our website at www.maryknoll.org.

Published by Orbis Books, Maryknoll, NY 10545-0308.

Manufactured in the United States of America.

Library of Congress Cataloging-in-Publication Data

Just war, lasting peace : what Christian traditions can teach us /
[edited by] John Kleiderer, Paula Minaert, and Mark Mossa.
    p. cm.
  Includes bibliographical references and index.
  ISBN-13: 978-1-57075-652-8 (pbk.)
    1. War – Religious aspects – Christianity. 2. Just war doctrine.
I. Kleiderer, John. II. Minaert, Paula. III. Mossa, Mark.
BT736.2.J875 2006
241'.6242–dc22

                                        2005033075

Contents

Foreword

Peace is possible. This belief has been at the heart of my preaching and ministry in the land that Christians, Jews, and Muslims all call "holy." Peace is possible because it is God's desire for the world. I believe this with every fiber of my being.

But for peace to be realized men and women of good will everywhere must turn to one another — and to those not yet conscious of the need for peace — and engage in an authentic dialogue of the mind, the heart, and the spirit. Such a dialogue will recognize and honor the demands of justice; such a dialogue, writes Pope Paul VI, "will make us wise" (*Ecclesiam Suam*).

The times are perilous. Wars, large and small, blaze in many parts of the world. And yet I hold on to my conviction that peace is possible. Furthermore, I believe that the world's religions have a crucial role to play in constructing a successful transition from the prevalent culture of war to a culture of justice, love, and hope. They can bring to the conversation the wisdom embedded in their traditions, articulating clearly and simply the ethical grounding of their religions where justice is cultivated and where peace can grow. Still, we all need resources to move the conversation and dialogue along.

Just War, Lasting Peace is an attempt to do precisely that. It takes readers into the history of the three Catholic positions regarding the characteristics of a just war and then looks at them through the complexities of public policy. Other Christian traditions are part of the book's dialogue, as are Judaism and Islam. The book's dynamism lies in how it will be used, for it has the potential to educate various publics about the extent of evil that wars let loose. I once again echo Dr. Martin Luther King Jr., who reminded us so many years ago that "wars are poor chisels for carving out peaceful tomorrows."

We are called by our faith in the God of life and by the gravity of this point in history to read the signs of the times and to act in a manner that is explicitly shaped by the Gospel. All of us, Christians and others, are on a pilgrimage of forgiveness and reconciliation; *Just War, Lasting Peace* is an intelligent and enlightening resource for this journey.

Michel Sabbah, Latin Patriarch of Jerusalem
President of Pax Christi International

Acknowledgments

If one had to choose a single word to express the hope and energy of the twenty-first-century church, I submit that word would be "collaboration." In so many places throughout the world, the reality of day-to-day ministry, whatever its form, is communitarian — *communio* — with men and women, laity and ordained, working together on behalf of the church's mission. This is true of parish life and it is also true of publishing life. *Just War, Lasting Peace* is an example of the latter. Collaboration characterized every stage of the book's becoming.

The U.S. Jesuit Conference and the Woodstock Theological Center *together* organized the one-day invitational forum that is the basis for the book's exploration of questions of peace and war. In particular, Richard Ryscavage, SJ, and James Stormes, SJ, of the Jesuit Conference, and Gasper LoBiondo, SJ, of Woodstock provided the institutional support needed to transform the forum into a book.

Participants in the forum, and especially the panelists, have been essential to the heart of the project. It should be noted, however, that panelists' comments were taken from the transcript of the forum; for the most part, they have not had the opportunity to rewrite their contributions. Their voices are present throughout, and some have contributed additional breadth and depth to particular chapters. William Bole authored the chapter on forgiveness, and Maryann Cusimano Love contributed the chapter on terrorism. Others served as consultants: Drew Christiansen, SJ, gave indispensable advice and direction to the chapter on parallel traditions; without his expertise it would have been impossible to navigate the complexities of just war positions. Al Pierce graciously read chapter 1, "A Sketch: The World and War," and his careful critique helped sharpen our focus. Others from outside the forum were also generous collaborators: Joseph Kane offered insights into chapter 1, as did Angelique Hauggrud; Dr. John Borelli of Georgetown University, an expert participant in interreligious dialogue worldwide, helped shape the chapter on that topic. John Paul Lederach reviewed chapter 7. To all these collaborators who tried very hard to help us "get it right," I extend my deepest gratitude. Whatever might *not* be "exactly right" is not because of their lapses, but mine.

The Sisters of Mercy of the Americas, who have an abiding commitment to justice and peace, awarded a grant to the project, which, in effect, gave life to this book. Without their collaboration we would still be pondering interesting ideas and wishing we could share them.

As always, Woodstock's Maria Ferrara's administrative assistance was invaluable. And finally, Michael Leach of Orbis Books was a patient, knowledgeable, and cheerful editorial guide. His enthusiasm surely has been a touch of grace.

Dolores R. Leckey,
Woodstock Theological Center
General Editor

Introduction

In the months before the U.S. intervention in Iraq in 2003, when everyone was talking of war — would it happen? should it happen? — the Jesuit provincials of the United States were having a similar conversation. They understood that, in light of the shifting geopolitical realities since the end of the Cold War, the just war theory was fraught with complexities. The provincials had a desire to further educate themselves and those with whom they work and serve, and thought it would be helpful to explore the different Catholic perspectives on issues of war and peace. They thought that a wider circle might also benefit from a conversation that sought to clarify and understand the different perspectives from the Catholic Christian tradition. This conversation among the provincials became the impetus for a one-day forum held at Georgetown University in November of 2003, jointly sponsored by the U.S. Jesuit Conference and the Woodstock Theological Center.

The forum gathered a group of scholars and experts (including policymakers) and featured more than a dozen presentations, as well as conversations among the fifty participants. The one-day dialogue gave birth to this book, *Just War, Lasting Peace: What Christian Traditions Can Teach Us*.

From the beginning, the Jesuit provincials hoped that the fruits of the forum could be made available to a wide spectrum of Catholics and perhaps to others as well. They felt, as did the participants in the forum, that men and women of all ages and all political positions could benefit from exposure to the underlying questions. Furthermore, they believed that correct information could help form a correct conscience, and that communities of conscience might possibly impact the decisions of our nation and perhaps of the world. *Just War, Lasting Peace* is a contribution to that process of decision making.

The book is designed for use by a variety of groups: college classes, parish adult education and justice groups, retreat participants, and even older high school students. It can also be used for individual reflection.

While Jesuit spirituality is at the heart of this project — a spirituality that promotes contemplation in action, with justice at the center — its basic teachings about war and peace transcend any single spiritual pathway.

The truth is that today's peacemakers are many. Some of them are recognized internationally; many of them labor quietly and steadily. Some of their voices were distinctively heard during the forum. Michael Baxter, theology professor at the University of Notre Dame, Joan Chittister, OSB, director of Benetvision, and Rev. Jim Wallis, the evangelical leader of the Sojourners movement, movingly articulated the little-heard historical roots and development of nonviolence in Christianity. The contemporary just war position was presented by Jesuit Drew Christiansen of *America* magazine, Catholic University of America political scientist Maryann Cusimano Love, and George Lopez of the Joan Kroc Institute for International Peace Studies (University of Notre Dame). The more traditional or "classical" just war position[1] was stated (and espoused) by Gregory Reichberg, a philosopher with the Oslo-based International Peace Research Institute, and Robert Royal, president of the Faith and Reason Institute in Washington, DC. These three positions are presented in the book and offer a starting point for a more extensive discussion of these complex issues.

As the book took shape, it became clear that a brief overview of the place of war in human history was needed, so we begin with that sobering reality in chapter 1. This chapter is not meant to be comprehensive but simply to illustrate the prevalence of war across time and culture. From there, we turn to the heart of the matter, the three major Catholic positions on what is known as "just war." Chapter 2 explores the history of the church's stance toward peace and war, and chapter 3 looks at how the traditions are being developed and applied today. Chapter 4 focuses on the current situation in the world and the struggles that responsible policymakers have in confronting decisions of war and peace. Policymakers were among the forum participants and their experience was and is critical for a deeper understanding of both war and peace. Their struggles to be discerning and responsible members of society are laid before the readers, who themselves are invited to grapple with similar decisions. In chapter 5, Dr. Maryann Cusimano Love asks the question: Does the just war tradition apply to the "war on terrorism"? She urges clarity of language about this subject.

Reflections from the other Abrahamic traditions (Judaism and Islam) enriched the forum and further enrich the content of the book; chapter 6 looks at them. Contemporary thinking on how best to build a just and lasting peace encourages conversation with the historic peace churches, and so we have chapter 7, which traces the history and contributions of the Quakers, the Brethren, and the Mennonites. Indeed, in recent years there have been official (and fruitful) dialogues between the Catholic Church and the Mennonite Church.

As the book moved toward its conclusion, it became evident that we needed to explore dimensions of forgiveness and reconciliation in the lives of peacemakers. William Bole, a Woodstock fellow who has written about forgiveness in international politics, authored chapter 8, "The Power of Forgiveness."

And what of the future? What questions arise from such serious dialogue? Where will they lead us? In chapter 9, William Bole, Fr. J. Bryan Hehir, and Margaret O'Brien Steinfels offer their analyses and reflections and, in so doing, evoke our own. Stories from Jesuit missions in Colombia, South America, and from the Sisters of Mercy of the Americas leave us with seeds of hope that study, prayer, and action can, bit by bit, erect places of peace on earth.

What can Christian traditions teach us about defining a just war and constructing a lasting peace? A great deal, but we must be willing to struggle with the complexities and subtleties and to continue learning. At the end of the book, we have included a far-ranging assortment of resources, from scholarly to popular. We pray that *Just War, Lasting Peace* will help communities everywhere faithfully continue their learning, attentively and intelligently, and to stay with the struggle. Therein lies our hope. What we offer is not a final word, but an invitation to dialogue.

Chapter One

A Sketch

The World and War

Ongoing conflict in Iraq, even though officially the war has ended, still fills the media. We hear in the news names of places such as Baghdad, Fallujah, Tikrit, Mosul, and Ramadi. The United States invaded Iraq in March of 2003. Technically, the war lasted only about five weeks. Iraq's leader, Saddam Hussein, was captured in December of that year; elections for a new government were held in January 2005. But as of the writing of this book, coalition forces, led by the United States, still occupy Iraq and are struggling against ongoing insurgent attacks. The country is by no means stable or secure, with constant mortar attacks, car bombs, assassinations, and kidnappings. The U.S. Department of Defense notes growing numbers of U.S. military dead and wounded — and most of these occurred *after* the official end of hostilities was declared on May 1, 2003. The figures also do not include Iraqi civilians or any contractors or journalists.

American opinion on the war and its aftermath is sharply divided; the country is more polarized today than it has been in many years. The media talks about the "blue" states and the "red" states, the liberals and the conservatives. According to this admittedly rather simplistic hypothesis, the blue states opposed the war and our presence in Iraq and the red states support them. The war has had a real impact on our society, culturally and socially as well as politically and economically, and the long-range repercussions are yet unknown.

Unfortunately, in our precarious world the chances are good that we may be confronted with a similar situation in the future. Conflicts are taking place all around the globe. Struggles have erupted between various parts of the former Soviet Union, most notably between Russia and Chechnya, where war has been endemic since 1991. In Africa, the civil war in the Congo is technically over, but opposing groups continue to fight for control of resources, killing and displacing thousands of people and causing widespread starvation and disease. Militias also are active in Sudan, in the Darfur region, again causing massive killing and displacement on a scale some call genocide. We hear rumblings of dissension between the People's Republic of China and Taiwan and talk of nuclear weapons in North Korea. And the fighting in the Middle East always seems to be

in the news. Not that long ago, we were hearing different names: Mo-
gadishu, Rwanda, Eritrea. The names change, but conflict seems to be
never-ending.

It is well that war is so terrible, else we
should grow too fond of it.

—General Robert E. Lee

Moreover, in our interdependent world, conflict and instability in one
place will have repercussions in other places. The political, economic,
and social ties that link us make it inevitable. War tends to reach out far
beyond its source of origin.

It is essential, then, that we try to learn something about this important phenomenon we call war. When are we justified in going to war? In
any given situation, are there options we can take to prevent war from
happening? If preventive measures fail, and we do find ourselves in a war,
how can we conduct ourselves honorably? More generally, how *do* we see
war? A potential force for good, to ensure justice? An evil necessity, for our
self-defense? A corrosive wrong, which is never acceptable? As we explore
questions such as these, we can come to understand our attitudes toward,
and perceptions of, war. War is a critical issue; we need to approach it
carefully, thoughtfully, and intelligently.

This chapter will take a brief look at warfare as it has played out in
human history. It is not a comprehensive treatment, but a sketch. We
need to have some idea of where we have been and to examine our own
viewpoints, to create a context for our current situation—and a basis for
future decisions and actions. This overview also will provide a background
for understanding what, in the Christian tradition, constitutes a just war.

THE ROOTS OF WARFARE

Perhaps the first question to ask is this: What exactly is war? We might
think this question is unnecessary, that everyone knows the answer. Yet
definitions vary. For centuries, the accepted definition came from Karl von
Clausewitz, author of the seminal work *On War*. In it, he argued that war is
the continuation of politics by other means. The philosopher Jean-Jacques
Rousseau believed that war happens not between individuals but between
states (*The Social Contract*). This view of war has the effect, though, of
making war a rational, organized activity. As we shall see later in this
chapter, war has often been very different in our history. Other thinkers
saw war in an all-encompassing, not to say gloomy, light. Voltaire called
famine, plague, and war the most famous ingredients of the world (*The
Philosophical Dictionary*).

More recently, a definition that seems to include the different forms that war can take comes from anthropologist R. Brian Ferguson. He sees it as purposeful group action against another group, which involves the use — at least potentially — of lethal force (*Warfare, Culture, and Environment*). This definition distinguishes war from other collective actions such as riots, which tend not to be purposeful, yet is broad enough to include types of war that do not fit the traditional mold, but which have become all too familiar to us, such as guerilla warfare and terrorism.

Next, we ask: Has war always been part of human history? Have people always fought? What does our distant past — human prehistory — tell us about this? The short answer is we don't know. Some archeological evidence exists, but it's unclear what it means, and scholars draw contradictory conclusions from it. Archeologist Steven LeBlanc, for example, in *Constant Battles: The Myth of the Peaceful, Noble Savage*, posits a primitive world that was very violent and warlike, more so than later times. He believes that prehistoric warfare in all places was both common and deadly and that its fundamental cause was competition for scarce resources. He insists that the notion of a peaceful, Eden-like time in early human history is a myth.[1]

War is the mother of everything.
—Heraclitus, Greek philosopher

Other scholars disagree with LeBlanc's hypothesis. R. Brian Ferguson believes that warfare was *not* prevalent in early prehistoric times and that the evidence points to it appearing no earlier than about ten thousand years ago. In analyzing the reasons for its appearance, he offers a list of five preconditions: the move from a nomadic to a sedentary life, population growth, the development of a social hierarchy, growing long-distance trade, and severe climatic change. Overall, however, his research leads him to theorize that war has not always been part of our human condition; rather, it emerged from a warless background.[2]

Military historian John Keegan takes a slightly different approach. He defines war as an expression of culture and states that all civilizations owe their origins to the warrior.[3] He does not believe that war is, as Clausewitz said, a continuation of politics by other means. War, he points out, predates the state. He adds, however, that war in its early form was rather different from what it later became. For one thing, war in the distant past sprang from causes that may not be familiar to us today. The Aztecs, for example, saw war as a duty they owed to their gods. They went to war to take captives for these gods, who demanded human sacrifice on a massive scale. "Human sacrifice was a religious necessity, warfare the principal means to acquire sacrificial victims."[4]

Primitive warfare differed in other ways from what we modern people think of as war. Early war, Keegan says, tended to be endemic and had no real beginning or end. It did not consist of sharply defined battles with winners and losers. Fighters often simply retreated to carry on the fight another time. All men were warriors, so there was no distinction between lawful and unlawful bearers of arms. Warfare was filled with looting, rape, extortion, and systematic vandalism. No mercy was shown to the enemy, to prisoners, or to noncombatants. Discipline and obedience to authority were not valued. This, he writes, was the "form of warfare which had prevailed during long periods of human history."[5] What we know of as the way of war is what European civilization developed over the two millennia since the time of the Greek city-states. It is "a style of conflict that achieved results by face-to-face struggle on a defined battlefield and within a narrow time-frame." It was what became "gentlemanly warfare, [which] honoured courage in combat to the point of death itself, but also honoured respect for the vanquished and execrated cruelty towards the captured. It deprecated deceit, cunning, expedience and anything that smacked of cowardice." War became collective combat, bound by accepted codes of laws and practices.[6]

WARFARE IN CHRISTIAN EUROPE

With the rise of Christianity came the beginning of a long and complicated relationship between the church and the practice of warfare. The writings of some of the early Christians — St. Cyprian of Carthage, Arnobius, Justin Martyr, and others — reveal a strong stand against war. And for the most part, Christians in the first two centuries avoided joining the military, because the military was connected to the Roman Empire and its pagan gods. They could not reconcile their beliefs with serving the pagan state.[7] This situation changed gradually, and particularly after Christianity became the state religion of Rome, when the church and the empire were linked. We can see this reflected in the thinking of Augustine, who concluded that complete peace is not possible in this life, and therefore a place needed to be made for war.[8] It was also Augustine who laid the foundation for the church's concept of the just war. (For a detailed discussion of his contributions, see chapter 2.)

This did not, however, mean that the church uncritically accepted warfare and all that went along with it. The church made many attempts over the centuries to limit the ravages of war. In fact, by the ninth century, war was seen as something that defiled those who engaged in it, and the church required participants' purification by doing penance. And up until the eleventh century, penance was required of all soldiers who killed during war. Twice in history, the church imposed a general penance on everyone who participated in a public war: first after the Battle of Soissons in 923 and then again after the Battle of Hastings.[9]

One interesting development that occurred in the early Middle Ages was something called the Peace of God. The weakening of the Carolingian dynasty led to a breakdown of society in what is modern-day France. There was no real central authority, and there was nothing to rein in the ambitions and aggression of the feudal lords. The result was a sharp rise in conflict, plundering, and violence. Local lords acted like brigands, robbing church property and attacking clergy and peasants with impunity, and the higher lords did nothing to restrain them. The Peace of God was an attempt to restore order in the face of widespread instability.[10]

The bishops in the region of Auvergne called a council of all the people. Monks brought relics from their monasteries. Then, in a solemn ceremony, the bishops called upon the lords to swear an oath of peace in the presence of the saints and the people. The oath meant that the lords were forbidden to violate the rights of clergy or peasants or to take church property. Several other such assemblies were called in the years leading up to 1000. The movement declined in the following decades but there was a revival in the 1020s and 1030s.[11]

> As, then, there may be life without pain, while there cannot be pain without some kind of life, so there may be peace without war, but there cannot be war without some kind of peace.
>
> —St. Augustine of Hippo

Around the same time came another attempt to limit violence called the Truce of God. The church outlawed all fighting from Saturday night (later extended to Wednesday night) to Monday morning and also during certain seasons of the church year. It began in France and later spread to Italy and Germany; eventually, it applied to the whole church. One scholar has commented that because the Truce suggested that the very shedding of Christian blood was sinful, it is not surprising that the knights saw the possibility of taking arms against the church's enemies attractive, since they were restrained from warring against their fellow Christians. Later, this is indeed what happened. In 1095, Pope Urban II called the First Crusade, proclaiming a renewal of the Truce of God.[12]

With the Crusades we see the rise of the concept of the holy war. Historian George Dennis, SJ, lists three criteria of holy war. "A holy war has to be declared by a competent religious authority, the obvious examples being a Christian pope or a Muslim caliph. The objective must be religious; again, two obvious examples are the protection or recovery of sacred shrines or the forced conversion or subjection of others to your religion. . . . Finally,

those who participate in the holy war are to be promised a spiritual re-
ward, such as remission of their sins or assurance of a place in paradise."[13]
Fr. Dennis points out that the Crusades started out as pilgrimages, rather
than a holy war, though they certainly assumed a warlike character as
time went on.

The other example of holy war that emerged during the Middle Ages
was the Muslim jihad. Interestingly, even though the Crusades were called
originally to help the Byzantine Empire resist attacking Muslims, the
Byzantine church completely rejected the concept of holy war. This is
not to say that the Byzantine Empire did not engage in war; it did. But the
Byzantine church concentrated on the struggle to save souls for the next
world, and left war in this world to the imperial government.[14]

This was not the case with the Western church. The Crusades began at
the behest of, and with the blessing of, the church. Urban II told Christians
"they should leave off slaying each other and fight instead a righteous war,
doing the work of God; and God would lead them. For those that died in
battle there would be absolution and remission of sins. . . . Here they were
poor and unhappy; there they would be joyful and prosperous and true
friends of God."[15] The Crusades — there were four of them — took place
from the eleventh to the thirteenth centuries, and caught the enthusiasm
of people all over Europe. Peasants, lords, clergy, and even children eagerly
went off to wrest the Holy Land back from the "infidels." *Deus le volt* —
God wills it! — was their cry.

The Crusaders attained their goal, the recovery of the Holy Land for
Christians, but it was later taken back by the Muslims. On their way
east, the Crusaders stopped and massacred Jewish communities wherever
they found them. They took the city of Jerusalem in a bloodbath in 1099.
In 1204, they sacked Constantinople, the center of the Eastern church,
thus sealing the division between the Eastern and Western churches.[16]
The Crusades are a grim chapter in the church's history.

The fourteenth and fifteenth centuries sowed the seeds of significant
change in Europe. The period was filled with warfare: the Hundred Years'
War between England and France, the struggle for control of the Holy
Roman Empire, rebellions in Bohemia and Switzerland. In some places,
war must have felt like the norm. In France during the Hundred Years' War,
even in those periods when a truce existed (it was an on-again, off-again
event) the people still had bands of unemployed and penniless mercenaries
roaming the countryside, taking what they wanted by force. From the
perspective of the common person, peace was no better than war.

These centuries saw the decline of mounted warfare as the dominant
style of fighting and the resurgence of the infantry, as well as the introduction of gunpowder.[17] The wars of this period were also significant in
that, for the first time, we see a developing sense of nationalism. It was
the beginning of the rise of the modern nation-state.[18]

The impetus for the next major series of conflicts was the Reformation and the Counter Reformation. These conflicts began with the rebellion of the Dutch — who were Protestants — against their Spanish Catholic rulers in 1566. This led into the Thirty Years' War (1618–48), which involved much of Continental Europe, including Bohemia, Denmark, Sweden, the German empire, and France. It is often called a war of religion, but politics and economics were also major influences. Catholic France, for example, (with the approval of the pope) supported the Lutheran Swedes in an effort to forestall the formation of a united Catholic Germany.[19] Whatever the label, it was one of Europe's most devastating wars, with the death toll reaching about 7 million.

WAR AND EMPIRE

Beginning around 1500, Europe entered into a new phase in its history: the Age of Exploration, when European explorers circled the globe, looking for gold, spices, slaves, and the new lands that would offer such wealth. What they also found, of course, were the people who inhabited those places. It was the start of the European domination of Africa, Asia, and the Americas. What made it possible was, in part, what is called the Western way of war. This way of warfare is marked by the use of technology, an emphasis on discipline, a focus on total victory, the ability to adapt to changing conditions, and the power to finance this new and expensive way of fighting.[20]

This method of warfare was wildly successful in enabling the West to expand its power to the rest of the world. To look at just one measure of this success, Europe in 1800 controlled 35 percent of the earth's land surface. By 1914, it controlled 85 percent.[21] Over the course of this period of the West's colonial expansion, France controlled areas in Africa and islands in the West Indies and on the Indian Ocean, as well as Louisiana in North America. Spain's rule covered most of Latin America. Germany had settlements in Africa and the South Pacific, Portugal in South America and the Indian subcontinent. Belgium had the Congo, after it took it over from King Leopold II, who had run it as a private fiefdom for his own profit. And the British Empire, of course, stretched across the globe.

Some might argue that the conflicts that took place during the building of the Western empires should not technically be labeled wars. There would not necessarily have been a formal declaration of war. Some of the contestants could not be considered states in the modern political sense, and there were not always clearly defined battles. Moreover, the fighting usually did not conform to what we think of as accepted practices of war. Yet these clashes did cross national borders; they were not civil wars or genocide by a people's own rulers. More importantly, the numbers of casualties resulting should put them in the category of significant conflicts.

For example, estimates of the number of indigenous people killed during the European conquest of the Americas vary dramatically, with some estimates at around 20 million. In the Congo, it is estimated that up to 8 million people have died.

The essence of war is violence. Moderation in war is imbecility.

— Sir John Fisher, Admiral, British Navy, early twentieth century

---

This is not to say that only the Western world engaged in wars. Over the centuries, non-Western peoples certainly fought with each other as well, sometimes with massive casualties. The Mongol conquests of Asia, Persia, and southern Russia in the thirteenth century are ranked as one of the worst cataclysms in human history, with the number of deaths estimated around 20 million. The same is true of the Manchu conquest of China in the seventeenth century and the campaigns of Tamerlane in Asia and the Middle East in the fourteenth. And there were numerous wars on a smaller scale as well. Overall, however, we don't have as good a record of them as we do of Western wars.

WAR IN THE TWENTIETH CENTURY

The twentieth century has been described as the most violent one in history. Some sources put the number of deaths in the First World War at 20 million and in the Second World War at 50 million.[22] These, of course, were the major wars. But there were others, including those in Korea, Vietnam, Iran-Iraq, Russia-Afghanistan, and the Middle East. And there were wars within nations. There were revolutions in Russia and Spain, uprisings in Armenia and Laos, and civil war in Nigeria, Indonesia, and Mexico, and these are only the beginning of a very long list. The years from 1900 to 2000 have been called ones of unrelenting conflict.[23]

One suggestion for why this was so comes from John Keegan, who writes that the competition for empire occupied the West until the early 1900s, but after that, with the territory available for empire shrinking, it turned on itself,[24] with the two world wars the result. The struggle for independence of the European nations' colonies also produced widespread conflict, and some historians attribute much of the current unrest and violence in Africa, Asia, and Latin America to the effects of their colonial past.

We must also add to this mix the phenomenon of mass killings not directly connected to warfare, such as the Great Famine and the Cultural Revolution in Mao's China and the purges of Joseph Stalin in the Soviet

Union. These killings range in size from the very large, such as the ones just listed (which are estimated to have taken more than 20 million lives each), to the slightly smaller, as in Rwanda in 1994 and Kosovo in 1998. Some result from deliberate policies by governments; some are ethnic or tribal conflicts. They did not necessarily occur more often in the twentieth century than in the past, or affect greater numbers of people, proportionately (although some scholars do believe this). But there were a great many of them in the past century. (More information on mass killings is found in chapter 4.) One very revealing statistic tells us that 90 percent of the conflicts since 1945 have been civil wars fought with simple weapons. And there seems to be a link between civil wars, low technology, and brutality.[25] We have only to read accounts of these conflicts — such as in Cambodia, Sierra Leone, or the Balkans — to see the truth of that statement.

CONCLUSION

If nothing else, this brief look at warfare in history tells us that it has been part of our human experience for as long as we can remember. We don't know if it has always been with us — this point is unclear — but it has certainly played a major role in our existence over the centuries. It has affected how we govern ourselves, the goods we produce, our health and our relationships, and even the art, literature, and music we create. We cannot deny its centrality in our lives.

An Abbreviated Timeline of War in Human History

In a science fiction book by Robert Heinlein, *Glory Road,* a woman from another galaxy mentions to the protagonist — a human — that there is something that people on Earth do that has no counterpart anywhere else in the universe. "You mean war?" he asks her. "Oh, no," she says. "You find war wherever you go." The timeline below shows just a sampling of the wars that have taken place on our planet.

1469 BC	First Battle of Megiddo
550–530 BC	Persian Empire formed
490–350 BC	Magahda wars in India
498–272 BC	Roman conquests
431–404 BC	Great Peloponnesian War
336–323 BC	Conquests of Alexander the Great
58–51 BC	Gallic wars
350–453	Conquests of the Huns
632–732	Arab conquests
1097–1291	Crusades
1190–1297	Mongol conquests
1298–1337	Scottish wars
1302–1326	Ottoman Empire founded
1337–1453	Hundred Years' War
1494–1559	Italian wars
1560–1584	Japanese civil wars
1503–1529	Moghul Conquest of India
1500s–1700s	Spanish conquests in the Americas
1618–1648	Thirty Years' War
1618–1650	Manchu conquest of China
1754–1763	French and Indian wars
1775–1783	American Revolution

1792–1815	French Revolution and Napoleonic wars
1808–1828	Latin American wars of independence
1848–1866	Italian wars of unification
1861–1865	U.S. Civil War
1870–1945	European colonial wars: Africa, Asia, the Pacific
1870–1871	Franco-Prussian War
1904–1905	Russo-Japanese War
1914–1918	World War I
1918–1922	Russian Civil War
1936–1939	Spanish Civil War
1939–1945	World War II
1945–1949	Chinese Civil War
1948–1991	Cold War
1950–1953	Korean War
1954–1962	Algerian FLN against France
1955–1972	First Sudanese Civil War
1961–1975	Vietnam War
1961–1991	Eritrean War against Ethiopia/Cuba
1975–1991	Lebanese Civil War
1975–1979	Cambodian War/Khmer Rouge Killing Fields
1979–1989	Afghanistan War against Soviet Union
1979–1992	El Salvador Civil War
1980–1988	Iran-Iraq War
1982–1984	Mozambique Civil War
1983–	Second Sudanese Civil War
1990–1991	First Gulf War
1992–1995	Bosnian War
1994–1996	First Chechen War
1996–	Congo Wars
1998–1999	Kosovo War

QUESTIONS FOR REFLECTION
AND DISCUSSION

1. Do you think human beings are inherently violent? Is violence necessary for survival? What evidence do you have for your viewpoint?

2. How do you define war? Is it always between countries? Where do civil wars and rebellions fit in?

3. If war is an expression of culture, as John Keegan suggests, what do the wars that the United States has fought say about us? What do you think of the idea of "gentlemanly warfare"?

PRACTICAL APPLICATION

Watch the movie *Platoon* (or *Good Morning, Vietnam*), which is about the Vietnam War. Then watch *Bridge on the River Kwai* (or the *Guns of Navarone* or *Hart's War*), which is about World War II. What images of the two wars do these movies present? Are they different images? How? Discuss them.

Chapter Two

War and Peace
Parallel Traditions

BACKGROUND

Our cursory look at the role of war in history is a grim reminder of the toll that warfare has taken on human lives and the human spirit through the centuries. Like it or not, we are forced to recognize that in the history of the world, there was almost never a time when war was not an immediate reality for some peoples. As Christians, what should be our attitude toward this historical reality, as well as toward the continued existence of war? Most people, no matter what their faith, agree that war is not desirable, that the world would be a better place without it, and that what we all want most of all is peace. But when faced with the practical reality of war's continuing existence, many conclude that war is an inevitable result of our human nature. Even some Christians believe that our sinfulness and our free will inevitably lead to conflict with others. Why not be realistic, they suggest, accept war as necessary, and forget about hopeless dreams of peace? Often this seems to be the reasonable attitude.

But this sort of hopeless fatalism is not our Christian tradition. Jesus said, "Blessed are the peacemakers." In saying this, he wasn't just expressing an idealistic hope, but giving all Christians a concrete mission. Jesus calls us to be peacemakers always, not just when it is "realistic" or when we believe we can succeed. It is a Christian imperative, as realistic and important as the related demand that we love one another, as Christ loves us. These two difficult tasks are integral to the Christian life. As Christians, we must love all people and, because of that, we must all be dedicated to achieving peace in our lives, our communities, and our world. In this way, peace becomes not just a naïve ideal, but a very real hope.

What is our Christian tradition with regard to this call to peace? To begin with, we must understand that the views of Catholics fall along a continuum, where total pacifism forms one end of the continuum and a belief in the acceptability of war under certain conditions forms the other. A whole range of positions is acceptable within the church. The official teaching authority of the church, however — the magisterium — holds a composite position: nonviolence as the basic Christian position, with provision for a limited use of force when nonviolence fails. In this book, that position is called the contemporary just war position; it is explained in detail later in this chapter.

In order to better understand both the diversity of views within the church today, as well as its official stance, it is necessary to look at its history. How did we get to the current situation? In doing this, it is helpful to speak of three positions, or traditions: the *nonviolent* or *pacifist* tradition, the *classical just war* tradition, and the *contemporary just war* tradition. Not everyone today agrees completely with these designations or definitions, but they will be used for the purposes of this book.

JEWISH ROOTS

The place of war and peace in the Jewish tradition will be explored in chapter 6. Here, it is important to point out one element of that tradition that had a particular impact on the Christian tradition that developed later. The Jews have a long history of *midrash*, a process by which the dictates of scripture are applied to the practical challenges of everyday life. As with many other teachings, the Jews developed a *midrash* concerning the Fifth Commandment, the commandment that forbade killing. An important part of it related to Exodus 21:24 — "an eye for an eye, a tooth for a tooth" — a passage often used to justify vengeance on one's enemies. There is, perhaps, still an element of vengeance here, but within the Jewish tradition it has been interpreted to be a means of ensuring justice: no one was to inflict more harm on another than the other had inflicted on him. And, indeed, given the difficulty in fulfilling this mandate, many in the Jewish tradition came to see it as applying only to financial damages given in reparation for a crime committed. It has never been understood, as some claim, as justification for vengeance. This concept of equal justice, we shall see, will play a part in the Christian tradition on war.

THE NONVIOLENT/PACIFIST TRADITION

Jesus also challenges the interpretation of "an eye for an eye, a tooth for a tooth" as a justification for revenge. In the fifth chapter of Matthew, where he proclaims, "Blessed are the peacemakers" (5:9), he goes on to say:

> You have heard that it was said, "An eye for an eye and a tooth for a tooth." But I say to you, offer no resistance to one who is evil. When someone strikes you on [your] right cheek, turn the other one to him as well. If anyone wants to go to law with you over your tunic, hand him your cloak as well. Should anyone press you into service for one mile, go with him for two miles. Give to the one who asks of you, and do not turn your back on one who wants to borrow. You have heard that it was said, "You shall love your neighbor and hate your

enemy." But I say to you, love your enemies, and pray for those who persecute you, that you may be children of your heavenly Father, for he makes his sun rise on the bad and the good, and causes rain to fall on the just and the unjust. For if you love those who love you, what recompense will you have? Do not the tax collectors do the same? And if you greet your brothers only, what is unusual about that? Do not the pagans do the same? So be perfect, just as your heavenly Father is perfect. (Matthew 5:38–48)

Jesus seems to be saying not only that we should be peacemakers, but that we should not meet violence with violence, and that we should love our enemies. Impractical advice perhaps, but Jesus says that this is not only what we should do, but that this is the way of Christian perfection. When it comes to making decisions about war, Christians have an obligation to take Jesus' teaching into account.

Does this mean that Christians are not to make war? Historical evidence suggests that this is how some early Christians interpreted Jesus' teaching. Some of those who became Christians in the first three hundred years after Christ claimed an exemption from military service and, during the early persecutions, even refused to resist violently. Some soldiers who became Christians either retired from soldiering or took an oath not to obey an order to kill another person. They didn't see Christ's teaching about nonresistance and loving one's enemy as impractical; it was imperative. It was an important mark that they were followers of Christ, peacemakers in the midst of an empire prone to making war.

> He shall judge between many peoples
> and impose terms on strong and distant nations;
> They shall beat their swords into plowshares,
> and their spears into pruning hooks;
> One nation shall not raise the sword against another,
> nor shall they train for war again.   —Micah 4:3

Yet there were compromises and tensions. For example, what obligations did Christ's injunction to "love your neighbor as yourself" bring in this regard? Moral philosopher James Childress points out that there were three "moral pressures" to participate in war, even in this early community: "(1) the recognition of prevention or removal of harm as a requirement of neighbor-love, (2) the related sense of responsibility, fault and guilt for omissions [for not coming to the aid of another], and (3) the generalization test proposed by Celsus [an influential third-century critic of the early Christians], who asked Christians to consider what would happen if everyone did what they were doing, i.e., refrained from military service."[1] These moral pressures demonstrate that not everyone completely embraced nonviolence, but also that the majority did. Indeed, Childress signals his agreement with religious historian Roland Bainton's observation: "The age of persecution down to the time of Constantine was the age of pacifism to the degree that during that period no Christian author to our knowledge approved of Christian participation in battle."[2] This is the first of the traditions in the newly formed Christian church about war and peace.

This tradition of nonviolence, closely tied to Christ's life and teaching, has been espoused by some portion of the Christian community throughout the church's history. It has not always been considered a legitimate moral stance within the church, though. During the time between the Council of Trent in the sixteenth century, and the end of the Second World War in the twentieth, nonviolence was not seen as an acceptable position for Catholics by moral theologians or church authorities. Only with Vatican II and the issuing of *Gaudium et Spes* (*On the Church in the Modern World*) did nonviolence and pacifism become acceptable again.

Only without the sword can the Christian
wage war: for the Lord has abolished the
sword.   —Tertullian, early Christian writer

Because pacifism was the first tradition, and because of its identification with Christ himself, many have claimed (and still do) that this is the only authentic tradition for a Christian. This first tradition is called the *pacifist tradition*. It holds that Jesus himself did not engage in violence and, indeed, preached the opposite — that one should refrain from taking vengeance, that one should not meet violence with violence or do violence to anyone, that one should love one's enemies. Therefore (as most of the early Christians seemed to believe), Christians did not involve themselves in war and, when persecuted, were not permitted to resist violently, but only in loving, nonviolent ways. Christians who hold to the pacifist tradition, therefore, believe that it is not permissible for them to participate in war under any circumstances and that peace must be brought about in nonviolent ways.

THE CLASSICAL JUST WAR TRADITION

In the year 313, Christianity became the official religion of the Roman Empire, with the result that most citizens of the empire, including the soldiers, were now Christians. One could not very well maintain an empire without an army, so the Emperor Constantine called meetings to decide how Christian belief and the needs of the empire would be reconciled. By the year 416, this reconciliation was so well established that soldiering became an occupation exclusive to Christians; non-Christians were not allowed.

What is reflected in this shift is a struggle with the implications of successful evangelization. While they were a persecuted minority, it was much easier for Christians to hold certain convictions contradicting those of their oppressors. Now, as a majority, there were practical implications of being citizens as well as Christians, implications that needed to be faced. It is here where the moral pressures that Childress outlines above "contributed to the legitimation of Christian participation in war."[3] How could the empire defend itself from its enemies if its citizenry refused to serve as soldiers or go to war? Some practical scheme needed to be arrived at that did not violate the spirit of Jesus' teaching. After three centuries of adhering closely to the letter of the scriptures, Christians were forced to engage in some *midrash* of their own.

St. Augustine, then bishop of Hippo, made a significant contribution to this effort in his masterpiece, *The City of God*, and in letters to Roman officials charged with the defense of the empire. In them, he lays the foundation of the church's just war theory, outlining the conditions he believes necessary for the Christian state to engage in a war. Augustine begins his discussion by saying: "Whoever gives even moderate attention to human affairs and to our common nature will recognize that if there is no man who does not wish to be joyful, neither is there any one who does not wish to have peace.... It is therefore with the desire for peace that wars are waged, even by those who take pleasure in exercising their warlike nature in command and battle. And hence it is obvious that peace is the end sought for by war."[4]

The presumption, then, at the foundation of the just war theory is that all human beings desire peace, and if it becomes necessary to have recourse to war, its only goal can be to achieve peace. Augustine defines peace as "the tranquility of order," an order in which the just prosper and the unjust suffer. So, for him, a war may be fought for the restoration of the just order, which is peace.

Augustine affirmed the duty of the magistrate to defend the innocent and maintain the public order. He emphasized that this duty to defend the peace must be altruistic. In the case of a city or state under attack, Augustine also allowed for the use of force, if necessary, since it is the responsibility of legitimate state authorities to protect their citizens by whatever proportionate means necessary.

Augustine recognizes as well that, on occasion, war may be necessary for other reasons in order to restore the peace and defend the innocent: to inflict punishment for a wrong suffered or to recover something unjustly taken. But he is emphatic that the intention must be pure; it cannot be vengeance, lust for power, or the desire for some undeserved benefit. It may be only the restoration of order, the achieving of peace. To help assure this purity of intention, he says that war may be declared only by a legitimate authority, recognized by the citizens as being charged with their protection.

Thomas Aquinas, drawing on Augustine some eight hundred years later, briefly treats peace and war in his great work, *Summa Theologica*, in the portion that deals specifically with charity. Peace he treats as one of the acts of charity. War, clearly, is a vice opposed to this peace. But he also recognizes with Augustine that war is sometimes necessary to restore the just order and thus bring about peace. So his answer to the question of whether it is always sinful to wage war is *no*.

Indeed, Aquinas refers to one of Augustine's sermons in which, citing Luke 3:14, Augustine explains that Jesus did not forbid soldiering. Rather, Jesus said, "Do violence to no man... and be content with your pay." Aquinas then goes on to explain what he sees as the three things necessary for a just war: it is commanded by a legitimate authority; the cause is just; and the intention is right. Aquinas draws support from Augustine's writings to back up each claim. And, like Augustine, he emphasizes in particular that the intention must be right: "For it may happen that the war is declared by the legitimate authority, and for a just cause, and yet be rendered unlawful through a wicked intention."[5]

Aquinas is careful to make some important distinctions. Acknowledging injunctions in scripture to resist evil and not take revenge, he says that "it is necessary sometimes for a man to act otherwise for the common good, or for the good of those with whom he is fighting."[6] He also reiterates that those who wage a *just* war have peace as their goal "and so they are not opposed to peace, except to the evil peace" (i.e., the false peace of an unjust order).[7] He also holds that participation in war is not permissible for everyone, specifically not for bishops and clerics.

Later theologians and philosophers — Francisco de Vitoria, Francisco Suarez, Hugo Grotius, and others — also played a part in the formation of the just war tradition. Their contribution was twofold: they added to the criteria to be met before going to war and also focused on the rules for fighting justly once a war has begun. Vitoria, Suarez, and Grotius added to (or reemphasized in) the just war tradition the principles of *last resort* and *proportionality*. Last resort, a concept implied in Augustine, demands that all nonviolent means of averting war and achieving peace be exhausted prior to engaging in a war. Proportionality, which we saw in the Jewish tradition ("an eye for an eye, a tooth for a tooth"), demands that the harm done in a war be no more than the harm originally suffered. Yet another principle espoused by these later thinkers is related to proportionality: that if a war is to be fought, it must have a *reasonable chance of success.*

To sum up, the classical just war tradition holds certain principles that are the foundation of its rules for engaging in a just war:

- There is a "tranquility of order," in which the just are rewarded and the unjust are punished. This order constitutes the peace for which all human beings naturally strive.

- All people, especially Christians, should strive to achieve this peace.

- Evil done by unjust persons or nations can so disturb order that some just action must be taken for the sake of peace.

If war is deemed necessary, then there are certain requirements that must be fulfilled in order for it to be a permissible, or just, war. The rules for engaging in a just war are listed in the box below.

The Classical Just War Tradition

- **Just Cause**. The acceptable reasons for going to war are:
  - legitimate defense
  - restitution: the regaining of things wrongfully taken
  - redress: the seizing of things owed that have been wrongly withheld
  - punishment: restoring the balance of justice by punishing wrongdoing

- **Legitimate Authority**. It must be commanded by the legitimate authority responsible for the common good.

- **Right Intention**. It cannot be engaged in for some undue benefit, such as domination of others, malice, or vengeance. It must be only for the just cause and to achieve peace.

- **Last Resort**. Other nonviolent means of achieving the peace, such as diplomacy and negotiation, must first be exhausted.

- **Reasonable Chance of Success**. Arms may not be used in a futile cause or in a case where disproportionate measures are required to achieve success.

- **Proportionality**. The harm done in the course of the war must not exceed the harm originally suffered that led to that war.

This tradition of just war formed a major current in the Christian world, up until around the time of the Reformation in the sixteenth century. It was not the only current; there were also during this same period church-led and officially sanctioned peace movements. With the advent of the Reformation, however, the predominant tradition in Catholicism —

as well as in the Anglican, Lutheran, and Calvinist churches — became the classical just war position, and it remained dominant until well into the twentieth century. It must be noted, though, that another current also developed in the Reformation, as some Anabaptist groups and other movements adopted a more radically nonviolent stance with regard to war (a more in-depth discussion of some of these churches can be found in chapter 7).

THE CONTEMPORARY
JUST WAR TRADITION

The nineteenth century saw the end of the close connection between the Christian church and the state that had existed up until that time. The Vatican became progressively more isolated and less involved in the day-to-day affairs of countries where for centuries it had wielded powerful influence. At the time, it seemed to be a crisis for the church, but it paved the way for the much different understanding of the church in the world that we have today. This separation inspired the beginnings of the modern social teaching of the church, giving the church a more objective perspective from which to speak to the world, especially given the challenges of industrialization and a changing world order. Pope Leo XIII gave voice to this in the first of the social encyclicals, *Rerum Novarum* (*On the Condition of the Working Classes*) in 1891.

The horrors of two world wars, the second ending with the use of the most deadly weapon humankind had ever seen at Hiroshima and Nagasaki, prompted a reconsideration of the possibility of a just war. The morality of war, the just war tradition, and the participation of Catholics in war began to be questioned in ways they hadn't been for centuries. This was helped by the fact that the Catholic Church now stood outside empire and state and thus felt less need for compromise. The shifting tide of Catholic thought first became officially apparent in the 1963 encyclical *Pacem in Terris* (*Peace on Earth*), where John XXIII declared, "Men are becoming more and more convinced that disputes which arise between states should not be resolved by recourse to arms, but rather by negotiation" (no. 126). Significantly, this encyclical, the first addressed not only to Catholics but to the whole world, takes an optimistic look at the world's potential for peace. It does so, however, by reflecting seriously on where the world stood at that time. World War II was still a fresh memory and the world was only months removed from the brink of nuclear conflict after the Cuban Missile Crisis: "We grant indeed that this conviction is chiefly based on the terrible destructive force of modern weapons.... Therefore, in an age such as ours which prides itself on its atomic energy it is contrary to reason to hold that war is now a suitable way to restore rights which have been violated" (no. 127). This bold statement was and is interpreted by many as signaling a shift in the church's teaching on war, away from "justified" conflict and toward a more general prohibition.

Similar statements in other church documents also reflected this change in emphasis. The Second Vatican Council, in *Gaudium et Spes*, affirmed the just war tradition while feeling compelled "by the addition of scientific weapons ... to undertake an evaluation of war with an entirely new attitude" and warned, "The men of our time must realize that they will have to give a somber reckoning of their deeds of war" (no. 80). It also recognized and praised "those who renounce the use of violence in the vindication of their rights and who resort to methods which are otherwise available to weaker parties too, provided this can be done without injury to the rights and duties of others or the community itself" (no. 78). Thus the council affirmed a new attitude and legitimized conscientious objection to war.

Gaudium et Spes marks a significant shift in the Catholic traditions regarding war and peace. In the face of contemporary weaponry, the church not only called for a stronger commitment to peace, but it relegitimated for Catholics the tradition of nonviolence that had been practiced by many early Christians. The documents of the Second Vatican Council and the encyclicals of both Pope John XXIII and Pope Paul VI that addressed war and peace did so with this new attitude.

When Pope Paul VI addressed the United Nations in 1965, he demonstrated that attitude, saying, "It is enough to remember that the blood of millions of men, numberless and unprecedented sufferings, useless slaughter and frightful ruin are the sanction of the covenant which unites you, in a solemn pledge which must change the future history of the world: No more war, war never again."

Out of this new attitude was born what might be considered a new tradition in the church about war and peace — what we call the *contemporary just war tradition*. This new tradition is not, as some suggest, a move back to the more strictly nonviolent stance of the early Christians. It is clearly a just war tradition, but one that is in some ways a departure from the classical just war tradition as understood until Vatican II. The first reason for this is historical. Anyone who grew up during the 1950s through the 1970s knows the great anxiety of those years. There was the memory of two world wars, the tumult of the Vietnam War, and the constant threat of nuclear holocaust occasioned by the Cold War. One need only watch movies like *War Games* or the more recent *Thirteen Days* (see Appendix B, page 148, for more about films) to get a sense of what those times were like. There was a growing conviction that any future war could mean the end of the world. And even now, when that threat seems less imminent, if we look at the death toll of the wars of the twentieth century, it's hard not to be convinced of the wisdom of starting our reasoning about whether to engage in a war with a strong presumption against the use of force, which is where the contemporary just war tradition starts. The U.S. bishops' *Challenge of Peace* comments: "While the

---

The Contemporary Just War Tradition

The distinctive qualities of the contemporary just war tradition are:

+ **A strong presumption against the use of force**, based on a consciousness of the destructive power of modern weapons, especially nuclear weapons.

+ **Just cause**: There is only one acceptable reason a sovereign state can independently engage in a just war: legitimate defense.

+ **Legitimate authority**: For all other reasons — restitution, redress, punishment — only the United Nations can authorize war.

+ **Right intention**: This remains the same as in the classical tradition. War must be engaged in only to achieve peace.

+ **Last resort**: This criterion is, arguably, even stronger in the contemporary tradition, which has a stronger confidence in and promotion of nonviolent means of avoiding conflict.

+ **Reasonable chance of success**: This remains the same as in the classical tradition. The cause must not be futile and disproportionate measures must not be necessary.

+ **Proportionality**: If war *is* deemed necessary, there is in the contemporary tradition a greater emphasis on proportionality and avoiding noncombatant casualties (also due to the awareness of the destructive power of modern weapons). There has been in recent years an articulation of noncombatant immunity. For a more extensive discussion of it, see the *Harvest of Justice Is Sown in Peace* and *Centesimus Annus*.

---

just-war teaching has clearly been in possession for the past 1,500 years of Catholic thought, the 'new moment' in which we find ourselves sees the just-war teaching and non-violence as distinct but interdependent methods of evaluating warfare. They diverge on some specific conclusions, but they share a common presumption against the use of force as a means of settling disputes" (no. 120).

The twentieth century, more positively, was also a century of increased international cooperation, which led to the formation of first the League of Nations and then the United Nations. One of the changes this occasioned in the church's stance is that in the contemporary just war tradition, it limited the reasons for which a state may declare it necessary to go to war. The authority to demand redress and restitution, and the authority to punish, have largely been ceded to international bodies like the United Nations. This is, in fact, the view of the Holy See. Thus the tradition has evolved to the point where, in the contemporary just war tradition, legitimate defense is now seen as the only reason for a nation to mount a just war. Indeed, in terms of international law and politics, the buildup to the recent war in Iraq seemed to reflect an understanding that if you want to go to war for other than purely defensive purposes, and you make the claim that it is just, then you must do so with the cooperation and/or approval of an international political body. The United Nations becomes the "legitimate authority" in these cases. This is a limitation that the United States, and those who claim that the classical just war tradition is more authentic, question; they do not see the UN — only the nation-state — as the legitimate authority in issues of war and peace.

The Catechism of the Catholic Church can be said to ascribe to the contemporary just war tradition. The subject heading in the *Catechism*, "Avoiding War," suggests the presumption against war characteristic of the contemporary view, and the text outlines the conditions for a just war, saying: "The strict conditions for *legitimate defense by military force* require rigorous consideration" (no. 2309). These conditions are that the damage inflicted by the aggressor be lasting, grave, and certain, that all possible nonviolent means of avoiding the conflict are exhausted, that there be a serious prospect of success, and that the evil inflicted (keeping in mind modern means of destruction) not be greater than that to be eliminated. As has always been the case, this decision is left to the "prudential judgment" of the legitimate authority.

Certain documents of the U.S. bishops also can be seen as key in the development and support of the contemporary just war theory. In *The Challenge of Peace* (1983) the U.S. bishops say: "Catholic teaching begins in every case with a presumption against war and for peaceful settlement of disputes. In exceptional cases, determined by the moral principles of the just war tradition, some uses of force are permitted" (Summary, I.A.1). In 1993, in *The Harvest of Justice Is Sown in Peace,* the bishops assert: "The devastation wrought by these recent wars reinforces and strengthens for us the strong presumption against the use of force.... The presumption against the use of force has also been strengthened by the examples of the effectiveness of nonviolence in some places in Eastern Europe and elsewhere" (I.B.1).

Pope John Paul II also strongly advocated the new attitude, especially in promoting peacemaking and nonviolent resistance. In 1995, he said in *Evangelium Vitae (The Gospel of Life),* "Among the signs of hope we should also count the spread, at many levels of public opinion, of a *new sensitivity ever more opposed to war* as an instrument for the resolution of conflicts

Comparing the Classical and Contemporary Just War Traditions

A presumption against the use of force is key in the contemporary just war tradition.

Just cause in the classical just war tradition: There are several valid reasons for which a nation may go to war in this tradition.

+ Legitimate defense. Someone has attacked a country and it goes to war to defend itself.

+ Restitution. A country goes to war to take back something another country wrongly took from it.

+ Redress. A country goes to war to seize something owed to it that the other country has wrongly withheld from it.

+ Punishment. A country goes to war to punish a wrongdoing done by another country and thus restore the balance of justice.

Just cause in the contemporary just war tradition: The only reason for which a nation may go to war in this tradition is legitimate defense. However, Pope John Paul II has also indicated that recourse to war may be allowed for humanitarian reasons when whole populations are at risk.[8]

Legitimate authority in the classical just war tradition is the individual or body recognized by a nation's citizens as being charged with their protection — the governing authority of that nation.

Legitimate authority in the contemporary just war tradition has, in all instances except for legitimate defense, been ceded to the United Nations. Thus, it falls to the UN to approve any war for other causes, such as redress, restitution, or punishment.

between peoples, and increasingly oriented to finding effective but 'nonviolent' means to counter the armed aggressor" (no. 27; emphasis added). In 1991 and again in 2002, he was one of the strongest opponents of what he determined to be an unjust war in Iraq.

Some Catholic philosophers and theologians believe that the present situation, with the "war on terror" and some critics questioning the usefulness of the United Nations, calls for a shift in the tradition toward a more classical just war position. But the church is still holding to the more contemporary just war viewpoint. The church also continues to encourage those who, for reasons of conscience or interpretation of the Gospel, choose to adopt a nonviolent stance toward war. In *Centesimus Annus* (*On the Hundredth Anniversary of Rerum Novarum*), John Paul II spoke in particularly strong terms affirming this: "I myself, on the occasion of the recent tragic war in the Persian Gulf, repeated the cry: 'Never again war!' . . . Just as the time has finally come when in individual States a system of private vendetta and reprisal has given way to the rule of law, so too a similar step forward is now urgently needed in the international community" (no. 52).

So when we speak of the contemporary just war position, we speak of a tradition that does not differ markedly from the classical just war position. The differences lie in its consciousness of recent history — the shattering events of the late twentieth century — and the resulting greater emphasis on a presumption against the use of force. This has led to some practical limitations on the conduct of war not found in the classical just war tradition.

SUMMARY OF
THE THREE TRADITIONS

We see then, that when it comes to war, we Christians have three parallel traditions, not just one. Even many non-Christians throughout the world subscribe to one of those traditions. In more recent church teaching, the tendency seems to be to emphasize both the contemporary just war tradition and the tradition of nonviolence, the presumption being that the classical view is not sensitive enough to the demands and practicalities of recent history. In *The Harvest of Justice Is Sown in Peace,* the U.S. bishops give priority to nonviolence, and also establish the public duty of nonviolence for both individuals and governments.

However, in *The Challenge of Peace,* they point out: "Throughout history there has been a shifting relation between the two streams of the tradition [nonviolence and just war] which always remain in tension." And we can see this tension in the fact that, since the terrorist attacks of September 11, 2001, and the subsequent "war on terror," some theologians are starting to question the marginalization of the classical view. They are arguing that the classical just war tradition is more suited to the changed global situation occasioned by the intensification of terrorism in recent years. The Holy See, on the other hand, has stated that recent events actually call the just war theory into question.[9] Also, the work of various grassroots Catholic peace movements in many countries, such as Focolare and San Egidio and, in the United States, the Catholic Worker Movement and the Catholic Peacebuilding Network, indicates the strength of the church's nonviolent tradition. One of the oldest and most widely respected movements is Pax Christi International.

In addition, there is also some disagreement about what actually constitutes the classical just war position. Some theologians are arguing that, contrary to what many people believe today, the classical tradition did indeed have a presumption against the use of force, that even Augustine and Aquinas held that recourse to war should be allowed only with great reluctance and after all nonviolent alternatives had been explored. Augustine said in one letter: "It is better to secure peace by a word than by the sword" (229.2). In this view, the contemporary tradition then is seen as a retrieval of a fuller just war tradition, with a presumption against the use of force and *for* the use of nonviolent means of conflict resolution. It is an ongoing discussion.

However, we ought always to move forward, attentive to the words of Pope John Paul II, who, though not a pacifist, spoke strongly against war. Echoing Pope Benedict XV and Paul VI, he said in *Centesimus Annus,* "No, never again war, which destroys the lives of innocent people, teaches how to kill, throws into upheaval even the lives of those who do the killing and leaves behind a trail of resentment and hatred, thus making it all the more difficult to find a just solution of the very problems which provoked the war" (no. 52). He also reminded us at the World Day of Peace in 2002 that there is "no peace without justice, no justice without forgiveness.... Peace is essential for development, but true peace is only made possible through forgiveness."

QUESTIONS FOR REFLECTION AND DISCUSSION

1. Can someone both be a pacifist and also allow for a just war? Explain your thinking.

2. Is it legitimate for individuals to fight back if they are attacked? Can a country fight back if it is attacked? What role do you think national self-interest should play in discussing the ethics of war? Put another way: Are we Americans first or Christians first?

3. Which of the three traditions most resonates with you? Why?

Chapter Three

The Three Traditions Today

We have traced the history of the church's three traditions in war and peace: their roots, influences, and development. Now we will look at them as they are today. What do they mean in today's world? How do they apply to our current situation? What are the issues and controversies surrounding them? The November 2003 forum, in bringing together people representing these three positions, explored these questions in depth and raised important questions about them. The following remarks are taken from the taped proceedings of the forum.

First, however, it is important to make a distinction between pacifism and nonviolence. These terms are often used interchangeably, but they are not synonymous. The definitions below come from the Nonviolence Training Project.

> Pacifism is generally taken to mean moral opposition to war, refusal to bear arms or adopting a policy of non-resistance. Nonviolence is an active confrontation of injustice which excludes violence for principled and/or pragmatic reasons. The critics of nonviolence, and some of its more naive advocates, often falsely equate nonviolence with passivity or non-resistance.

THE NONVIOLENT PACIFIST POSITION

Michael Baxter, *associate professor of theology,*
University of Notre Dame

We were given the assignment of speaking about pacifism, which, I suppose we could say, began in the upper room when Jesus greeted his disciples: "Peace be with you" (John 20:19–20). It's renewed every time Catholics go to mass. That greeting is given to us all the time. It certainly shaped the life of the early church in its practice. There's no record of any Christian in the military before the late second century. And there's clearly a strong record of Christians who, upon baptism, left the military, partly because of idolatrous practices but partly because of the violence, which was seen as out of character with being a Christian. In fact, one of the proofs for the divinity of Christ (given by Athanasius) is the fact that Christians are peaceable. And one of the strongest criticisms against Christians was that the prophecy wasn't being fulfilled when there was violence detected in the community. But there is a strong presumption for peace in the life of the church, a kind of gravitational pull. Jesus reveals our nature to us and that nature has power in us because of our desire for peace.

When Augustine proposes the exceptional use of violence in some cases, it doesn't overturn that presumption for peace. You go to war for peace, according to Augustine, with a great sense of sorrow, with love in your heart, and so on. And we see the foundational nature of this presumption in the many ways in which war was limited by church teaching and practice in the Middle Ages.

> Peace is a gift from God, given by Jesus
> Christ to the apostles in the upper room
> with the greeting, "Peace be with you."
> This gift of peace is intrinsic to. the
> church's mission to forgive sins.
>
> —Michael Baxter

By and large, in modern times with the rise of the modern nation-state, just war principles have received less and less attention; the influence of Catholic teaching in international politics waned. This became evident with the onset of total war. After World War II, at the Second Vatican Council, the church voiced sharp criticism of total war, specifically of the disproportionate destruction and indiscriminate weapons associated with modern war. The council also affirmed Christian pacifism and conscientious objection. In the years since, the church has issued statements along these lines.

Pacifism is in a unique position to articulate and embody the church's long-standing commitment to peacemaking patterned after the teaching and example of Jesus, and also to use just war principles to criticize the waging of war from a perspective extending beyond the policy concerns of particular nation-states.

We offer two policy perspectives and five policy recommendations.

Perspective #1: We urge meetings with Christian political and religious leaders from the Middle East, in order to gain otherwise unavailable facts and insights about political and religious dynamics there.

Perspective #2: We urge meetings with peacemaking groups in the Middle East, indigenous and international, in order to gain insights about conditions there.

Recommendation #1: That the rights of total conscientious objectors (COs) in the U.S. military be restored and that the rights of selective conscientious objectors (SCOs) be established and protected.

Recommendation #2: That U.S. policymakers make monetary support of Israel subject to the following reforms in Israeli military policy: protection of the rights of Israeli SCOs, cessation of terrorist retaliations aimed at civilians, and cessation of targeted assassinations.

Recommendation #3: That U.S. policymakers allocate funds for NGOs working to enhance the living conditions of Palestinians and other groups in the Middle East.

Recommendation #4: That U.S. occupation of Iraq be terminated and that government of the country be gradually handed over to Iraqi groups under the supervision of the United Nations.

Recommendation #5: That any U.S. military action against Iran or Syria, including an economic embargo, first be approved by the United Nations.

Jim Wallis, *publisher,* Sojourners *magazine*

To begin with, wars are not ceasing. In fact, war is becoming more and more the primary instrument of foreign policy, particularly in this country. And I'm operating from the assumption that from a Christian point of view, this is not a good thing. I would suggest that all of our Christian traditions, all of them, need to be reexamined and pushed and challenged and held accountable, both to gospel and to context.

Jesus did not say, "Blessed are the peace lovers."
He said, "Blessed are the peacemakers."

— Jim Wallis

I don't particularly like the word "pacifist." It's not a biblical word, and I'm an evangelical. But I am in that gospel tradition of peacemaking often called nonviolence, and I believe that that tradition must be challenged too, for its frequent failure to address context. All of our traditions need some scrutiny, in my view. So let me just challenge mine, instead of the others.

If nonviolence is to be credible, it must answer the questions that violence purports to answer, but in a better way. It cannot underestimate the questions or say they aren't real questions. It must take them seriously.

I suggest that protest is simply not enough. And here's my evangelical influence: the problem of evil must be taken seriously.

It is good to say *no*. It is better to have an alternative. And the pacifist position needs not to just say no faithfully out of witness, but in fact to construct alternatives. Some of you know that some of us were involved in meetings with Prime Minister Blair and the British government before they went to war in Iraq, and we presented something called a six-point plan. It was an alternative to war with Iraq, based on the assumption that Saddam must be removed and any weapons of mass destruction must be found and eliminated. This plan was too late. But I want to testify that it was being seriously considered at the highest levels of the British government and cabinet. And I had many nonadministration hawks tell me this should have been tried. And it wasn't tried.

What are those things that can be done before war breaks out, as an alternative to war, to solve the problem in a way other than war?

What about conflict resolution? Peacemaking is a difficult task. It can't be undertaken just by faithfulness to the gospel, as if context doesn't count. Incarnation is at the heart of my notion of peacemaking, and context is very important.

Joan Chittister, OSB, *co-chair, Global Peace Initiative of Women, Religious, and Spiritual Leaders*

Women bear the greatest cost of the wars we wage in their so-called defense. And we never ask women as a class if that's the way they want to be defended. No amount of smart bombs or technological precision will reduce the cost of the way women go to war. When we wipe out an electrical grid that we call a military target, we wipe out the food-making capability of women throughout that entire area. When we wipe out the water system of a country and call it a military target, we never bother to count the number of babies who are drinking dirty water. We don't call them the victims of war. We count only the soldiers and then only ours, with deep, deep distress.

We can't have any complete theological tradition or position on war unless we do two things. We must recognize the effects of war on the other victims of war, who are the other half of the human race. And we must understand that women, who never as a class are included in the decision making that leads us to war, must at least be included in the class that negotiates the peace.

These three voices point to the fact that the nonviolent/pacifist positon has serious policy implications. For specific examples, see chapter 5 of this book.

THE CONTEMPORARY
JUST WAR POSITION

Drew Christiansen, SJ, *editor-in-chief,* America *magazine*

In the context of our paper on the presumption against the use of force as it affects contemporary Catholic social teaching, my job is to set the Catholic context on the relationship of just war to the body of Catholic social teaching on peace.

I think that in the time since the Second Vatican Council, there's probably been no area in which the church's teaching has evolved so quickly, where things that were incipient grew and have become dominant themes. In World War II, conscientious objectors were denied official backing by the church; the church refused to give them approbation. As late as 1962, just at the beginning of the council, the Holy Office was sending around prescripts telling people that Catholics could not be conscientious objectors. The council broke with that practice. It praised nonviolent resisters and it supported conscientious objection and selective conscientious objection.

The U.S. bishops' *Challenge of Peace,* some twenty years later, brought about change, particularly by articulating common ground between the nonviolent and the just war positions, saying that they both shared a presumption against the use of force. But while *The Challenge of Peace* accepted nonviolence, it denied that it was a state ethic or could be a state ethic.

In 1991, in *Centesimus Annus,* John Paul II gave his clear endorsement of nonviolence. It was a result of his interpretation of the events in Eastern Europe in 1989 and the overthrow of the Communist regimes there. This document articulated a position that said, "Nonviolence ought to be the alternative, both in domestic and international disputes." Two years later, the U.S. bishops also endorsed the status of nonviolence as a public ethic. Reformulating and summarizing the position of the church, the bishops declared that the ordinary Christian position is to address conflict nonviolently, but when repeated attempts fail, then they allowed that force may be utilized under the terms of the just war.

Today, the church's position is a composite of nonviolence, but with provision for just war when repeated attempts at nonviolence fail. The coherence of this position, it seems to me, resides in the notion of resistance to evil. That is, all people — not just Christians, but all people — must resist — not just avoid, but resist — large-scale evil, nonviolently if possible, by legitimate and limited means if necessary.

Accordingly, the context of the just war in Catholic social teaching has changed. The just war has to be read in the context of an official theology of peace with a strong critique of war as a public policy. There is in that critique a presumption *against* the use of force and *for* the development and utilization of nonviolent alternatives to war.

And there's an explicit rejection, as seen in the debate of recent years, of preventive war. Vatican denunciations of preventive war have been a bit too preemptory. There has been very little argument. But I think the reason for this is evident. Preventive war overrides an underlying principle of Christian just war, namely, the notion of necessity.

What we have in the national security doctrine of the United States are doctrines of preemption, prevention, and preeminence, with war as an option for choice. Just wars are never wars of choice, and for that reason, there's a direct conflict between the national security strategy of the United States and Catholic social teaching.

Maryann Cusimano Love, *professor of international relations,*
Catholic University

Some have been arguing since September 11 that because we are facing a totally new kind of war we need a totally new kind of ethics. The just war tradition is either obsolete or needs to be radically altered to accommodate weapons of mass destruction, terrorists, nonstate actors, the whole post–September 11 landscape. This argument is overblown and untrue. Terrorism is a centuries-old tactic of asymmetric warfare, nothing new there; weapons of mass destruction have been around for centuries. And nonstate actors are the norm, not the exception, in international politics.

Just war tradition was developed long before the sovereign state existed, with the Treaty of Westphalia in 1648. It was not originally oriented to the modern state system and it has often been applied to nonstate actors. So those are not really problems for the just war tradition. Globalization is also not new. It's how you and I are all here, how our country was formed with previous periods of colonization, trade, and missionaries.

What is new is the global megaphone: the 24/7 news cycle, with media and Internet that are instantly accessible and that are not filtered by governments or Western media outlets. This is why norms and just war tradition matter more, not less, in the post–September 11 scenario. The world is watching not just the terrorist attacks but our responses to them. The war on terrorism is an attempt to build a global prohibitionary norm against the tactic of killing noncombatants. Terrorism is a tactic used by lots of different ideologies to kill noncombatants. Osama bin Laden skillfully uses the global media to try to present al Qaeda's case, and al Qaeda makes moral arguments why they believe killing noncombatants is permissible in pursuit of their goals.

The Bush administration, in turn, is trying to create an international coalition against killing noncombatants. That laudable effort is like the attempt to get a ban on slavery, a ban on piracy; it's like the international campaign to ban land mines. These are types of global prohibitionary norms that we've seen in the past against practices of international politics deemed particularly barbarous, such as killing noncombatants.

That effort to create a global prohibitionary norm against killing non-combatants cannot proceed if we take the killing of noncombatants lightly with the global media watching. So just war tradition is not an obstacle to fighting the global "war on terror"; it is a very essential tool to limiting and checking our actions as we go forward.

Finally, Augustine and Aquinas grappled with the problem of the use of force by armed bands not authorized by public authorities. Vitoria and Suarez discussed the clash of civilizations and what to do about the use of violence in those situations. Grotius examined how international law and international communities should factor in the decisions over the use of force. We have a very rich tradition that gives us lots of tools to deal with the present situation. We should not abandon that tradition or seek to radically alter it at the time when it is needed most.

> The just war theory exists to discern, not necessarily to legitimate, the preferences of policymakers.
> — position paper by Christiansen, Lopez, and Love

To respond to the policy questions raised, it is simply a false choice to argue that our choices are either preventive war or catastrophic terrorism and catastrophic casualties. It's immoral to suggest that those are our only choices, rather than developing the vast territory between these two extremes. Research and experience show that preventive war doesn't work, and that other means of countering terrorism and the spread of weapons of mass destruction have been successful. This is where we need to expand international efforts and attention.

Some examples would be the cooperative threat reduction program, arms control, efforts of preventive proliferation programs, public diplomacy, the development and strengthening of a variety of international institutions for all, not simply the United Nations. To weaken those types of approaches and then argue that our only choice is preventive war is not only disingenuous, it is, I think, an immoral way to proceed.

George Lopez, *senior fellow, Joan B. Kroc Institute for International Peace Studies, University of Notre Dame*

I am going to present a "case" about Iran, based on certain assumptions. I am going to do this as a way to test the presumption against the use of force within a just war tradition. Ethicists claim that beginning with "tough cases" makes the task of developing viable ethical principles of action more cumbersome. But whether the United States should use preemptive force against Iran is too timely an issue to worry about its degree of difficulty. In fact, to ensure that the case is tested at its most difficult level, we will assume that the U.S. government is engaged in the debate about whether to employ preemptive force against Iran during the summer and early autumn of 2003, the time of deepest suspicion and highest rhetorical attack. In this time period the knowledge available to policymakers reflects considerable uncertainty about the scope, direction, and intention of a potential Iranian nuclear arms program. The policy atmosphere in Washington is a combination of the continuing sense of insecurity after 9/11, and self-congratulations for having pursued successfully the course of preemptive action against Iraq.

To this we add the final framing of the case: we accept the Bush administration's characterization, as stated in its January 2002 National Security review, that the greatest threat facing the United States [thus that which would comprise a *causus belli*] is the volatile combination of rogue or failed states, which seek to acquire weapons of mass destruction, and which also support terrorism. Those who would (and did at that time) argue for preemptive force against Iran claimed that (*a*) Iran fit these criteria perfectly; and (*b*) the United States had surgical air strikes or war for regime change as its only alternatives. Did Iran fit the fears? Could a presumption against the use of force have changed the dialogue about war options?

The Bush team defines rogue nations as those that subvert international law and demonstrate ongoing hostility toward the United States. In a seminal article about Republican foreign policy in the January–February 2000 issue of *Foreign Affairs*, Condoleezza Rice wrote of the need to pursue an aggressive posture against such rogue states and made particular mention of Iran. The castigation of Iran continued, as Iran was designated part of an "axis of evil" in the president's State of the Union Address in January 2002.

Ironically, in the same issue of *Foreign Affairs*, there appeared an article by Robin Wright, then of the *Los Angeles Times* and author of *Sacred Rage*, the well-known book about Iran's politics and society. Citing quite different evidence than that articulated by Bush and Rice, Wright portrays an Iran of vastly contradictory forces in politics, religion, and society. She notes that the challenge facing a new U.S. administration would be how it chooses to influence the forces of moderation within Iran, especially regarding terrorism, regional security, and peace with Israel. In Wright's analysis appeared a theme that would be underscored over the next eighteen months in reports from the Council on Foreign Relations and the Carnegie Endowment for International Peace: Iranian positions on foreign policy issues would be heavily influenced by the style and substance of U.S. policy toward Iran.

The claim from Washington became that no state that seeks peace needs to acquire nuclear weapons. This is a very plausible assertion and one worthy of support. But there also exists the principle used by the U.S. Catholic bishops in *The Challenge of Peace*: that there might be a strictly conditioned, temporal, moral acceptance of a policy of nuclear deterrence under conditions of serious external threat. There are some who consider that this still comprises the operative policy and moral rationale for the United States to hold its own nuclear weapons stockpiles. Therefore, we ask: between the mid-1990s and 2003, did Iran face legitimate national security concerns that might warrant a nuclear deterrent?

We believe that the evidence suggests that at least three nuclear-related and well-documented security concerns might prompt the Iranians to hold or develop nuclear weapons. First, the emergence of the Taliban in Afghanistan, and their alignment with al Qaeda, were not developments welcomed by the Iranians. Second, Iran expressed deep concern about the "Talibanization" of Pakistan and that nation's acquisition of nuclear weapons. A third major Iranian security concern is not well documented in the United States, but caused a major news story in Europe and the Middle East: the presence of nuclear weapons in Israel. In ending UN sanctions against Iraq, former U.S. Ambassador Negroponte proclaimed "the final triumph of Security Council Resolution 687." But the Iranian foreign minister quickly suggested that there was still one provision that hadn't been operationalized in SCR 687: the establishment of a nuclear-free zone in the Middle East. He underscored the hypocrisy Iran saw in the willingness of the United States and the West to leave this situation unchallenged.

No serious analyst of terrorism in the Middle East can come to a conclusion other than that, historically, Iran has been one of the major sponsors of terrorism. Its support for Hezbollah in Lebanon has been consistent, while aid to Palestinian groups and others elsewhere in the Middle East has varied. But many of the same analysts would note the difference between Iran's sponsorship of terrorists within the regional context of the Palestinian struggle against Israel, and the lack of an Iranian alliance with global terrorists who directly threaten the United States. And, again in reference to specialists on Iran, like Robin Wright, the future of such support for Hezbollah and the role of Iran in Palestinian strategies are also subjects of intense internal debate.

Conflicting evidence about and interpretation of Iranian support for terrorism is reflected in a pronounced manner in the mid-2003 disagreement between the United States and Iran regarding the latter's treatment of al Qaeda members in Iran. For their part, the Iranians claimed that they had, consistent with their international obligations, regularly detained, questioned, and when appropriate tried and convicted members of al Qaeda. The portrayal by the U.S. government, echoed in U.S. news sources, was that Iran was "harboring" al Qaeda. Portrayal in Middle

Eastern and European newspapers was that Iran's detention with limited judicial action was much like the style employed by the United States in dealing with al Qaeda suspects. The controversy continues even now.

As we add up the three U.S. concerns — rogue state status, weapons of mass destruction, and aiding and abetting of terrorism — we believe that the evidence for making a case for a preemptive strike against Iran in the summer of 2003 was mixed. If allowed to run its course, we suspect that the arguments on the political and military side by those eager for war would probably have focused on the extent to which Iran constituted an "imminent threat" due to the mixed evidence.

As we now know, as the military situation in Iraq deteriorated, the calls for similar preemptive war against Iran became less politically viable. Moreover, and of considerable import, by early 2004 a quite different set of possibilities was created by increased Iranian cooperation with the International Atomic Energy Agency (IAEA) and the success of a European economic incentive package embraced by Iran. The crisis that would have meant preemptive war had been — to a certain extent — resolved without resort to force.

What role might have the articulation of a presumption against the use of force played in this case? It would have demanded of citizens and policymakers that, even in uncertain and insecure times, a much higher standard of proof governing "evidence" and a strict burden of proof of ethical rightness would have to be met. The Iranian case shows definitively that to pursue the preemptive war that some called for against Iran was ultimately unnecessary *and* that the possibility of achieving U.S. objectives short of this was not sufficiently explored by the war proponents. Only a strict holding to a presumption against force can, consistent with just war thinking, forestall such disregard for nonwar options.

We must acknowledge that the case for preemption has not been willing to deal with the bitter ironies of the Iraq and Iran cases. The former is a case of actual preemption that went wrong, the latter a proposed preemption that was unnecessary and would have been equally wrong. The balance, prudence, and higher standards that the presumption against the use of force pushes us to employ simply must be the prevailing rubric, even in these dangerous and uncertain times.

THE CLASSICAL JUST WAR POSITION

Gregory Reichberg, *senior researcher, International Peace Research Institute, Oslo*

Certain forms of wrongdoing are so grave that they merit a vigorous armed response. This response is not merely justifiable or allowable, because in some circumstances countering grave injustice is positively called for. This is the medieval notion of *bellum justum*, or just war.

Those of us in the classical tradition object to the idea that there is a presumption against war in the church's tradition, because it tends to put all the weight on making the tradition a standard of criticism of government policy and almost no weight on the concept that sometimes the use of force is morally obligatory.

In the classical understanding, defense from attack is not the only rationale for just war. In addition to legitimate defense, the tradition recognized three other just causes for the use of lethal military force: restitution, regaining things wrongly taken, such as land or honor; redress, seizing things owed that have been wrongly withheld; and punishment, restoring the balance of justice by avenging wrongdoing. Together, these three causes constitute the ground for what Vitoria termed "offensive war," *bellum offensivum*. This stands in contrast to the other just cause mentioned, defense against attack, which Vitoria termed *bellum defensivum*.

The classical just war thinkers construed legitimate defense quite narrowly: repelling armed attack. Their definitions correspond closely to the famous Webster definition of defense as "a necessity of reaction, instant, overwhelming, leaving no choice of means, and no moment for deliberation." This conception allowed for acts of interceptive defense. If, for example, the Japanese war planes that were flying toward Pearl Harbor at the onset of the Second World War had been shot down, even before entering U.S. air space, this would have been a legitimate act of self-defense, since the attack was in some sense already underway.

The narrow definition of self-defense also allows for some preemptive defense: military strikes to counter an attack that, from clear and manifest signs, is about to begin. But the classical tradition forbids, on moral grounds, preventive military strikes, strikes that aim purely and simply to hinder or eliminate an adversary's capacity to do future harm.

But, as already noted, aside from defense, there are three other just causes for war. Is there a role for preventive force in them, particularly in punishment? Punishment looks backward: a wrong has been done and the fabric of justice must be restored. Yet punishment also looks forward: it aims to deter the same party from repeating acts of wrongdoing in the future. In other words, a wrong done in the past can be the ground for preventive action in the future. Vitoria argues that if a certain regime has engaged in a particularly unjust action that is clear and documentable, then preventive action can be taken to the point of deposing that regime's rulers.

However, this broadening of just cause to include preventive military action is counterbalanced by an accompanying narrowing. This narrowing has two aspects. First, if a state is going to use preventive action to address a wrong, something like due process of law will be needed (a requirement that does not apply for self-defense). The second aspect is that only duly authorized leaders have the license to wage war for restorative or punitive ends. For the classical just war thinkers, this authority resides in the sovereign (whether a single ruler or a council); it is not a prerogative of private individuals or subordinate rulers.

Preemptive War: Going to war to counter an attack that is imminent.

Preventive War: Going to war to counter an attack that is foreseeable or conceivable at some time in the future.

—Yoram Dinstein, *War, Aggression, and Self-Defense*

Let's leap forward three centuries to 1945 and the founding of the United Nations. An argument can be made that the UN Charter follows the classical just war schema of defensive and offensive war — the schema just outlined — except what the tradition openly termed *bellum offensivum* the charter euphemistically termed "enforcement action." Another difference, more substantive, is that the charter severely narrows the authority condition required for offensive war. Under the new legal regime created by the charter, the authority to wage war for restitution, redress, or punishment is vested solely in a multinational body, the UN Security Council.

Let's assume we adopt the UN Charter as a normative text for the present application of classical just war principles, particularly the condition of legitimate authority. Does this rule out any unilateral resort to offensive force, including preventive military action based on a prior wrong? Well, the classical thinkers, Vitoria in particular, did recognize the possibility that those holding legitimate war-making authority might be derelict in their duties. They might be unwilling or for some reason unable to prosecute injustice, to resist evil. In such a case, Vitoria maintained that the authority to wage war could, by virtue of necessity, pass from a higher to a lower authority, so injustice would not go unchecked and the rightful order of the world would not come undone. Suarez, however, did not agree. He believed it better for injustice to go unpunished so the rightful lines of authority would be upheld, because these lines are essential to international order.

Robert Royal, *president, Faith and Reason Institute*

I want to make three brief points. First, I disagree with Professor Cusimano Love. There is something new in front of us. I think it's only a verbal similarity to say that there have been terrorism and weapons of mass destruction in the past. But not like what we're facing now. This truly raises the ante.

And I want to point out that the whole issue of weapons of mass destruction, that Iraq had them — this is not simply a fantasy of the administration and its supporters. There are things that we — all of us — thought we knew back then. In 1990, Iraq told the UN that it had two thousand gallons of anthrax and several tons of the nerve agent VX. As recently as earlier this year [2003], Hans Blix, the UN weapons inspector, told the Security Council that there is no convincing evidence that these were ever destroyed. This was not just something that the "Bushies" invented whole cloth. Even President Clinton, Al Gore, their secretary of defense, and their CIA director said that the weapons were there and were dangerous. So, essentially, did Jacques Chirac, Gerhard Schroeder, and many others in Europe, again not only Tony Blair and close American allies. This is something that everyone believed, that Iraq posed a threat to the region and potentially to the United States as well. And it's important in retrospect not to lose that yardstick.

> One hundred million people were killed in the twentieth century by governments not in conditions of warfare.
>
> — Robert Royal

The second point. I believe that, quite rightly, the church began to emphasize in the twentieth century a presumption against war because of the unprecedented nature of weapons that now exist. But the question we have to ask ourselves is this. Those wonderful men, Augustine, Aquinas, Vitoria, Suarez, were not only brilliant thinkers but were shrewd and wise observers of the world in which they existed. If they were alive today, would they think: Ah, this is something new that needs to be analyzed within the tradition? I think in fact it is. It isn't a retreat from the central tradition of just war, but an application of it to our own circumstances.

My last point is this. If we don't have criteria in advance by which to say that something crosses the line of what we will tolerate — development of weapons, support for terrorists — if we don't have criteria that help us to limit when states are going to go to war in these circumstances, then we will truly live in a Hobbesian world. In my view, it is best that we start developing such criteria now, when we have the leisure for reflection. Developing those criteria would not be, as is often claimed, establishing rules for making aggressive war more likely. On the contrary, they would provide us with principles arrived at in conditions of calm and rational reflection rather than in the wake of pressures following another terrorist attack. So better now than in the predictably massive public pressure then.

QUESTIONS FOR REFLECTION
AND DISCUSSION

1. One criterion of how to fight a war justly — after the decision has been made to go to war — is proportionality. The damage inflicted in a war must not exceed the harm originally done that was the cause of the war. Today, one element of that criterion has come to be the protection of innocents, the noncombatants. A point raised at the forum was that modern warfare meets this criterion because of technology — precision bombing, for example. Elements of the infrastructure — electricity and water, for example — can be targeted to good effect; they can be destroyed but casualties will be limited. But what happens afterward, if there is no electricity or no clean water and people die as a result? Is this just?

2. One criticism of pacifism is that it is passive. Jim Wallis said that it is not enough to say no to war, that pacifism, to be effective, must offer concrete solutions in place of war. Think about the lead-up to the war in Iraq. What things could have been done to prevent the war? What avenues were not explored? What wasn't tried? Brainstorm some possibilities.

3. The classical just war position holds that there are occasions when the use of force is necessary to restore justice. Are there times when a nation must intervene somewhere in order to right a wrong? If one accepts this idea, then what are the limits to such a use of force?

4. Professor and well-known commentator on just war theory James Turner Johnson maintains that the use of force is inherently neutral and that force can be used for good as well as evil. He takes issue with the contemporary just war position's presumption against the use of force as a foundation for their position. What do you think?

PRACTICAL APPLICATION

In what ways can you contribute to the promotion of peace and the avoidance of war?

Chapter Four

The Current Situation

Chapter 2 examined three parallel traditions within the church in peace and war. Chapter 3 looked at how these traditions are playing out today. There has been a renewed interest in recent years in these traditions. The devastations of the last century, with the far-reaching effects of two world wars and the horrors of weapons of mass destruction, have led many people to look again at the role of the church and individual Christians in peacemaking.

However, the church and the world are, for many people, two separate arenas. What can the world do with the insights and teachings of the church? The issue of how these traditions actually interact in the world today is crucial. How are they regarded by the people charged with making decisions in matters of war and peace? Do they have a role to play at the level of policymaking?

One of the goals of the November 2003 forum was to bring together the thinking of the church on these issues and the world of public policy. Leading scholars, theologians, and activists wrote papers that explained the pacifist position and the two just war traditions and how they relate to the current international situation. At the forum, three people involved in the policy world responded to these papers and shared their perspectives on the different traditions.

AMERICAN POLICYMAKERS SPEAK

Albert C. Pierce, *director, Center for the Study of Professional Military Ethics, U.S. Naval Academy*

> *Dr. Pierce addressed the ways in which each of the three positions influences, or might influence, policymaking.*

With regard to the *pacifist tradition*, policymakers tend to see it as an inevitable feature on the political landscape, usually in the form of demonstrations, but usually a minor factor on the political landscape, one policymakers generally feel comfortable ignoring. Policymakers perceive pacifism as representing an ideal, but one that is of little practical use to them in trying to solve pressing problems in the real world.

45

Among the issues the three groups were asked to address, the pacifist position would resonate most in the use of nuclear, biological, and chemical weapons; UN authorization for military action, including economic sanctions enforced by military means, on Iran; and peacekeeping and conflict resolution. In this last area, the pacifist tradition might have something useful to say to policymakers in the context of today's Afghanistan and today's Iran in trying to build a peace within fractured, fragmented societies.

> If we have to use force, it is because we are America. We are the indispensable nation. We stand tall. We see further into the future.
>
> —Madeleine Albright, former secretary of state

A typical reaction from policymakers on one point made in the pacifist paper [see Recommendations 2 and 3 listed by Michael Baxter in chapter 3] might be, "You criticize Israel for attacks on noncombatants, but for the Palestinians all you say is that we should spend more to improve their living conditions." But the paper is silent on Palestinian violence, and this would lead most policymakers to see this position as biased and therefore largely irrelevant.

The approach taken in the paper from the *contemporary just war tradition* is largely consistent with international law, including the law of armed conflict, which is woven into the fabric of policymaking. This position's point, that the just war tradition is not a mathematical formula but something that requires judgment, would also resonate with policymakers because judgment is the essence of policymaking.

There are also interesting ways in which the just war tradition parallels political-military-strategic considerations. For example, the just war idea of probability of success would translate into "feasibility" in military language. Last resort can be linked with the strategic-political argument of "Let's give sanctions a chance."

One important contribution of this articulation of the just war tradition is to remind people that just cause is not the only criterion involved in war; there are five other *ad bellum* criteria as well [legitimate authority, right intention, last resort, reasonable chance of success, and proportionality]. At the same time, what constitutes just cause is a central issue for policymakers.

As for the *classical just war tradition*, that position's paper has considerable resonance in the policymaking world, for example, with the Bush administration's strategy on preemption, Madeleine Albright's posture on the use of force (see the quotation above), and the Reagan administration's strategy in Central America (see the quotation below). In particular, the paper discusses America's "unique capability for leadership": the idea that someone has to do something about this; no one else will; we can; we should; we will. This fits in well with Madeleine Albright's description of the United States as "the indispensable nation."

The linkage between terrorism and weapons of mass destruction lies at the heart of the policy debate today, and it should lead us to rethink the traditional distinction between preemptive and preventive war in the light of new and contemporary realities. The paper's emphasis on America's special responsibilities and "certain prerogatives" points, though, to another problem — that of having, in effect, one set of rules for one nation and another set for everyone else. One policy issue that was not addressed by this position is the problem that arises from the fact that U.S. decisions and actions have the potential to set precedents in customary international law, precedents that could well be invoked in the future by other nations.

The United States was heavily involved in wars in Nicaragua, El Salvador and Guatemala in the 1980s in what [President] Reagan described as an effort to stem Soviet influence in the hemisphere.
— *Washington Post,* June 10, 2004

Finally, all three papers were largely or wholly silent on national interest, which is always central in any policymaking debate on the use of force overseas.

Pamela Quanrud, *U.S. Department of State*

Pamela Quanrud described the three traditions as three different toolboxes and presented them as ways to approach and solve the problem of war.

Pacifism is not used as a national security strategy by any nation in the world with a population over a hundred thousand. However, many early prevention tools should come from this toolbox, such as education and aid, because these things help national security by making the world a peaceful place through nonviolent development.

The second toolbox — the contemporary just war position — contains within it the pacifist toolbox. It can use anything in the pacifist toolbox, but it is bigger because it admits that going to war may be necessary. The difference between them is that there exists in the contemporary just war toolbox a threat and the potential for violence.

The third toolbox — the classical just war position — is the biggest, because it contains within it the other two. It has a much stronger presumption that war could be used.

The pacifist position is grossly underdeveloped. It could be useful not just for governments but also for nongovernmental organizations and civil society. Even though pacifism is associated with protests and conscientious objection, it is actually a very active stance; it is not passive. It is important to learn how to activate it.

The contemporary just war position could also be made more applicable. In particular, its tools must be developed and made appealing to policymakers; it cannot rely on theory but must become more concrete. It must demonstrate where its ideas have been used, where it has been put to work.

For both the contemporary and classical just war positions, a relatively new arena that presents a challenge is that of the human rights movement. The classical just war presentation said very little about what to do in a situation where a horrible wrong was happening or was about to happen. The boundary between that which is the sovereign right of a country and that which is the obligation of the international community has blurred over the last forty years or so, which offers opportunities to think about intervention in the cause of peace and justice.

Frank Sullivan, *former staff director for the Senate Armed Services Committee and the Senate Appropriations Committee*

> *Frank Sullivan described how American military thinking resembles just war principles and how our society and military face new challenges today.*

First, the principles of the just war theory are embedded in Western and American society, especially in the military. For example, noncombatant immunity is called in Pentagonese "the CNN effect." We do not want civilian casualties; we should not target civilians or destroy them accidentally. Proportionate means translates into "smart targeting": using precision weapons and information technology to avoid civilian casualties. Reasonable chance of success in Pentagonese is "overmatching strength": making sure we can really do something and making sure we can win. The protection of innocents is accepted by most people. Helping the Kurds against Saddam Hussein — the military mission — was called just cause. Right intention is exit strategy. An exit strategy indicates that we're not in it for ourselves, not doing it for our own gain, but for other reasons. Last resort was shown in the original Kuwait battle in Desert Storm [in the early discussion about whether or not to go to war]. That was about the question: Have we done everything we can before we use force?

We live in a changing world, and it presents new problems. First, there has been an explosion, at the end of the twentieth century and the beginning of the twenty-first, of the destructive power available to small groups. This power includes weapons of mass destruction, but also biological weapons, like the anthrax attack on Capitol Hill, and dirty bombs, and even conventional explosives.

Second, there is a globalization of technology, information, and finance. This means that almost anyone can obtain this destructive power. We're having to deal with different people than we did in the past.

Third, we have the growth of nonstate actors, failed states, and rogue states.

Fourth, is the growth of radicalism: suicide bombers in the Middle East, child soldiers in Africa, drug lords in South America. They all operate in a radical way, and this is something we're not used to dealing with.

Finally, there is the growing vulnerability of complex Western life and society. We depend on power, on water supplies, and on information technology. Our whole society and form of government would be changed if these were attacked.

TODAY'S DANGERS
by J. Bryan Hehir

Fr. Hehir, formerly director of the U.S. Catholic bishops' Office of Social Development and World Peace and currently on the faculty of the Kennedy School of Government, Harvard University, makes the following observation of the current international situation. He sees it as having three distinguishing characteristics: weapons of mass destruction, terrorism, and issues of humanitarian intervention. Each of these phenomena will be explored, along with some other elements in the world today that also affect warfare.

Weapons of Mass Destruction

Weapons of mass destruction fall into three categories: biological weapons, chemical weapons, and nuclear weapons.

When we speak of *biological weapons*, we are looking at some of humanity's most-feared diseases, such as anthrax, plague, and smallpox. All of these diseases have touched human history. The Black Death seems to have arisen in China. It then decimated the population of Europe, once in the fourteenth century and again in the seventeenth. Smallpox was a scourge all over the world until recent years; the last U.S. case was in 1949 and the last naturally occurring case was in Somalia in 1977. Both diseases — plague and smallpox — killed millions of Native Americans when they came into contact with European adventurers. As for anthrax, some scholars believe that the fifth Egyptian plague described in the Bible was anthrax. The disease was later responsible for killing thousands of cattle in Europe in the 1600s.

Some of these diseases were also used as weapons in the past. The first known use of a biological weapon was in 1346, in the Genoese city of Kaffa. Attacking Tartars had laid siege to the city but were then stricken by a mysterious and deadly disease: the plague. The Tartars had to retreat, but before doing so, they used catapults to throw the bodies of infected soldiers over the city walls. Kaffa, too, succumbed; the disease then spread to the rest of Europe. During the French and Indian War in North America, in Pennsylvania, the British gave smallpox-infected blankets to Indians who were allied with the French. An epidemic broke out among the Indians, allowing the British to capture a strategic fort. More recent years have also witnessed biological warfare. Between 1937 and 1945, it is estimated that Japan killed more than three hundred thousand Chinese with biological weapons such as anthrax and plague. And, finally, in the United States, a still-unknown person or group killed five people with anthrax spores in the fall of 2001.

A factor that adds to the uncertainty today are the suspicions that some nations still have bioweapons programs, despite the 1972 Biological Weapons Convention that prohibits making, storing, or using biological weapons.

Chemical weapons were first used during the First World War, in 1915, when the Germans used chlorine gas against French, Algerian, and Canadian troops at Ypres. Five thousand soldiers died and ten thousand were disabled, some of them permanently. The British soon began using poison gas in retaliation, and by 1916 gas was used routinely by both sides. Two other gases, phosgene and mustard, were added to the arsenal. At the end of the war, it was estimated that gas had killed about a hundred thousand soldiers and maimed a million more.

The Geneva Protocol of 1925 banned the use of chemical warfare, but after the war several countries developed these weapons secretly: the Soviet Union, Germany, Japan, Italy, Britain, and the United States. A new kind of chemical weapon was produced: nerve agents, among them tabun and sarin. However, chemical weapons were not used during World War II; what one study calls "a fragile stalemate" appears to have prevented it.

During the Cold War, chemical weapons continued to be developed and stockpiled. Certain nonlethal but toxic chemicals were used in a few instances. The British used a herbicide, a form of Agent Orange, against Communist rebels in Malaya in the 1950s, and the United States used it in Vietnam. In later years, nations other than the major powers developed chemical weapons. In the 1980s, Iraq used poison gases in its war with Iran, and later used them again battling Iraqi Kurds. In both cases, thousands of people died.

Now, even some organizations — what are called nonstate actors — have acquired chemical weapons. In 1994 and again in 1995, the doomsday cult Aum Shinrikyo released sarin gas in Japan.

The Chemical Weapons Convention was approved in 1993, banning the development, production, and possession of chemical weapons. More than 140 countries signed it. Despite this, Libya, Syria, and North Korea have these weapons, and it is possible that other nations do as well.

We all know at least some of the history of *nuclear weapons*. The United States opened the nuclear age with the bombs it dropped on Hiroshima and Nagasaki to end the Second World War. After that, in the atmosphere of the Cold War, other countries rushed to attain nuclear capability. The Soviet Union tested its first nuclear weapon in 1949, the United Kingdom in 1952, France in 1960, China in 1964, and India in 1974. For years, the world lived with the fear that a nuclear attack could occur at any time; the Cuban Missile Crisis in 1962 was probably the closest this came to happening.

In some ways, the prospect of nuclear disaster seems less likely today. Many countries have signed the Nuclear Nonproliferation Treaty and, with the breakup of the Soviet Union, the tensions of the Cold War have abated. However, other tensions have taken their place, and some of them are nuclear. Some of the countries that have nuclear arsenals today are ones that are engaged in long term, sometimes violent, feuds with other countries. India and Pakistan have nuclear weapons, for example, and their feud is volatile. Some experts feel that the threat of disaster is even greater now that nuclear weapons are added to this unstable mix.

> Through the release of atomic energy, our generation has brought into the world the most revolutionary force since prehistoric man's discovery of fire. This basic force of the universe cannot be fitted into the outmoded concept of narrow nationalisms.
>
> —Albert Einstein, January 22, 1947

Another factor affects the current international situation with regard to all types of weapons of mass destruction. It is true that the arms race of the Cold War is over and that many countries have dismantled their weapons programs. However, this very fact has created a new and alarming situation. With the dismantling of these programs comes the problem of what to do with the leftovers: deactivated nuclear warheads, closed production plants, and nuclear material. In some places, such as Russia, the necessary security to protect these things is not in place. There have been attempts to smuggle fissile material out of the country; some of the thieves were caught, but not all. It is not known where the stolen material went, but the fear is that it fell into the hands of terrorists. Similar danger exists in other countries, where biological labs and chemical facilities have material attractive to terrorists.

Terrorism

Terrorism has a history; it is not new to our time. (Dr. Maryann Cusimano Love makes this point as well, both in chapter 3 and chapter 5.) The *sicarii* were Jewish Zealots in first-century Palestine who fought Roman rule. They assassinated people, burned granaries, and poisoned water supplies to try to force people to join them in their struggle. From the eleventh to the thirteenth centuries, a Muslim group called the Assassins killed political leaders in the Middle East.

According to experts, modern terrorism began during the French Revolution, when Robespierre justified the use of violence and terror by the state in order to protect itself.

One expert, Audrey Kurth Cronin of Georgetown University, outlines what she calls three ideological catalysts for modern terrorism — democratization, decolonization, and spiritual motivation — which led to three kinds of terrorism in more recent history.

The first kind, linked to democratization, expressed itself in a wave of democratic rebellions against long-established empires in Europe in the nineteenth century, particularly in Russia, Armenia, Macedonia, Serbia, and Ireland. Even today, we see this kind of terrorism in places like the Balkans and Kashmir. The second kind of terrorism, associated with decolonization, arose after World War I and is linked to the efforts of former colonies to attain independence. This occurred in countries such as Algeria, Vietnam, South Africa, and Israel. Related to this is the leftist terrorism we saw in Europe in the late twentieth century. Finally, a different form of terrorism is active in the world today, epitomized by the September 11, 2001, attacks: terrorism arising out of religious motivation. It is ironic, as Cronin points out, that we seem to be going full cycle, in that this kind of terrorism is akin to the type practiced by the sicarii almost two thousand years ago.

The definition of terrorism varies, depending on who is giving the definition. Even within the U.S. government, the experts don't always agree. The State Department defines terrorism as "premeditated, politically motivated violence perpetrated against noncombatant targets by subnational groups or clandestine agents, usually intended to influence an audience." Most experts agree that terrorism's goals are fundamentally political ones — aimed at changing the existing order — rather than criminal ones.

Divergence of opinion arises when one considers who can be a terrorist. Some experts believe that states can — and have, and still do — engage in terrorist activity, and call it "terrorism from above." To support their position, they use examples such as Hitler's Germany, Stalin's Russia, Khomeini in Iran, Pol Pot, Chile, and Argentina, among others. Further, they argue that this kind of terrorism — terrorism by the state against its own people — has been more widespread and more deadly, especially over the last century, than terrorism by nonstate actors.

However, a strong sentiment does exist that terrorists are strictly nonstate actors, that terrorism is something else when engaged in by states. And one characteristic of terrorists today that is particularly alarming is that they cross national boundaries. Modern technology has allowed them to create a network that can operate in countries all over the world.

Humanitarian Intervention

Humanitarian intervention is something else that is not new. There are examples of it as far back as ancient times; for example, Syracuse was freed from Carthaginian oppression by the Corinthian Timoleon. A later instance occurred in the early 1800s, when France, Britain, and Russia intervened militarily to liberate Christian Greeks, who were suffering brutal oppression under the Muslim Turks. The intervention led to an independent Greece in 1830. Also in the nineteenth century, France intervened in Syria on behalf of Christians and the Russians intervened in the Balkans for Christians under Turkish rule. The United States, in 1898, did the same for the people of Cuba, who were suffering under Spanish oppression. Cuba gained its freedom shortly thereafter.

No one can demand that you be neutral toward the crime of genocide. If there is a judge in the whole world who can be neutral toward this crime, that judge is not fit to sit in judgment.

— Gideon Hausner, chief prosecutor, Eichmann trial

However, it must also be said that these interventions, whenever they have occurred, happen for a variety of motivations and the interventions themselves proceed in different ways. Clearly, not all are purely — or even primarily — carried out for humanitarian reasons. This is true for the earlier interventions, and also for subsequent ones. Not everyone agrees that all military actions launched under the label of humanitarian intervention actually deserve that label. One expert has commented that actions having

A Sudanese woman cooks sorghum, her family's only meal of the day, at the Bredjing refugee camp in northeastern Chad, August 29, 2004. In Bredjing, the number of refugees has swelled to more than 40,000, with new refugees arriving every day. Catholic News Service photo/ Steven Steele.

other motivations but claiming humanitarian ones risk giving humanitarian intervention a bad name. It is therefore important to look more closely at exactly what we mean by this term.

Human Rights Watch is an international nongovernmental organization dedicated to protecting the rights of people around the world. Unlike most such organizations, it does have a policy on humanitarian intervention. Its criteria for what constitutes a valid reason for such intervention follow, and it must be recognized that these criteria are particularly crucial when the intervention is not invited by the government in question.

First, and most important, humanitarian intervention is justified only in the presence of ongoing or imminent genocide or comparable mass slaughter or loss of life. Tyranny in and of itself is not enough to warrant military action. If this criterion is met, then Human Rights Watch outlines five other factors that must be considered. First, military action must be the action of last resort, used only after other alternatives have been tried. Second, the intervention must have a primarily humanitarian purpose. Third, the means used in the intervention itself must respect international human rights and law. Some abuses cannot be accepted in order to stop others. Fourth, it must be reasonably likely that military action will do more good than harm. Finally, Human Rights Watch prefers that the UN Security Council or some other body with significant multilateral authority endorse the intervention.

This definition gives us some tools with which to analyze various interventions. It makes it clear, for instance, that hostage rescue attempts, or a government's attempts to rescue its own nationals, whatever their other benefits, are not humanitarian interventions. The U.S. action in Grenada in 1983 falls into this category. Neither are interventions motivated primarily by issues of national self-interest, even if a humanitarian crisis does exist and is relieved by the intervention. This was the case in some other actions, such as India's invasion of the former East Pakistan in 1971 and Vietnam's invasion of Cambodia in 1978. In both instances, harsh repression and suffering existed in the invaded country—but alleviating it does not seem to have been the main reason for the action (and, in fact, the invaders did not claim that it was). So these, too, should not be considered humanitarian interventions.

The interventions of the 1990s are most familiar to us, and their legacy is mixed at best. In Somalia in the early years of the decade, a UN effort began as a mission to oversee food delivery in a famine brought on by a civil war. But it turned into a military campaign led by U.S. troops — a campaign that ended in a U.S. withdrawal — with many casualties resulting.

Civil war broke out in Bosnia in 1992, followed by ethnic cleansing carried out by Serbs. The UN Security Council authorized the use of force to help the distribution of relief supplies to the people. In 1993, the UN set up safe areas in Bosnia for Muslims. But one of those safe areas, Srebrenica, was attacked by Serbs in 1995 and thousands of Muslims were massacred. UN peacekeeping forces were nearby but did nothing to prevent it.

In 1994, in the African nation of Rwanda, more than eight hundred thousand people were slaughtered in a matter of a few months, by other Rwandans, in a political and ethnic cataclysm. No one in the outside world intervened, despite clear indications that something terrible was being planned.

In these three interventions, and in others, such as in Angola, Sierra Leone, and Kosovo, it is easy to lay blame, to point out where things went wrong and what should have been done differently. It is much harder to learn from what happened and apply these lessons to the future. But it is crucial that we do this, for, unfortunately, such crises will arise again.

What new elements of war do these policy makers and commentators suggest?

Technology

Warfare today looks nothing like it did in the past. Some military theorists believe war has changed in the use of manpower, in tactics, even in overall strategy. One of the main reasons modern war looks different, though, is *technology*. Prehistoric people used slings and stones; later warriors used swords and bows and arrows. In medieval battles, the horse, the mace, and the longbow were crucial. More recent times witnessed the appearance of muskets, barbed wire, tanks, bombs, and airplanes. Technology is certainly the most visible way in which the face of warfare has changed over the centuries. The most immediate example, of course, is nuclear weapons, but staggering developments have been made in many other areas as well.

Computer technology — undreamed of not that long ago — lies behind many of these developments. Some of them are used in what are called precision weapons: weapons that can locate very specific targets miles away. Cruise missiles are unmanned airplanes that take bombs to distant areas. Fighter pilots use sidewinder missiles, which can find their targets by themselves in air-to-air combat. Stinger missiles, employed on the ground, can automatically find and destroy attacking planes. Patriot missiles can detect and hit incoming missiles.[1]

Technology is also used for navigation; the Global Positioning System, developed in the first Gulf War, uses satellites to help troops find their way when visibility is difficult. Surveillance is another area expanded with the use of technology. Something called portable unmanned aerial vehicles are small devices, remote controlled, that can take pictures and detect chemical agents, all from a distance. Finally, in scenes that seem to come right out of science fiction movies, remote-controlled robots were used to explore caves to search for Osama bin Laden in Afghanistan and to look for signs of ambush in Iraq.[2]

Computer technology has found another use in warfare: gathering information. Military leaders now can use computer and digital technology — sensors, data bases, networks — to get information on enemy locations and the movement of weapons and supplies. They have the ability to communicate in real time with their forces to make decisions. All this is relatively new. Some military thinkers have written articles that talk about "the exceptional lethality gained by linking real-time information to precision guided weapons and controlling them with digital command and control."[3] They argue that information, rather than manpower or firepower, has become the critical element of modern warfare; the group that can effectively gather and use information will have a decided advantage over its opponents. According to writers John Arquilla and David F. Ronfeldt, the implications of this are far reaching. It means that wealth and size will become less important than technological prowess and flexibility in using it, thus leveling the playing field. They point out that groups such as drug cartels, guerrillas, terrorists, and racial gangs have already learned this lesson.[4]

The Media

Yet technology is not the only new element in warfare. The *media* play an increasingly dominant role in war today. They report it — again, almost in real time — using e-mail and digital and video cameras. These reports reach millions of people around the world, who can keep up with a war's progress almost on a minute-to-minute basis. Maryann Cusimano Love, in her presentation at the forum, called it "the global megaphone: the 24/7 news cycle." Every insurgent attack, every car bomb, every assassination, is beamed back to the United States almost instantly. This was certainly not the case in earlier wars.

In one sense, this means that there is, indeed, a spotlight on the progress of our wars, both politically and militarily. It would seem that everything comes under this media spotlight, and that it would be difficult for hard issues, such as corruption and malfeasance, to go unnoticed. The reports on the abuses at Abu Ghraib prison would appear to confirm this. However, some sources claim that the U.S. media, while they saturate the public with information, are not always providing thoughtful analysis or evenhanded coverage. A March 2005 *Washington Post* and ABC News poll revealed that a majority of Americans still believe that Iraq possessed weapons of mass destruction, even though the facts do not bear this out. Some critics blame this erroneous belief on the media being unwilling to ask hard questions about the war, a refusal to actively investigate and report important issues. To sum up, the role of media is very obviously a major one, but serious questions remain about it.

On the other hand, Americans do not have to get their news from U.S. outlets. If they have access to the Internet, they can get the BBC viewpoint, or the perspective from Chile, New Zealand, India, and many other countries. They can go to the Al-Jazeera network and get that particular perspective from the Arab world. The coverage of the war by these sources — even in countries that are U.S. allies — can be very different from that of the U.S. media. In a grisly development, Americans can, if they wish, even watch the video clips made by the kidnappers of some contractors in Iraq — clips that actually show their prisoners' beheadings. This is also something that was not possible during past wars.

What are we to conclude?

Some scholars believe that warfare has changed dramatically in recent years. They point to developments such as the ones just mentioned — in technology and in the media — to make this argument. Others disagree, asserting that the changes have been a long time coming. For example, what we call insurgency warfare in Iraq was called guerilla warfare in Vietnam. It was also in Vietnam that the media started to bring the war right into our living rooms, and to take on the major role they play in warfare today. Some of the new weapons and instruments used today were developed in the Gulf War, and weapons of mass destruction, as mentioned earlier, go back many years.

One scholar, Mary Kaldor, believes that war has changed, but attributes the change to other causes, such as the effects of globalization and the decline of the nation-state.[5] Another theory, set forth in a recent book by Thomas X. Hammes, holds that war has evolved into something he calls "fourth-generation warfare." He characterizes this kind of war as one that uses social networks (political, economic, social, and military) to "attack the minds of enemy decision makers to destroy the enemy's political will," rather than trying to overcome militarily.[6] Hammes sees the conflict in Iraq as this type of war.

It is true that some elements of contemporary warfare present us with particular moral questions. How do we deal with enemies who don't play by what we consider the rules of fair combat? How do we use the new precision weapons in ethical ways? Does the need to deal with lethal dangers mean that we can't abide by the old restrictions on just war? However we view warfare today, it is crucial that we face and explore these kinds of issues.

QUESTIONS FOR REFLECTION AND DISCUSSION

1. When should the United States intervene in another country's affairs for humanitarian reasons? What grounds would you think are valid for such intervention?

2. The growing role of technology in warfare raises some critical questions. One is this: Just because we *can* do something — create a new weapon, for example — does this mean we should? What guidelines should we follow in developing technology?

3. Do the media have a role in times of crisis, such as humanitarian disaster or war? What should this role be?

PRACTICAL APPLICATION

Using the definition of humanitarian intervention given by Human Rights Watch, discuss whether or not the U.S. invasion of Iraq fits the criteria for such an intervention.

Chapter Five

Effective Ways to Fight Terrorism While Retaining Our Values

The Lord Has Not Given Us a Spirit of Fear

MARYANN CUSIMANO LOVE

The last chapter presented a rather grim picture of the nature of war-fare today. Weapons that can wreak unimaginable havoc, genocide, terrorism: it would be all too easy to conclude that there is little we can do in the face of these threats. Yet there are things we can do. In this chapter, Dr. Maryann Cusimano Love, professor of international relations at Catholic University, outlines some of them. Specifically, she analyzes how we can face the challenge of terrorism by holding on to, and living out, our values.

Today's headlines are disheartening. Terrorists kill innocent civilians, burning, beheading, and mutilating people on live television with instantaneous Internet broadcast. U.S. troops torture detainees in Iraq and Afghanistan, so proud of their deeds that they took reams of digital photos to show off to their friends. The U.S. government will spend nearly $500 billion on the military in 2006, yet despite this high investment in the military means of fighting terrorism, we still feel insecure. We remain "America the Vulnerable,"[1] with police and fire departments that cannot talk to one another, with ports, public health, and other critical infra-structure still open to attacks. As Catholics, we are challenged to view the daily headlines through the eyes of faith. But are our traditions up to the task of meeting these twenty-first century challenges?

The words of 2 Timothy 1:7 are worth remembering: "God has not given us a spirit of fear; but of power, and love, and of a sound mind." If we begin there, then the questions are these: What kinds of power are at our disposal (such as the power of ideas, diplomatic power, and infor-mation power, not merely military power)? How do we appropriately and effectively use our power to combat terrorism, protect civilians, and build the kingdom?

Too often since September 11, we have spent our time erecting barricades, reacting to Code Orange alerts, duct-taping ourselves into seclusion and separation from the world, fearful and suspicious of foreigners and strangers, especially Middle Eastern men. If we believe that we meet Christ in unlikely places, it's important to remember that Christ was a thirty-three-year-old Middle Eastern male and a radical itinerant preacher — precisely the type of person who these days would trigger racial and intelligence profiles and set off alarms as a suspicious person. If Christ were to return to us today, would we let him in? Or would we search him at the airport and detain him without charges?

The United States is the world's most powerful country, yet since September 11, we live in fear and a heightened sense of vulnerability. If we believe that the Lord has not given us a spirit of fear, then we have a moral responsibility not to succumb to fear, not to partake in the politics of fear. Instead, we need to use our reason, our faith, the strength of our communities, and our traditions to wield our power responsibly in the world today, while recognizing the limits of our power and the vulnerabilities to which we are all subject.

We'll look at the war on terrorism, how best to fight it, and whether we are combating it in ways that are consistent with Catholic social teaching and our just war tradition. Since the war on terrorism is primarily a battle of ideas, we'll examine how our means and our morals matter greatly in a 24/7 news and information world. I'll discuss how a layered, multipurpose approach that focuses greater attention on nonmilitary means of international cooperation can give us greater security in line with our values at a fraction of the price of military means and help move us away from an impossible, quixotic quest for 100 percent security from terrorism and threats of weapons of mass destruction. We'll see how the just war tradition is still relevant and necessary, although insufficient to guide the morality of the war on terrorism. We'll conclude with suggestions for what we can do to practice policies in line with our values.

DISPELLING MYTHS: WHAT IS TERRORISM AND THE WAR ON TERRORISM?

First, the war on terrorism.[2] What is it? "One man's terrorist is another's freedom fighter" is a common cliché used to argue that there are no clear definitions of terrorism. But this cliché is wrong. Terrorism is a tactic, not an ideology. It is the tactic of clandestine groups deliberately targeting and killing noncombatants (in violation of the laws of armed conflict) in order to generate a psychological reaction disproportionate to the physical damage inflicted. Fear, shock, and overreaction are the terrorist's goals, more than the destruction of a nightclub or a housing barracks. Thus the war against terrorism is a war against a tactic, not a country or a particular group.

Common usage of the word "terrorism" in media and politics can vary widely and is often imprecise. The term is frequently used as an insult, describing any use of violence with which one disagrees as terrorism. But beyond the variations found in particular treaties by different organizations, there is much core academic and legal agreement about the definition of terrorism. Terrorism is an illegitimate use of force (by non-state, clandestine groups); terrorism is illegitimate specifically because it intentionally and deliberately targets violence against noncombatants, in violation of centuries of natural law and international law regarding the rules of war.[3] Terrorism is a tool, not an ideology. It is a means, a strategy, not an end or a belief system, unlike other "isms" — communism, fascism, and socialism. It is a tactic used by groups with nothing else in common ideologically, politically, or geographically, from separatists in Ireland to Maoists in the mountains of Peru to conservative Islamic extremists in the Arabian desert.

God has not given us a spirit of fear; but of power, and love, and of a sound mind.

— 2 Timothy 1:7

Terrorists target noncombatants *because* doing this is a violation of deeply held moral and legal convictions. Killing noncombatants generates a greater response than killing soldiers, who expect personal risk in their line of work. Terrorists are minority groups without the conventional means to attack their enemies. They deliberately break conventions against killing noncombatants in order to cause a psychological reaction (fear, shock, panic) that is out of proportion to the magnitude of the attack in order to perpetuate political or other goals.[4] For terrorist tactics to gain attention and generate fear, surprise is key. Thus, terrorists must vary their means or they will lose the power to shock. If terrorist violence becomes routine, attacks will no longer reverberate, receive attention, or generate pressure for change toward the terrorists' goals. Surprise and shock are force multipliers, ways of compensating for lesser forces and size. This is why terrorist attacks generally occur in peacetime, not wartime; violence is less shocking during war. Looking to generate big returns with small resources, terrorists look for soft or symbolic targets. Victims are useful only if society likes and empathizes with them, if their deaths cause outrage or fear that "it could be me." In this regard, terrorist tactics have changed over the years. Terrorist groups used to assassinate political leaders, but now rarely do so, as this method fails to generate much public outcry or the fear that any citizen could be next.

The press and political rhetoric often describe terrorists as "madmen." They are not. However heinous their tactics, they are rational and calculating. Their behavior is premeditated, controlled, and intentional, not random. Terrorism is an inherently political act, generally done to bring public pressure to bear on government decisions. For example, al Qaeda studied U.S. military withdrawals after sustaining casualties from surprise attacks in Lebanon in 1984 and Somalia in 1993. They calculated that terrorist attacks that raise the costs of U.S. military presence in the Middle East and the costs of U.S. support of the Saudi, Egyptian, and Israeli regimes would undermine support and encourage change of U.S. policies in the Middle East. Terrorism is distinct from mass uprisings or spontaneous, chaotic violence. It is planned, purposeful political violence, organized by small clandestine groups.[5]

> Terrorism is a tool, not an ideology. It is a means, a strategy, not an end or a belief system. ...It is a tactic used by groups with nothing else in common ideologically, politically, or geographically.

The term "war on terrorism" has been criticized for many reasons. How can a country be at war with a tactic? The slogan is open-ended and ambiguous, and incorrectly identifies war as either the only way or the best way to combat terrorism (more on this point later). Whatever the merits of these criticisms, the war on terrorism refers to a concerted global effort to curtail the use of a specific method of violence.[6] If understood as an international campaign to delegitimize the tactic of terrorism, then it follows in the footsteps of some previous successful efforts to stop a specific tactic of global politics as being particularly barbarous. The International Campaign to Ban Landmines and the prohibitions against slavery and piracy are similar efforts to prohibit certain tactics as being morally reprehensible. In this light, the war on terrorism can be seen as an effort to bring international politics more in line with core values of protecting innocent lives.

ENGAGING THE BATTLE OF IDEAS

Ultimately, terrorism is a battle of ideas more than a battle of competing militaries. Groups choose terrorism to try to compensate for their small numbers and their military inferiority by using the power of ideas and the power of fear. While terrorism is a tactic used by groups with varying ideological agendas, it is always a tactic of asymmetrical conflict used by

militarily weaker parties.[7] The reactions that terrorists seek to provoke —
fear, shock, panic, and attention to their views or goals — are the real
weapons, regardless of whether guns, bombs, or airplanes are employed.
Surprise magnifies the psychological reaction to a terrorist attack, and the
media amplify the message. If the larger population empathizes with the
victims of the terrorist attack, the attacks will produce a disproportionate psychological reaction compared to the actual damage done. After the
September 11 attacks, the real estate market for Manhattan skyscrapers
plummeted. The idea that it could have been anyone in a plane, on their
way to work, or in or near a skyscraper did more damage to the U.S.
economy and society than the initial damage done by the planes to the
buildings. Only in 2005, four years after the 9/11 attacks, is air travel in
the United States returning to pre-9/11 levels.

Military efforts abroad largely do not engage the terrorists on their real
battlefield, the war of ideas. We must cut the flow of recruits willing to
lay down their lives for al Qaeda's ideas, the financiers willing to bankroll
terrorism, and the governments willing to overlook terrorist activities so
long as the terrorists are not conspiring against domestic targets. To do
this, we must counter al Qaeda's ideas and the power of fear with more
attractive and powerful ideas and norms. Missing this values battle in
fighting terrorism leads the United States to turn its back on some of
the most powerful tools at its disposal: ideas, moral persuasion, moder-
ated responses that protect innocents, and the ability to effectively craft a
message and then disseminate it and persuade others of it abroad.

In contrast, Osama bin Laden and his network astutely use the tools
of global media to broadcast their ideas, attract members, and generate
sympathy for their cause. Al Qaeda is fighting for its own moral ideas.
It is fighting against what its members perceive as the violation of the
sanctity of Islamic holy sites by the presence of U.S. troops and the sub-
jugation of the Islamic community and fundamentalist Islamic values by
the preeminence of Western power and influence. In response, the United
States attempts to build an international coalition around an antiterrorism
norm. The United States also is engaged in a war of ideas, and also fights
for its moral ideas — specifically, the protection of noncombatants. But
therein lies a problem: the United States cannot create a global coalition against the killing of noncombatants while it uses means that are
insensitive to noncombatants. The war on terrorism will not work if, in
constructing a global norm to protect innocent noncombatants, means
are used that knowingly and intentionally harm innocents. U.S. security
cannot effectively be considered or sought in isolation. The protection
of innocents and noncombatants is not merely a Catholic, Christian, or
Western concern, or a nicety of international law that can be easily dis-
regarded when inconvenient. It is a widely held norm across cultures and
borders internationally. Protecting U.S. noncombatants by endangering
foreign noncombatants, for example, is not only bad morality, it is bad

militarily. U.S. troops are stationed all over the globe. Actions that under-mine the legitimacy of the U.S. military engender greater opposition to U.S. forces and expose U.S. troops abroad to greater risks.

It is essential to realize that we are not forced to choose between uphold-ing ethical norms or pragmatically advancing U.S. power. Ethics versus power politics is a false choice. Ethics are not opposed to power politics, but are an important and underutilized tool of power in the war on terror-ism, and must be embraced as such. Ethics and just war tradition are power politics assets. They help discredit terrorists; assuage negative pub-lic opinion of the United States in the Arab and Muslim world; prevent the self-defeating overreactions that terrorists seek to create; maintain legitimacy for the effort at home and abroad; retain military ethos and professionalism; build international support for the war on terrorism; and construct a global prohibitionary norm against terrorism.

Particularly in an era of globalization, means matter. The global mega-phone, the 24/7 global news media and Internet news media, casts a wider broadcast net for terrorists to spread their messages, a net not filtered by governments or Western media outlets. This is why norms and just war tradition matter more, not less, in an age of global terrorism — because the world is watching not just the acts of terror, but our response. Any U.S. violations of ethical standards are broadcast immediately and glob-ally, undermining international support and creating greater sympathy for terrorist causes. Because of disproportionate U.S. power in the world, U.S. behavior is held to a higher standard than the behavior of its ad-versaries, who are perceived to have fewer choices in combating such a powerful foe. Additionally, the U.S. military enjoys a global reputation for superb training, discipline, professionalism, morale, and ethos, yet these very characteristics are degraded by divergence from ethical codes in fighting the war on terrorism.

Moral arguments are the basis of al Qaeda's case against the United States. They argue that the U.S. military presence in Saudi Arabia dese-crated the land of Mecca and Medina, holy sites in Islam. This is despite the fact that Muslims serve in the U.S. military, and that U.S. troops were invited in to protect Saudi Arabia from invasion, were stationed far from these holy sites, and are now being withdrawn. Bin Laden believes that ideas matter and has conducted an active global media campaign to promote al Qaeda's norms through videotapes, town hall meetings, and active outreach to the Arab and Muslim press. Polls show these efforts are succeeding. A troublingly high percentage of the Muslim world be-lieves al Qaeda's representation of events. In hour-long polling interviews of ten thousand people in nine mainly Muslim countries that together ac-count for half of all Muslims worldwide (Indonesia, Iran, Jordan, Kuwait, Lebanon, Morocco, Pakistan, Saudi Arabia, and Turkey), only 18 percent of those polled believed Arab men carried out the September 11 attacks; 61 percent did not believe Arabs were responsible.[8] Al Qaeda and other terrorist organizations also seek to win the "hearts and minds" of local populations by "good works" in the Arab world, providing humanitarian, educational, and social service aid and outreach.

By attacking the United States, al Qaeda has attempted to open a new forum for politics blocked by the local Arab governments. Al Qaeda, which considers the Egyptian and Saudi governments to be hypocrites who collaborate with infidels in the desecration of Islam, seeks to overthrow these governments and replace them with a fundamentalist Wahhabi Islamic theocracy that rules by their interpretation of Islamic law. But they do so by attacking the United States, believing it is a better target than Saudi Arabia or Egypt. Since Saudi Arabia is a closed society, attempts to attack the Saudi regime are brutally put down, and their messages do not make it past the heavily state-censored Saudi media to the outside world. More importantly, the killing of Muslims would appear illegitimate and immoral to the Muslim audience al Qaeda addresses. Knowing that morality matters in what they pose as a moral crusade, they use means that are morally acceptable within the context of their brand of Wahhabi Islam. In a dramatic departure from Islamic tradition requiring the protection of noncombatants, al Qaeda argues that since U.S. citizens elect, fund, and cooperate with the U.S. government, they are not noncombatants but are acceptable targets of violence.

Just as al Qaeda attempts to build a global base for its ideals, the United States also attempts to spread global norms. The Bush administration, however, is trying to construct a global norm against terrorism with its hands tied. The administration has placed great emphasis on the military prosecution of the war, at the cost of over a billion dollars a month in Afghanistan[9] and in Iraq.[10] U.S. military support has also been extended to fight terrorists in the Philippines, Georgia, and Yemen. But by emphasizing the military tools to prosecute the war, with insufficient attention to the public diplomacy and moral tools, the United States tries to construct global norms with a muzzle on the means to establish such norms. The State Department spent only $685 million on all public diplomacy efforts around the world in 2004, with only a small portion targeting the Muslim world. U.S. public diplomacy efforts are in disarray;[11] the position of undersecretary for public diplomacy has been vacant for nearly a year, and the previous office holder was in place for only one year.[12] The ineffectiveness of U.S. public diplomacy shows, as support for the United States across the Muslim and Arab world has plummeted, even among U.S. allies such as Egypt, Saudi Arabia, and Indonesia.[13] Writing three years after the September 11 attacks, the 9/11 Commission urged the United States to "engage the struggle of ideas. . . . We should offer an example of moral leadership in the world, committed to treat people humanely, abide by the rule of law, and be generous and caring to our neighbors. . . . Just as we did in the Cold War, we need to defend our values abroad vigorously. . . . If the United States does not act aggressively to define itself in the Islamic world, the extremists will gladly do the job for us."[14] Edward S. Walker, former assistant secretary of state for the Near East, concurs that "public diplomacy . . . has been a critical missing link" in U.S. policy toward the Islamic world. "The basic reason we're not very effective," Walker said, "is we don't even try."[15]

The ideas war has been a poor stepchild to the military conduct of the war, in part because the U.S. diplomatic and public diplomacy infrastructure has been so badly degraded over the years. Arab linguists are in critically short supply throughout the government, undercutting the government's effectiveness in the Arab world. Weakened by budget cuts throughout the 1980s and 1990s, the U.S. Information Agency was disbanded as a separate agency in 1999 (after the concerted campaign by Senator Jesse Helms, who called the Voice of America "a rogue agency").[16] Public diplomacy functions were folded into the State Department and were allocated fewer staff and resources. While bin Laden routinely has media access in the Arab world, the Broadcasting Board of Governors discovered in its study of media in the Arab world that "there certainly was a media war going on in the region, and that U.S. international broadcasting played absolutely no role" in it.[17]

Private-sector U.S. actors are masters of communications, marketing, advertising, and diverse cross-cultural exchanges. The United States dominates world movies, music, advertising, and culture. The United States soundly won the struggle for hearts and minds during the Cold War. Communist totalitarianism is nowhere an attractive system today; North Korea is a struggling, isolated pariah, while China and Cuba seek hybrid reforms, to liberalize their economies while maintaining some political controls. The United States engaged and won the ideas war in the Cold War, and as George Kennan predicted, the Soviet system was eventually "unable to stand the comparison." Ideas compel more completely than military force. When the arms are withdrawn, ideas remain. Long after the empires fall, their ideas continue. At the dawn of the U.S. republic, the fledgling United States wielded far more power than its nearly nonexistent armed forces could project due to the force of U.S. moral claims — that all are created equal, with inalienable rights to life, liberty, and the pursuit of happiness. Rather than distancing ourselves from this code, the fight against terrorism would be much more effective if we drew on this touchstone to make the case for why the tactic of terrorism is wrong and should be curtailed. Given U.S. strengths in the information and communications industries, it is crazy that, as Richard Holbrooke noted in 9/11 Commission hearings on bin Laden, "a man in a cave outcommunicate[s] the world's leading communications society."[18]

Some argue that since terrorists fight dirty, so must we. The United States has to be willing and able to respond in kind, and in war the United States must not let moral considerations over means constrain its pursuit of foreign policy ends. As Thomas Friedman put it, "We have to fight the terrorists as if there were no rules."[19] Robert Kaplan argues that "leadership demands a pagan ethos."[20] But this approach is not only bad morality, it is bad politics, short-sighted and self-defeating behavior that undermines rather than advances the fight against terrorism. Why would the United States fight terrorism in ways that degrade U.S. military, political, and ethical assets?

No terrorist group has ever successfully overtaken a democratic state. But terrorists seek to overcome their minority status by provoking an overreaction by democratic states. This is typically how democratic states lose ground to terrorist organizations. Overreactions by democracies that are at odds with core democratic values bring greater legitimacy, support, and followers to the terrorists' cause while delegitimizing the state fighting terrorism. Terrorists try to capitalize politically on governments' increased use of violence to combat terrorism. For example, increased violence by British and Protestant forces in Northern Ireland, including the British Army's firing into a crowd of unarmed Irish Catholic demonstrators in Londonderry on "Bloody Sunday," January 30, 1972,[21] led to the establishment of the Provisional Irish Republican Army and increased sympathy for the IRA cause overall for a time, as many asked "who are the real terrorists here?"[22] The limiting logic of just war tradition is a useful protection against this terrorist gambit. Using ethical principles to constrain the use of force helps deny terrorists their goal of provoking ethically compromised and ultimately self-defeating behavior from their adversaries.

If we seek to build an international coalition to delegitimize terrorism, our means matter, and certain counterproductive tactics ought to be taken off the shelf. We cannot effectively build an international coalition against terrorism while thumbing our nose at the international community. We cannot effectively build an international coalition against terrorism while undercutting international law and institutions. The United States cannot create a global coalition against the killing of noncombatants while using means that are insensitive to noncombatants.

THE BAD NEWS IN THE WAR ON TERRORISM: THE STRONGER THE UNITED STATES IS MILITARILY, THE MORE LIKELY WE ARE TO BE TARGETS OF TERROR

The bad news is that we will never be 100 percent safe from terrorism, due to the nature of terrorism. Terrorist attacks against the United States and U.S. interests are a direct result of the military superiority of U.S. armed forces. The lower the possibility that an enemy can strike the United States conventionally on the battlefield, the higher the probability that opponents will pursue unconventional, asymmetric warfare tactics, striking at targets of opportunity — from unprotected civilians, trade and transportation infrastructure, to other critical infrastructure. In responding to the terrorist strikes, the United States faces a target-poor environment, not knowing who or where the terrorists are. The terrorists, in contrast, face a target-rich environment. In the information age, the United States and its developed democratic allies have increasingly open societies, economies, and technologies. Through globalization, these open economic, technological, and societal infrastructures are actively accessible abroad.

The United States cannot prevent all terrorist attacks. Instead it must seek to curtail the number and lethality of such attacks, as there will always be more potential targets than resources to protect them. The United States can seek to deter large-scale attacks by protecting major targets so that terrorists will be compelled to go after softer targets, such as public buses or restaurants. Keep in mind, though, that if we are successful in protecting major targets, without building an international coalition or addressing root causes of terrorism, we may be like Israel, with bombings in smaller numbers in difficult to protect public places like buses or restaurants. This is the new face of U.S. containment policy against asymmetric threats. Israel is a cautionary tale of fighting terrorism militarily without engaging the ideas war or winning the battle for hearts and minds. Because this type of terrorist asymmetric warfare is cheap and its means are easily available to a wide variety of individuals and groups, even success against al Qaeda would not make the United States safe from global terrorism. Terrorism is not only a cheap and easily available tactic, but also it is now globalized.

HOW GLOBALIZATION CHANGES TERRORISM: WHY MILITARY RESPONSES AND "DRAINING THE SWAMPS" DON'T WORK

While terrorism has existed for centuries, the modern period of globalization changes terrorism. If terrorism is a form of "advertising discontent,"[23] globalization offers terrorists the opportunity to easily and cheaply take their complaints to a global stage.[24] Globalization takes local fault lines farther afield. For example, Australian authorities arrested a Caribbean-born French citizen who they believe was sent by a little-known Pakistani group to scout possible targets for attacks. The group, Lashkar-e-Taiba, was previously thought to be focused only on the India-Pakistan border struggle in Kashmir, but now is thought to be working with al Qaeda, substituting training camps in Kashmir for the ones U.S. and coalition forces destroyed in Afghanistan. Terrorists easily operate globally. Governments must also operate globally, creating and maintaining international cooperation and coalitions to counter terrorism.

Today's terrorists have gone global and virtual. Terrorist organizations are not connected to one piece of land, and they can operate and move across borders easily and cheaply. This is important, because it lessens restrictions on casualties. Local terrorist groups in the past faced diminishing returns on increased bloodshed. If their activities caused too many casualties, it could decrease critical social support, recruitments, financial support, and legitimacy. The Irish Republican Army (IRA) often faced this dilemma. But today, since terrorist groups operate globally, increased deaths of one country's citizens may not reduce sympathy, support, and recruitment for the group in other countries.

Ideas compel more completely than military force. When the arms are withdrawn, ideas remain. Long after the empires fall, their ideas continue.

Terrorist groups are now decentralized, hydra-headed networks, so effectively combating a terrorist group in one area (such as Afghanistan) or eliminating some leaders (such as the arrest and killing of many key al Qaeda leaders) does not eliminate terrorism, but pushes it to other areas and facilitates the rise of other leaders. According to the UN Arab Human Development Report, Arab countries are the youngest on the globe, with almost 38 percent under the age of fourteen, significantly younger than the global average. Income and jobs are not growing commensurately with the population, however; the GDP growth rate is lowest except for sub-Saharan Africa. While oil income buffers the region from the abject poverty seen in other areas of the globe, the high unemployment rate and insufficient educational opportunities leave young people feeling helpless, hopeless, and frustrated, especially contrasted with the proud heritage of Islamic civilization in the past. Dissatisfied with current conditions and future prospects, today, more than half of Arab young people surveyed by a UN Arab Human Development Report want to emigrate outside the region. Such conditions provide a ready labor pool for terrorist organizations. There are no shortages of grievances, there are no shortages of groups recruiting for members, there is no shortage of hopelessness, and there is no shortage of potential recruits.

The administration has focused on "the away game" in the war on terrorism, citing the need to drain the swamps as a way to stop terrorism. But there are no shortages of swamps around the world, countries or regions with fragile or nonexistent governments where the arm of law and order does not reach. Further, terrorists do not need swamps to operate. The September 11 terrorists operated out of cells in the United States, Britain, Canada, France, Germany, Italy, and Spain, hardly failed states. Today's global terrorist networks do not need state sponsorship to survive,[25] so focusing on "rogue states that sponsor terrorism" is a failed approach to the war on terrorism. Thus, no matter how successful U.S. military operations abroad are, U.S. military actions alone cannot protect noncombatants from acts of terror. That's the bad news.

> The belief in the possibility of a short decisive war appears to be one of the most ancient and dangerous of human illusions.   — Robert Lynd, Anglo-Irish essayist

As an aside, this bad news could actually be good. The bad news is that we can never be 100 percent secure from terrorism, that we are always vulnerable. But scripture tells us Christ enters into the lives of the vulnerable, and that it is difficult for the rich and secure to enter heaven, not because the prosperous and peaceful are inherently bad folks, but because if you do not experience vulnerability it is difficult to feel a need for other people or for the presence of God. A sense of invulnerability can set you up for separation from others and God. But vulnerability experienced not in fear but through the eyes of faith opens a window for the spirit to operate, and creates an opportunity to experience greater empathy for others. Vulnerability approached in faith, not fear, presents a tremendous opportunity to stand in solidarity with our brothers and sisters around the world who daily experience risk to life and insecurity. It presents an opportunity to advance international cooperation, international law and institutions, as we are more aware of the need to work with others. So without being Pollyanna-ish about it, a sense of vulnerability could provide both good political and theological opportunities, if approached in a spirit of faith, not fear.

THE GOOD NEWS IN THE WAR ON TERRORISM: LAYERED, COOPERATIVE SECURITY WORKS

The good news in the war on terrorism is that there is much we can do to protect ourselves from terrorism and from the spread of weapons of mass destruction, without becoming a people of fear. We need to adopt a layered, cooperative approach to security, rather than looking for the single silver bullet. Consider how we secure our own homes. We get to know our neighbors and tell them when we are going to be away from home. While away, we have the newspaper and mail delivery stopped so they don't advertise our absence, or maybe we ask a neighbor to take those in for us. Our door handle has a lock. Because that doesn't deter a determined thief, perhaps we add a deadbolt and exterior lights. Perhaps we put our interior lights on a timer. Any one of those measures alone is not foolproof, and perhaps is only a 60 percent solution. But add enough 60 percent solutions together, and we have created a pretty secure environment,[26] not one that is guaranteed failsafe, but we have met our responsibilities to ourselves and those in our care to protect them from harm. Additionally, each one of these actions is multipurpose, that is, we enjoy the benefits of these measures whether or not our home is visited by burglars. We enjoy better relations with our neighbors, which helps to build community. Secure doors and windows help keep animals and the elements out as well as thieves. The layers serve several purposes every day, not just for the worst case scenario.

The same sensible layered approach is needed to safeguard the United States from terrorist attacks and weapons of mass destruction. We need to work with the private sector to upgrade and better protect critical infrastructure such as the electric grid, the public health system, the shipping system, the banking system, etc. As the blackout in New York City showed, our systems are antiquated and vulnerable. The value of investing in our critical infrastructure and domestic first responders is that the investment pays dividends right away, whether or not the nightmare scenario ever occurs. Because we use our critical infrastructure every day, we will enjoy the updates and improvements in them every day. For example, we would enjoy a stronger public health system whether or not terrorists ever strike with smallpox. A layered approach gives us multipurpose security; we are not only more secure from terrorists, we are more secure from thieves, smugglers, hackers, drug traffickers, disease, and international criminal organizations that already compromise our systems of daily life, our critical infrastructures, every day.

Focusing on a layered approach to security means devoting more resources to the homeland and putting less focus on fighting the war on terrorism abroad militarily. We spend about 500 billion dollars a year on the away game, on the military defense of U.S. positions abroad. We give them the best of high tech equipment, but here at home our fire departments and police departments don't even have radios that can talk with one another. Our hospitals and health care systems do not have effective means of tracking let alone containing the outbreak of infectious diseases. It's an artifact of the Cold War that we think of defense as something we do abroad, rather than something we do at home. We need to change our ways of thinking about national defense, and with it, change our spending priorities to be more in line with our values.

We also need to place more emphasis on the nonmilitary means of combating terrorism and the spread of weapons of mass destruction, such as international cooperative efforts to build international coalitions. One such effort is the Cooperative Threat Reduction (CTR) program, a bipartisan effort begun by Senators Nunn and Lugar to stem the flow of nuclear weapons and weapons materials from the former Soviet Union. The program has been incredibly successful, and the former Soviet states of the Ukraine, Kazakhstan, and Belarus are now nuclear weapons–free states. Coupled with programs from the Department of State and the Department of Energy to employ out-of-work Soviet scientists so they will not sell their expertise in weapons of mass destruction to potential proliferators, these programs provide an excellent basis from which to work. Senator Lugar argues that these programs need to be expanded globally beyond the former Soviet states, beginning immediately with Pakistan and India. The good news is CTR is a cooperative effort to build security that works, and it is very cost effective. All the government's Nunn-Lugar type nonproliferation programs combined per year cost less than one week of the war in Iraq.

The bad news is that even this modest budget is chronically underfunded and under attack. Before September 11, the Bush administration proposed 100 million dollars in budget cuts for these programs. After September 11, Congress restored the cuts, but funding has been repeatedly halted. While the green light has recently been given to expand the program to Albania (not India and Pakistan), this is being done by taking budget away from existing programs, not from new investments. One of the co-founders of the program, Sam Nunn, says, "In measuring the adequacy of our response to today's nuclear threats, on a scale from one to ten, I would give us about a three."[27]

Another innovative program to advance international and private sector cooperation in stopping the spread of weapons of mass destruction is the Proliferation Security Initiative. This Bush Administration-created program works later in the supply chain; it is designed to interdict the transfer or transport of weapons of mass destruction or related materials. The initiative began with "a coalition of the willing" of eleven countries who used existing national and international law to track and block suspect shipments.[28] Some sixty countries are now cooperating with the program in some measure. The initiative has already had some important successes. Remember the news reports that Libya agreed to give up its weapons of mass destruction programs and accede to international inspections? What got lesser billing in the news is why that happened. Through the cooperation of several countries and companies in Germany, Italy, and the United States, Libya was caught red-handed in October 2003. An illegal shipment of uranium enrichment (centrifuge) equipment headed for Libya's nuclear weapons program was seized. Less than two weeks after the successful international interdiction and seizure, international weapons inspectors were in Libya.[29]

Another piece of good news is that since the Iraq war and the failure to find Iraqi weapons of mass destruction, the Bush administration is giving less emphasis to the "Bush doctrine" of preventive war to stop the spread of weapons of mass destruction. In a speech at the National Defense University, Bush announced greater attention and funding for international cooperative efforts, such as strengthening and working with the International Atomic Energy Agency, the Nuclear Suppliers group, the Nunn-Lugar Cooperative Threat Reduction program, etc. The trick will be following the money trail to see whether these announced priorities are actually funded. (While announcing increased attention to the cooperative threat reduction program, the administration also has identified the program for 10 percent budget cuts).

Other positive developments that help build international cooperation are increased development spending, increased spending to combat HIV/AIDS, and the creation of the Millennium Challenge Account with the potential to help streamline aid to poor countries that meet the administration's good governance criteria. Again, it is important to carefully follow the money trail in tracking the effectiveness of these programs. Promising to allocate increased money in the budget outyears of the future is not the same as actually allocating money today. None of these efforts alone provide a silver bullet, a single solution to make the world more secure against terrorism, weapons of mass destruction, and the political instability that can facilitate terrorism. But taken together, these can work as the sort of layered security approach that provides concrete benefits today while also safeguarding against worst-case scenarios tomorrow.

DOES JUST WAR TRADITION APPLY TO THE WAR ON TERRORISM?

Since September 11, some have argued that the nature of warfare has been transformed. As Colin Powell put it, "It's a different world ... it's a new kind of threat."[30] Assuming warfare has been transformed, many believe that the ethics of war must be transformed, that just war tradition is obsolete or needs to be radically changed to handle terrorism, suicide bombers, holy war, nonstate actors, and especially weapons of mass destruction.

This is not true. The nature of the threat Americans have faced since September 11 is not new; what is new is the U.S. sense of vulnerability to these persistent and preexistent threats. Terrorism is a centuries-old tactic of asymmetric warfare. Nonstate actors are a standard feature of international politics, predating sovereign states and long vexing governments. The view that just war tradition does not apply because it describes the ethical responsibilities of sovereign states, while the war on terrorism entails fighting nonstate actors, is misguided. Just war tradition was developed long before the sovereign state system developed with the Treaty of Westphalia in 1648. Just war tradition was not originally oriented to the modern state system and has often been applied to nonstate actors. Augustine and Aquinas grappled with the problem of the use of force by armed bands not authorized by public authorities. Francisco de Vitoria and Francisco Suarez, SJ, discussed the clash of civilizations and what norms of warfare should apply when conflict occurred between governments and nongovernment groups from different continents and cultures. Hugo Grotius examined how international law and international community should factor in decisions by states over the use of force. And contemporary just war theorists have analyzed just war tradition's applicability to both weapons of mass destruction and low intensity, asymmetrical conflicts. Those who argue that everything is different post-September 11 would seem to bear the burden of proof. Why would just war tradition not apply to the very types of problems it has addressed over the centuries? Moral limitations also do not disappear in light of technological innovations. Weapons of mass destruction are not new. Chemical and biological weapons have been in use for more than a millennium (as noted in chapter 4). And of course, nuclear weapons have been a fact of the political landscape for sixty years, killing hundreds of thousands in Hiroshima and Nagasaki. Three thousand dead on September 11 are horrific, but sadly not unheard of, casualties.

While the nonmilitary means of fighting terrorism are and will continue to be the most successful, wherever troops are engaged with the rationale of fighting terrorism, just war tradition continues to be useful to assess, critique, and restrain the use of force in line with the values of peace and protection of civilians. U.S. forces are still engaged in fighting in Afghanistan and Iraq, and will be for some time to come. Are we fighting in a manner consistent with our Christian values? The good news is that U.S. forces did not systematically destroy infrastructure in these wars, which goes a long way toward protecting noncombatants and restoring normal life after the wars are over. Advances in intelligence and smarter weaponry and targeting also helped to reduce noncombatant casualties. Still, there is more we can do to ensure discrimination, proportionality, and the protection of noncombatants in the way the United States fights wars. Cluster bombs, even when used against military targets, leave behind a legion of unexploded bomblets that act like landmines. The use of cluster bombs near populated areas should be restricted until the Department of Defense can reduce the percentage of unexploded ordnance. U.S. troops also desperately need more linguists, greater training in ambiguous force environments, and more investment in nonlethal weapons technologies and their use so troops can better safeguard noncombatants. Troops in hostile situations should not be yelling "stop or we'll shoot" commands to noncombatants in English. We should not give our troops a choice between shooting and doing nothing. Noncombatants deserve better, as do twenty-year-olds in armed service, who do not deserve a lifetime of remorse over killing a noncombatant in a situation for which they were ill-prepared and ill-equipped. Better training, more linguists, and more nonlethal technologies give troops more options and more opportunities to do a better job of discrimination and proportionality, so they do not have to use the full and fierce firepower they have at their disposal.

No matter how we feel about whether the United States should have intervened in Iraq and Afghanistan, having done so, we bear responsibilities for post-conflict reconstruction. Catholic just war tradition tells us that peace must be our intention, and we must strive to do more good than harm through the use of force. This means no drive-by interventions. We must continue to work with the Afghans and Iraqis and the international community to build the peace in these regions.

While just war tradition is necessary and still relevant in assessing the use of force in fighting terrorism, it is not sufficient. It addresses the immediate pre-conflict and during-conflict conditions; it offers no moral guidance in post-conflict situations, and other than saying peace must be our aim, it gives no guidance on how to build a just peace. Just war tradition urges that war must be only a last resort, but offers little counsel on what prior measures would be effective for establishing peace and justice without resort to war. Fruitful and much needed efforts are currently underway to expand the concepts, tools, and practices of just peace, peacebuilding, and just policing.

VALUES AND POLICY: WHAT CAN WE DO?

What else can we do to promote policy in line with our values? One positive development is the initiation of the Catholic Peacebuilding Network.[31] This newly formed network seeks to bring together preachers, teachers, academics, missionaries, and practitioners involved in Catholic peacebuilding efforts around the world. Informed by Caritas International's training manual in peacebuilding, the effort reflects the church's orientation to go beyond relief and charity in its preferential option for the poor and move toward reconciliation and building more peaceful societies where the human person can thrive. Peacebuilding is not just negotiating peace treaties; it is avoiding conflict and recovering from it. As the Caritas manual describes it, it is "a longer process of overcoming hostilities and mistrust between divided peoples . . . and of promoting the consolidation of constructive social relations between different groups of the population, including parties to conflict." Rather than just activating our Catholic networks and coming together in opposition to particular wars or in response to acute crises, this network attempts to encourage community and collaboration in more proactive and regular ways. Joining or support-ing the Catholic Peacebuilding Network is one way to address security issues within the framework of Catholic social teaching.

If we believe Catholic social teaching is important, we must do a bet-ter job of teaching our Catholic traditions in war and peace in our own parishes, dioceses, schools, universities, and other Catholic institutions.

We must work to strengthen the bonds between Catholics and Mus-lims in each of our communities. Ending the Crusades mentality begins here at home. We have our faith tradition, our rich networks, our authen-ticity to speak on these issues because of our sister parishes and sister dioceses abroad, our global networks, and our global presence on the ground through Catholic Relief Services and Jesuit Refugee Service and other Catholic groups. All these give us a unique ability to walk with our brothers and sisters abroad and to advocate for them here at home. This will make solidarity not simply an element of Catholic social teaching to be preached, but an attainable daily practice.

Beyond all that, advocacy and lobbying government are also important, especially in overlooked areas like advocating for the refugees, who have been adversely affected by the war on terrorism and who have no voice otherwise. We must continue to lobby our government representatives, advocate for change, and educate ourselves and others in our values. Par-ticularly now, we must stand tall and firm as a beacon, so that others will come to associate the Catholic Church with more than the sexual scandals.

The world's problems are large, but the power of the Holy Spirit is far more expansive. Regardless of the actions and inactions of the U.S. government and international institutions, we can show through our own institutions and actions that "God has not given us a spirit of fear; but of power, and love, and of a sound mind." It's telling that in that verse from Timothy, power is not considered independent of love. The two go together. To exercise power responsibly, we must do it not in a spirit of separation, looking at U.S. interests in isolation from the rest of the world, but in a spirit of love and solidarity.

QUESTIONS FOR REFLECTION
AND DISCUSSION

1. This chapter asserts that terrorism is a tactic, not an ideology. What do you think of this?

2. This chapter also labels as wrong the cliché "One man's terror-ist is another's freedom fighter." Discuss this statement. Do you agree with it? What might be the differences between terrorists and freedom fighters?

3. Dr. Love, quoting 2 Timothy, says that God has not given us a spirit of fear, but a spirit of power, love, and a sound mind. If we accept this, what are its implications for how we react to the terrorist threat? Would it change how we resist terrorism? Does the threat of terrorism require that we start with a "strong presumption against the use of force," or does it require quicker and more decisive military action?

PRACTICAL APPLICATION

If you could design the memorial to honor the victims of the 9/11 terrorist attacks, what would you do? What would it look like? What would your specific goal be, and how would you achieve it?

Chapter Six

The Interreligious Dimension

We have been looking at the nature of warfare in human history and what warfare looks like in the modern world. We have also looked at Christian traditions of war and peace and what they mean to us today. How does our faith inform our attitudes and our decisions in these matters? What can we learn from our faith tradition to help us as we wrestle with these critical issues?

But we must remember that other religions are as heavily invested in these issues as we are. Judaism and Islam in particular are very much involved in the problem of war and the search for peace. One of the major areas of conflict in the world today (though by no means the only one) is the Middle East. This is the part of the world where the three major monotheistic religions — Judaism, Islam, and Christianity — originated and where they have long had a presence. In fact, all three are called Abrahamic religions, since they all trace their history back to Abraham.

Unfortunately, there has been a tendency recently to view certain aspects of the Middle East conflict — especially the recent spillover into conflict with the West that began with the 9/11 terrorist attacks — as a "clash of civilizations." We sometimes see this term used by the media to describe the situation. Yet this perspective is not really accurate. For one thing, it tends to paint both the Christian and Islamic traditions in very broad strokes and too monochromatically. The "other" tends to be viewed comparatively in a negative light, with Christians labeling Islam as inherently fundamentalist and violent and Muslims regarding Christians as greedy and rapacious Crusaders. These are obviously incomplete views of each other; they ignore the complexities of both the Christian and Islamic traditions. After 9/11, Muslims complained that their whole religion was being judged by the actions of a few extremists, who have misrepresented their tradition. It should also be pointed out, in reference to the clash of civilizations, that the Holy See and the Council of Patriarchs of the East reject the notion of a clash; their emphasis has been, rather, on a *dialogue* of civilizations.

What do the Jewish and Islamic traditions have to say about peace and war? What is their history in this regard? What are their most pressing issues today? How are their perspectives similar to that of Christianity, and how are they different? This chapter will briefly explore these questions.

As we start, it is important to bear in mind that there is no single stance on war and peace within either Judaism or Islam. It is all too easy for casual observers to make snap judgments. One cannot say categorically, for example, that Islam permits (or even encourages) offensive war and puts no limits on harming noncombatants. To the contrary, immediately after the 9/11 attacks, many prominent Muslim movements and scholars condemned the attacks, declaring them a crime against humanity and not permissible in Islam.[1] Similarly, one cannot say that pacifism does not exist at all within Judaism. Some Jewish scholars assert that Judaism strongly upholds nonviolence. There are also several groups of Israeli Jews working for a nonviolent defense of Israel — soldiers' groups, women's groups, cooperative groups.[2] Within both religious traditions, then, there are varying interpretations of how to deal with issues of peace and war.

A related characteristic of both Islam and Judaism is that these religions do not have a unified authority in the same way that the Catholic Church does, with its one teaching office and code of canons. The Catholic just war tradition, for example, was mostly the domain of theologians and canonists and later became associated with the magisterium. There are elements of just war teaching in the Augsburg Confession and the Westminster Confession, placing it in the official teaching of the Lutheran and Anglican churches as well. But in Islam and Judaism, there are several legal traditions and interpretations of the sources, and these interpretations can, and do, disagree. It is worth asking if there is a definitive teaching on critical issues such as war and peace.

THE JEWISH TRADITION

As with any tradition, the Jewish tradition on war and peace grew out of its history. That history is told in the Hebrew scriptures, what Christians know as the Old Testament. These scriptures are the first of the primary authoritative sources in Judaism. Of particular importance are the first five books — Genesis, Exodus, Leviticus, Numbers, and Deuteronomy — which are known collectively as the Torah.

The scriptures are more than just history, however; they tell the story of this people's relationship with God. The story begins with God calling Abraham to leave his home in Ur of the Chaldees and travel to a new land. God enters into a covenant with Abraham and his descendents: he will be their God and they will be his people; he will give them a land for their own and the people will form a great nation. This covenant forms the bedrock of the Jewish faith.

A pivotal event in Jewish history occurred when God freed the Israelites from slavery in Egypt and led them as they conquered the land that had been promised to them. Eventually, after a period of tribal leadership with times of peace and times of war, the Israelites formed a monarchy. David and his son Solomon were the greatest of the kings; they united the people and made of them a strong kingdom, equal to its neighbors. It was under Solomon that the Temple at Jerusalem was built.

After Solomon's death, however, the unity dissolved and the kingdom broke apart. Ten tribes together formed a new kingdom of Israel in the north and the tribes of Judah and Benjamin formed the kingdom of Judah in the south. The two kingdoms existed for several hundred years afterward, until two powerful empires conquered them. In 722 BCE the Assyrians destroyed Israel and scattered its people. In 586 BCE, the Babylonians invaded Judah and took most of its people into exile. These events marked the beginning of the Diaspora — the scattering of the Jewish people.

The Jews in exile were allowed to return to their land by Cyrus, the king of Persia, but they were under Persian control. Later, they came under Greek control and finally became a Roman protectorate. In 73 CE, after a Jewish uprising, Rome destroyed Jerusalem and forced all the people into exile; they went all over the world. Their history during their wanderings was marked by oppression and persecution; to name a few, they faced deportation in Spain, pogroms in Russia, and massacre in twentieth-century Europe. They held on to their faith and their traditions wherever they went; there were always Jewish communities, but there was no Jewish state until the formation of Israel in 1948.

Given this history, what does Jewish tradition say about peace and war? Turning to the Hebrew scriptures, one of the tradition's authoritative sources, we find first of all that God made human beings in the divine image (Genesis 1:27, 31). All people carry something of God in them. Therefore, life is greatly valued in the Jewish tradition, and this has profound implications for Jewish thinking. Genesis 9:6 says: "Whoever sheds the blood of a human being by human beings shall his blood be shed, for in the divine image did God make humanity."

Related to this focus on life, we also see a value placed on peace, perhaps most powerfully described in the prophet Isaiah: "[God] shall judge between the nations, and shall arbitrate for many peoples; they shall beat their swords into ploughshares, and their spears into pruning hooks; nation shall not lift up sword against nation, neither shall they learn war any more" (2:3–4).

Yet, as described above, conflict and war were part of Jewish history, so inevitably we find this element as well in the Hebrew scriptures. To cite one example, in Deuteronomy the Israelites are commanded by God to take possession of the land that they were promised, and they do so, often quite ruthlessly. "At the time we captured all his towns, and in each town we utterly destroyed men, women, and children. We left not a single survivor" (2:32–34; 20:15–18). Later in their history, the Israelites carried out a war of vengeance against the Midianites, an event related in Numbers (chapter 31).

Let's turn to another authoritative Jewish source, the Talmud, which is the centuries-long history of commentary by rabbis on the Hebrew scriptures. We find there the same juxtaposition of peace and war. In one place, the rabbinical commentary says: "When one destroys a single individual, it is as if that person destroyed the whole world" (Sanhedrin 4:5). Yet we also find the assertion that, in some cases, war is legitimate. The rabbis outline two kinds of legitimate wars. The first kind is obligatory war (*milkhemet mitzvah* or *milkhemet hovah*), and the wars described in Deuteronomy, which are wars commanded by God, fall into this category. Defensive wars — wars fought to protect the Jewish people — also belong in this category. The other kind of legitimate war is discretionary, or optional, war (*milkhemet ha-reshut*). These are wars fought to expand the boundaries of Israel. The rabbis put a limit on discretionary wars that they did not impose on obligatory wars, ruling that only the Sanhedrin, the equivalent of a legislature in ancient Israel, could call for these wars; the ruler could not do it on his own authority.

> All people carry something of God in them. Therefore, life is greatly valued in the Jewish tradition.

Jewish tradition also has rules governing the conduct of wars once they have begun. The first of these is that the people in a town to be attacked must first be offered terms of peace. Absent this offer, an attack would violate Jewish law. Additionally, residents of the town who wish to leave before the attack must be allowed to do so. A second rule applies once the battle has begun. Jewish law does not allow an army to surround and lay siege to an opposing army or civilization. Rather, they may only surround their enemy on three sides, allowing a means of escape for those who wish to flee. Still another rule forbids Jewish armies to destroy fruit trees when fighting, since it would be a wanton waste of something needed for life.

These, then, are the very basic elements of the Jewish tradition of war and peace as they appear in its sources. But it is not enough to merely know the tradition; we must also ask the question: How does the tradition apply to the contemporary situation? This is complicated by the fact that, as noted earlier, there have always been contesting interpretations of the sacred texts. Moreover, some experts even question "whether or not a focus on sacred texts makes for good public policy especially in matters of war."[3] There is, in fact, no general consensus in Judaism as to how to use the scriptural sources to address today's problems.

There does seem to be general agreement among Jewish scholars on some major points, however. First, the rabbinical category of obligatory war as applied to today does not include the wars commanded by God, such as the wars described in Deuteronomy. Professor Reuven Kimmelman of Brandeis University distinguishes between mandatory and discretionary war, saying that the only case of obligatory war today is a defensive war, when a nation is under attack.[4] Rabbi Yehudah Mirsky, Jewish scholar and former advisor to the U.S. State Department, asserts, "The only remaining category of legitimate war since the destruction of the Temple in 70 CE has been, and remains, war for the defense of the Jewish people."[5]

Second, there seems to be agreement that Judaism places a high value on peace. The word for peace is *shalom*, and *shalom* is also one of the names of God in the Jewish tradition. In any situation of conflict, peace should always be the goal.

Yet there is disagreement about what this embracing of peace means as a lived reality in the world today. Many scholars hold that it does not mean a stance of nonviolence. Professor Kimmelman asserts that the Jewish tradition focuses, rather, on the obligation to preserve life, one's life and the lives of others. The greatest obligation is to preserve one's own life, and this limits the obligation one has to preserve the lives of others. He also states that some scholars would include in the category of defensive war a preemptive strike against an enemy with a declared intent to attack your state.[6] And Rabbi Mirsky has stated that "although Judaism honors nonviolent action under some conditions, it permits and even enjoins the use of force in defense of the survival of the Jewish community."[7] Yet Naomi Goodman of the Jewish Peace Fellowship rejects the idea that Judaism does not emphasize pacifism. She sees "a pacifist tradition within Judaism that recognizes peace as the highest priority in Jewish life and as the essence of Jewish morality."[8]

In summary, most experts seem to agree that pacifism is not as strong an element in Judaism as it is in Christianity. Yet there is also agreement that in the Jewish tradition, peace is always the goal in any situation of conflict and that one should strive to avoid war.[9]

Rabbi Harold White

At the November 2003 forum, Rabbi White of Georgetown University had the following to say about the tradition of peace and war in Judaism.

In Judaism, we don't have encyclicals. We don't have bishops or cardinals. So, obviously, you would expect a great deal of diverse opinions.

What I'd like to do here is cover three areas. The first is the laments. I am very sad that media give a very low profile to the peace movements in Judaism. Hardly anyone would know from reading any of the major newspapers that there is a peace movement. I happen to belong to four rather important peace organizations. Yet they get very little press.

In Israel, you see demonstration after demonstration for peace, but they're never publicized. I think that's very tragic and sad, since these movements do exist. That's a lament.

When you're dealing with Judaism, you're dealing with a paradox. But in Hebrew the word for paradox is also the world for mystery. So that helps us in understanding that. Because if you look at the biblical tradition, the existence of war is obviously there. And there are various categories in terms of war. The first is genocide. And you have two examples of that within the Torah. They're both in the book of Numbers.

The first is in relation to the Amalakites. This is a genocide where, actually, the Amalakites attacked the children of Israel as they were leaving Egypt, with the intent of annihilating them. So, in that case it's very clear. You have the right not only to attack them (the Amalakites), but the Torah says to blot out their name from the world. That's a clear case of actual attempted genocide.

The other case is the case of the Midianites, in which the Midianite king, Balach, hires a soothsayer to curse Israel, with the hope that the curse would also result in their genocide. And the same law applied. In the case of attempted or proposed genocide, you could retaliate.

At the same time, you have in the Torah the case of going against the city and offering that city an overture of peace. If the city accepted, the inhabitants accepted the overture of peace, you were commanded to treat the people with respect. For example, in the book of Deuteronomy, if you wished to marry one of the women who live in the city, you had to treat her with respect (and of course she had to convert). And if you could not, you had to compensate her and return her to her family.

The other category is that of the seven Canaanite nations. Why was Moses commanded to fight against them, annihilate them? Basically because of their idolatrous practices, their inhuman practices. So that's another category.

I think the important thing, though, when we think about the Canaanite wars, and the commandment to Moses, is that Moses doesn't lead the children of Israel across the river Jordan. He's the prophet. Who leads them across? Joshua. And, in reality, Joshua doesn't engage in a holy war. What Joshua engages in is contacts.

His first contact is with Refa, who is a prostitute, when he promises to spare her and her family and then the Gibeonites. And we don't have a war. We actually don't have a war of annihilation, even though in the Torah it appears to come as a divine command. So we have a variance between what we find as the word of G-d in the Torah and what human beings actually do (which is actually more clearly understood in the *midrash*).

That's the second part. So if we use the biblical tradition, the tradition of the Torah, it's very clear that war is allowed. Actually, commandments are categorical imperatives in terms of genocide and the religious practices of certain people. When we turn to the Talmud, we come to a very different category. We really can't understand Judaism unless we go to the postbiblical tradition. And that's the case of permitted war and war that requires the approval of the Great Sanhedrin, the Council of Seventy.

In the case of a preemptive strike, where it's very clear that your enemy has stated that he wants to fight against you, you don't need approval. You don't need a declaration of war by the Great Sanhedrin. Or in the case of where your enemy has actually attacked you, you don't need a declaration of war.

But what about the case of where you want land expansion for safe borders? Your enemy has never, never indicated that he is going to attack you, but you want secure borders. There you need the permission of the Council of Seventy. (According to my understanding), that is a war which would be considered a permissive war.

Now in Judaism, you deal with a problem, many problems. But one specific problem is this: Who is your enemy? Because according to Talmudic Law, your enemy is the person who declares war publicly on you, who in the presence of at least two witnesses, declares that he or she is your enemy. And the issue is this: Do the leaders of a nation have the right to declare everyone living in another nation as your enemy? Clearly, according to the Talmud, they don't (according to my opinion).

You have in the Torah the case of going against the city and offering that city an overture of peace. If the city accepted, the inhabitants accepted the overture of peace, you were commanded to treat the people with respect. For example, in the book of Deuteronomy, if you wished to marry one of the women who live in the city, you had to treat her with respect.

Of course, that becomes a very, very important issue in the Jewish community. Are we allowed to hold all Germans who lived in Germany during the Second World War accountable for the Holocaust? (In my opinion), obviously, according to (my interpretation of) Talmudic law, we're not. So that becomes a very, very sensitive issue as far as Jewish ethical law is concerned.

One final point, and this is why I say there is a paradox. Even though you have these categorical imperatives in the Torah, in our liturgy, G-d is described as being the great creator of peace. Over and over again, G-d is described with the phrase, "May G-d who makes peace in the heavens grant peace unto us," one of the most important prayers in Judaism. It [the prayer book] also says, "Grant us peace, O G-d, your most precious gift."

So G-d is clearly portrayed in the liturgy as the pursuer of peace. And if you look at the names of synagogues and temples, one of the most common names is Rodef Shalom, the pursuer of peace.

So when I present (my perceptions of) Jewish views, yes, I look to the biblical tradition, to the Torah, but I also look to liturgy, because people who are not familiar with the Torah are familiar with the liturgy. And the liturgy is really one of the most important factors in determining what our position should be and what it is.

THE ISLAMIC TRADITION

Islam — which means "submission to the will of God" in Arabic — began in the Arabian desert, in what is now Saudi Arabia, in the seventh century CE. In 610, a merchant of Mecca named Muhammad received what he came to recognize as guidance from God, given to him in a series of revelations through the angel Gabriel. These revelations proclaimed that, as in Judaism and Christianity, there is only one God. In fact, Islam sees itself as a continuation of the revelation of God to humanity that began with those two religions. It considers all three to be religions descending from Abraham, their common father in faith, and thus honors Jews and Christians, calling them "people of the book" in reference to their scriptures as divine revelation.

The revelations to Muhammad form the Qur'an, which is the primary authoritative source in Islam. It is impossible to overestimate its centrality. It is not the history of a people and it is not viewed as written by divinely inspired authors. For Muslims, the Qur'an is, as one scholar says, "the word of God incarnate," eternal and uncreated;[10] its words were actually dictated by God to his prophet, Muhammad. Therefore, its words can never be changed or added to. The Qur'an is considered to be God's final revelation. Along with the Christian Bible, it is one of the world's two most widely read books.

On fire after receiving the first revelation, Muhammad began preaching this message: all people should renounce their pagan gods and worship the one true God, Allah. Humanity should follow the dictates of Allah, especially those mandating care for the poor and the weak. Some people heard and accepted the message, and they formed the beginnings of a community of believers. Yet most people in Mecca saw Muhammad's message as a threat to their way of life because the town was a pilgrimage site and had accommodated to the polytheistic religions of the Arab tribes of the area. Tension, conflict, and even violence resulted. Finally, Muhammad accepted an invitation to serve as judge among several tribes, some of which were Jewish, in a town called Yathrib, since renamed Medina, or "city," as in "city of the Prophet." His move there from Mecca in 622 CE marks the beginning of the Islamic calendar.

Under Muhammad's leadership, believers formed a community in Medina and defeated the hostile city of Mecca in 630. Muhammad died in 632, but the new religion he had formed in Arabia began to grow at a great rate, carried by Arab Islamic forces. By 647, these forces had conquered Damascus in Syria, Jerusalem, the Sassanian Empire in Persia, the city of Alexandria in Egypt, and cities in present-day Libya. The Muslim capital was moved from Medina to Damascus in 661 and from there, the reigning Umayyad Dynasty expanded into an Islamic empire. It moved across North Africa, into Sicily, and up into the Iberian Peninsula, where a great Islamic civilization was established. Eastward, it moved into what is now Pakistan and central Asia.

In 750, the Umayyads fell to another faction, the Abbasids, who moved the empire's capital to Baghdad. Under this dynasty, there followed the Golden Age of Islamic civilization. Many Islamic cities were great centers of learning; while European culture struggled during its so-called Dark Ages, Muslim scholars, artists, and scientists made lasting contributions that would eventually influence Western knowledge and civilization. For example, Muslim mathematicians developed the concept of zero and the system of decimalization. Their pivotal role in the field is seen in the fact that our word "algebra" comes from the word *al-jabr*, the title of an Arabic mathematical treatise. Muslim doctors invented innovative surgical instruments and procedures and expanded the boundaries of known medical knowledge. Muslim scholars also were responsible for recovering and preserving works from antiquity that later made their way back into the West accompanied by Muslim commentaries; otherwise, these works might have been lost.

The unity of the Abbasid Empire did not last, however. Conflict among warring factions, religious dissent, and the sheer size of the empire weakened it. In the tenth century, the Seljuks, a Turkic-speaking people originally from Central Asia and converts to Islam, gained power in Baghdad. Later, the Fatimid dynasty from Tunisia took control in Egypt and North Africa and eventually moved into Palestine and Syria. Abbasid rule in Baghdad ended in 1258, when the Mongols sacked the city. Muslim rule in Spain ended in 1492 with the final victory of the Christian *reconquista*, the fall of the city of Granada.

Another major Islamic empire, which held power from 1299 to 1923, was the Ottoman. Established by a tribe of Turks, it included the Middle East, portions of North Africa, Anatolia (in present-day Turkey), and southeastern Europe. In 1453, the Ottomans conquered Constantinople and ended the Byzantine Empire. Christian forces at the defense of Vienna eventually halted Ottoman westward expansion in 1683, though much of the Balkans remained under Ottoman rule and the empire continued to play a major role in European affairs for some time. It grew weaker as the nineteenth century progressed, suffered a crushing defeat in World War I, and was formally disbanded in 1923.

Space does not allow a more detailed presentation of the growth of Islam. Its spread to sub-Saharan Africa and South Asia, for example, are other stories entirely. The important thing to note is that by the early modern era, Islam had reached a significant portion of the globe. Today, there is no Islamic empire, although there are about sixty nations considered to be Islamic states. The world's approximately 1 billion Muslims are found in many different countries all over the world.

What generalizations can we make about Islam from this brief outline of its history? To begin with, it is clear that it is a story not primarily of oppression but rather one of triumph, growth, and cultural achievement and diversity. Some of these patterns may not immediately be obvious. For example, the image many people today have of Muslims being all the same throughout their history is not accurate. There were various states and peoples that made up the Muslim world. There were Arabs, of course; the religion was born in the Middle East. But there were also Persians, Turks, Mongols, and Mughals, not to mention Sicilians, West Africans, and people in the Caucasus. Today we find the same diversity. Arabs comprise only about 15 percent of all Muslims. The country with the largest Muslim population — 175 million people — is Indonesia.

We also find diversity in the style in which the different Islamic empires maintained power. There was the early colonial-style empire of a ruling Arab minority governing large populations of other peoples. The question arises, then, of how the conquering Muslims interacted with these other peoples. Some scholars hold that, at least in the earlier years, the Arabs were not interested in changing the order of things in the conquered lands because such unrest would jeopardize the tribute that could be demanded of them.[11] And, contrary to the image of invading Arabs forcibly converting their subject peoples, in some cases (such as the Coptic Christians in Egypt) these peoples actually welcomed the newcomers, seeing them as more merciful overlords than their current ones.[12] In ninth- and tenth-century Spain, under the rule of the Umayyads, an attitude of tolerance prevailed and adherents of all three faiths — Islam, Judaism, and Christianity — lived together in relative harmony.[13] There were also periods in the history of the Islamic world, of course, when the rule was harsh and oppressive, and Christian missionary activity could be punishable by death — but the same can be said for the harshness Muslims might experience if they entered Christian territory.

Turning now from Islamic history to the Islamic tradition, what does Islam have to say about peace and war? What does it believe about these critical issues? As we explore these questions, we must keep in mind what was mentioned earlier: there is more than one authoritative source in Islam, just as there is Judaism. The most authoritative source in Islam is the Qur'an, the revelation of God to humanity given through Muhammad. Another is what is called the *hadith*, the accounts of the words and actions of Muhammad. Because he was God's prophet, what he said and the way he lived out God's guidance is also regarded as authoritative. Still another source is the body of thought of Islamic jurists, especially during the time of empire. Difficulty arises because at times these sources seem to hold conflicting views. Contemporary Islamic scholars, in interpreting these sources, sometimes present opposing opinions. This is certainly the case with attitudes toward peace and war.

Another source of difficulty lies in the fact that, as mentioned above, there is no one Islamic authority in religious matters. The original unity of Islam broke apart shortly after Muhammad's death, when disagreement arose over who should be his rightful successor. Rival factions from that time still exist, the Shiites and the Sunnis, and many Islamic states have differing Islamic sects within their borders, occasionally leading to conflict. There are also various schools of Islamic law. In some Islamic states, the ruler appoints a chief or grand mufti to interpret Islamic law, but the decision of which school of law to follow is sometimes decided arbitrarily by the ruler. This can lead to the situation where some people may feel that what the mufti says is correct, but they do not follow that school of law. During the 1991 Persian Gulf War, a Baghdad group of scholars supported the Iraqi position and a Meccan group supported the anti-Iraq coalition. Sohail Hashmi, associate professor of international relations at Mount Holyoke, comments that if this was any indication, "Muslims are hopelessly divided on the Islamic ethics of war and peace."[14]

> Jihad refers to the individual's effort to live according to the will of God and to put into practice the message of justice in God's revelation.

What do we find in the Qur'an about war and peace? To begin, one of its major themes — just as in the Hebrew scriptures and in the Christian tradition — is a strong emphasis on the sanctity of life: "Slay not the life that God has made sacred" (6:152) and "If anyone slays a person — unless it be for murder or for spreading mischief in the land — it would be as if he slew all people. And if anyone saves a life, it would be as if he saved the life of all people" (5:32). Other passages show an emphasis on aiming for peace in any conflict. "But if the enemy incline towards peace, do thou (also) incline towards peace" (8:61) and "Therefore, if they leave you alone, refrain from fighting you, and offer you peace, then God gives you no excuse in fighting them" (4:90). There are also passages rebutting the notion of forcibly imposing Islam on anyone: "Let there be no compulsion in religion" (2:256).

However, other passages proclaim the need for Muslims to fight. One says: "To those against whom war is made, permission is given (to defend themselves), because they are wronged — and verily, Allah is Most Powerful to give them victory — (they are) those who have been expelled from their homes in defiance of right — (for no cause) except that they say, 'Our Lord is Allah'..." (22:39–40). Another passage says: "Fighting is prescribed upon you, and you dislike it. But it may happen that you dislike a thing which is good for you, and it may happen that you love a thing which is bad for you. And Allah knows and you know not" (2:216).

When we look at another authoritative source, accounts of the words and deeds of Muhammad, we also find seemingly contradictory approaches. In the early years in Mecca, his followers asked him for permission to fight back against the hostility and persecution they encountered there. He refused to allow it, counseling forbearance instead. But later, after the community had moved to Medina, they were still under attack from tribes near Mecca; then Muhammad allowed recourse to war. Under his leadership, they defeated the Meccans, and Islam became the dominant force in the Arabian Peninsula.

This leads to a crucial point: the later passages in the Qur'an were received during a time of violence. Bassam Tibi, professor of international relations at the University of Göttingen, says, "All Qur'anic verses revealed between 622 and the death of the Prophet in 632 relate to the establishment of Islam at Medina through violent struggle against the hostile tribes surrounding the city-state."[15] Reuven Firestone, a professor of medieval Judaism and Islam at Hebrew Union College in Los Angeles, explains: "Islam naturally includes a lot more material in its most classic, basic sources that are militant because that is the world they lived in — a world of successful military campaigns."[16] Muhammad himself was both religious leader and political leader, trying to proclaim and establish a faith in the face of violent opposition. This too must be taken into account in any attempt to understand Islam.

One element that causes a great deal of confusion today is the Islamic concept of jihad. Many non-Muslims believe it means a holy war or violent conflict. This definition is in fact often used in the media, especially in their accounts of the actions and statements of extremist Islamic groups, some of whom have chosen jihad as part of their identification. However, the word actually means "to strive" or "to struggle" and in Islam is an important element in Qur'anic-based spirituality. It refers to the individual's effort to live according to the will of God and to put into practice the message of justice in God's revelation. In fact, most scholars see armed combat as a secondary meaning for jihad. Armed conflict is often referred to as the lesser jihad, distinguished from the greater jihad of one's spiritual struggle. This distinction is rooted in a well-known hadith in which Muhammad, returning from the conquest of Mecca, told his companions,

"We have completed the lesser jihad but we now have the greater jihad to live."

Imam Dr. Abdul Jalil Sajid explains jihad this way: "The word Jihad finds its origin in the verb *jahada*, which means to struggle one's utmost effort to remain Muslim and to exert to establish peace and justice. The word Jihad has a few different connotations, since struggle can occur on several levels." He describes three levels of jihad. There is personal jihad, which is the struggle to cleanse one's spirit of sin and is the most important level. There is also verbal jihad, raising one's voice in the name of Allah on behalf of justice, and finally physical jihad, which is "combat waged in defence of Muslims against oppression and transgression by the enemies of Allah, Islam and Muslims."[17] Jihad, he asserts, has a much wider scope than mere fighting. In an interesting development, Professor Hashmi sees certain similarities between Western and Islamic thinking on war and peace, especially between the concepts of jihad and just war.[18]

Islam also has rules governing conduct during war, and they do not differ much from those of international law or other religions. The Qur'an requires notifying the enemy before attack, forbids targeting certain groups of people (children, women, and the elderly) and plundering and destruction, and demands humane treatment of prisoners.[19] After the 9/11 attacks, Muslim scholars and legal experts affirmed publicly that nothing in Islam allows the wanton killing of the innocent.

Many scholars, in fact, comment that it is all too easy to take selected portions from the Qur'an or from other Islamic sources and use them to justify a certain position, while ignoring the contexts of these passages and disagreements and contradictions. In addition, some legal scholars have expanded a distinction drawn from the Qur'an between the *dar al-harb* (house of war) and the *dar al-Islam* (home of peace). During the age of Islamic empires, *dar al-Islam* was the Islamic world governed by Islamic law and *dar al-harb* was the non-Islamic world; these two were considered to be in conflict. Some label Western civilization the *dar al-harb*, something diametrically opposed to Islam, and have adopted this distinction in recent years, and thus they attempt to justify war against non-Muslims. Bassam Tibi notes, "Islamic fundamentalists have emphasized the warlike aspect of jihad, while also emphasizing the dichotomy between the dar al-Islam and the dar al-harb."[20]

Yet a close examination of this notion shows that it never was an institutionalized system of indiscriminate violence against non-Muslims but a set of rules to govern relations between a Muslim political body and a non-Muslim one. In this system, war was always the last step. Some scholars today even question the distinction between the two spheres, seeing it "as an idea introduced by certain medieval legal thinkers in response to their own historical circumstances, but having no basis in Islamic ethics."[21]

One perspective on the place of war in Islam comes from Professor Hashmi, who explains that the traditional Islamic belief is that war is inevitable, the consequence of human beings choosing to violate God's commands. In response, "Muslims must always be prepared to fight to preserve the Muslim faith and Muslim principles.... The use of force by the Muslim community is, therefore, sanctioned by God as a necessary response to the existence of evil in the world."[22]

Most scholars do acknowledge that Islam does permit the use of force in certain situations. What are these situations that would allow recourse to war? Imam Sajid lists five such justified wars. The first is wars against oppression, where oppression is defined as a refusal to allow Islam to be practiced or communicated. The second is wars in defense of Muslims. The third is wars against foreign aggression, and the fourth is wars against rebellions. The last is wars for the cause of justice and truth, since Islam commands its followers to spread justice on earth.[23]

We see, then, that in the Islamic tradition there are occasions that actually call for war. A key reason for this, though, according to some scholars, has to do with Islam's focus on justice. According to Professor Abdulaziz Sachedina of the University of Virginia, "In Islam, true peace is not simply the absence of war but the achievement of justice.... For true peace to be attained, oppressive conditions must be removed, and sometimes this goal can only be accomplished through violence."[24] In fact, Professor Hashmi comments that people across the political spectrum in Islam seem to agree that "jihad is an instrument for enforcing human rights."[25] Proponents of this view point to the passage from the Qur'an that asserts: "Tumult and oppression is worse than killing" (2:191).

Yet this does not mean that Islam does not value nonviolence or does not prefer a nonviolent solution to conflict. Professor Hashmi also cites this Qur'anic verse: "But if one is patient in adversity and forgives, this is indeed the best resolution of affairs" (42:43) and states that this shows that Islam affirms the moral superiority of forgiveness over revenge.[26]

In summary, there is a great diversity of thought about the Islamic tradition of war and peace. Some scholars, such as Professor Tibi, assert that there is no Islamic tradition of nonviolence and no presumption against war. Yet there is an active Muslim Peace Fellowship, just as there is a Jewish Peace Fellowship. Most scholars do seem to agree that the pacifist element is not as strong in Islam as it is in Christianity, although it shares with both Christianity and Judaism a fundamental valuing of peace. Finally, Professor Sachedina notes one distinctive characteristic of Islam: "Muslims tend, particularly in the Middle East, to emphasize the impact of religion on public policy and on questions of war and peace in a way that sets them apart."[27]

In looking at all three Abrahamic faiths and their approach to these issues, Professor Michael Negler of the University of California at Berkeley sees "an impressive fundamental similarity among the people of the Book." He notes that all three wrestle with the problem of two seemingly contradictory tenets of their faiths: the requirement on the one hand to uphold life, which would call for nonviolence, and, on the other hand, the duty to fight injustice, which sometimes seems to demand violence.[28]

Dr. Amira Sonbol

Georgetown University professor of Islamic history Dr. Amira Sonbol offered the following observations on peace and war in Islam at the November 2003 forum.

Does the Islamic world have a just war theory? Yes, and I'd like to talk about this for a little bit, because there's a great deal of similarity between the just war theory of Islam and that of Catholicism. Most of the essentials are there. Most of the essentials are agreed upon. There are some differences, and repercussions of these differences, that I'd like to talk about.

This is just a small list, but it could go on. First, there is protection of life. Protection of life is essential in Islam. This is the first thing that we are taught. The Qur'an mentions it more than one time. Protection of life is essential.

There is protecting the helpless. If the Qur'an does anything, it talks about feeding the orphans and taking care of those who are the wayfarers, protecting them in every way possible, protecting the wealth of the children, protecting their property after they are orphaned, and so on and so forth. The protection of the helpless is ultimate.

Protecting old people is also there. In war, especially old people, children, the helpless, the handicapped — all those have to be protected and are not subject to war.

Even offering medical assistance to your enemy is in the Qur'an. It's something that is looked at with great appreciation as a way to heaven. The story of Saladin happens to be a true one, about him sending his doctor to Richard the Lionhearted when Richard was sick.

Treating prisoners in the right way is very important. People may not know this, but a great Muslim hero was removed just before the invasion of Iraq, the original one, because the caliph had heard that he had maltreated prisoners in one of the battles, and that he had butchered some. And so the caliph removed him completely and told him, "You can be one of the soldiers."

There is to be no poisoning of wells. This is very, very clear: no poisoning of wells or poisoning of food supplies. These are some things, again, that Islam speaks against. And there are to be no massacres and no destruction of homes.

So the idea is that we have a commonality. One should not be surprised because people of faith, people who think together, or people who want to find answers normally come to this kind of common moral tradition.

What about the types of war? Punitive war? Yes, Islam has punitive war. It's a concept that's there. The idea, as we talked about in the Catholic tradition, is of taking back what belongs to you. Yes, that's acceptable. Going to war for honor, that's also acceptable. That's why, though people may not have noticed, that Arab countries did join with the United States in the first Gulf War. Why? Because there was an attack against Kuwait. And the message was very clear: taking back what belonged to another.

Even in Afghanistan, there was not the kind of outcry you see now against the war in Iraq. Why? Because it was understandable that the United States had to go after al Qaeda because of what happened on September 11. That, of course, becomes different when it comes to the Iraqi war today.

What about jihad? Jihad is really self-defense. And I want to make this very clear. People think of jihad as offensive. It's really self-defense. But here it is extremely important to understand what we mean by self-defense. Self-defense simply means that not only do you protect yourself, but that it's your duty to do so. This is something people don't understand very well. I'm sure the United States knows this, because it has enough experts on Islam working here in Washington to tell it that once you take on one Islamic country, what you're taking on is all Islamic countries.

So once you begin going into war, especially if the war is not looked on as being justified, then you are really taking on several, if not all, Islamic countries. Today, the talk about Iran only acts to cause others to cause terrorism. And one wonders when one sits back and hears the constant talk about attacking Iraq, attacking Iran, attacking Syria, and so on. What they're calling for is a reaction to begin with. If you begin by attacking one Islamic state, what you are doing is putting something into action that could bring results that have to do with the duty of self-defense — the duty, not something that you merely do. You have to defend Islam in any way possible.

The third type of war we talked about today is preventive war. We don't have that concept in Islam, the idea of preventive war. You do not fight against somebody unless they fight against you. That is very important. And therefore, how are you going to be speaking to the Muslim public when they ask: Well, how do you know I'm going to come and hurt you unless I've already started to do so?

I think it is important to look at this, because today in the Islamic world we do not really have efforts like we have here today at this forum, to try and do this kind of meeting in which there is some sort of theology of war that is active. We are still using the classical idea that I have described.

Why? Because most of our clerics are state theologians. They belong to the state. And the problem is the question of the state and the interests of the state. What is the state all about? People are very skeptical toward the so-called state theologian. He can speak as much as he wants, but there's not going to be that much of a response within the population.

Then we have the anti-state theology. This is where people listen. The anti-state theologian comes through; there are the little mosques, the little broadcasts that come through the tape recorder. And it comes out publicly in popular writing and so on. The anti-state theologian is the one today that is formulating the meaning of preventive war or just war. It's very important to understand that, because it's a very complicated situation. It's a situation where the state is seen as an agent of the West. The state is seen as facilitating globalization. The Arab public in particular sees the West as sucking the oil wealth of these countries, with the countries not getting anything back from it. Therefore, there's a class conflict here, a class war at play, in which theology plays a very big role.

So when the theologian comes to talk about what the just war is, this theologian belongs to a particular faction within the class war. Then we can see that there's an acceptance of what is being said. So when a person like Osama bin Laden comes and talks about preventive war, what does he mean? What's he talking about? He's actually talking about the definition of war. What is war? And that's what they really talk about: What is war?

Here in the United States, we think that war is what you fight with a tank. Over there, they think that war is what you fight with the dollar. They're looking at economic war. They're looking at culture war. They're not looking at a just war that is being fought. They think they're already under siege.

What they are trying to prevent is a war that they see as a near-colonial war, which extends from colonialism. What they have is a war situation. They did not have to do what they did on September 11 to show that they are at war. They are already. They consider their actions defensive.

When you're poor, or you don't have a job, when you don't have any hope in the future, this makes a lot of sense to you. It's a question of what is war. I think if we ask this question, a lot of this could be understood.

Now for a couple of last things. Islam is against suicide, completely. You commit suicide, you go to hell. It's the first thing they teach you. So here again is evidence of the helplessness we've talked about. What would make young people actually go and blow themselves up when they know that in the hereafter they're going to go to hell? One after another, they do this, this atrocious act. And nobody asks the question why. Nobody cares. There's only condemnation. If anything, an insult was heaped on all of this by saying, oh, their families make money from their death, as if the families don't have a feeling of love toward their children. We're talking about complete cultural alienation, the idea of other that is less than myself.

The racist feelings that come through this, and the very fact that most of the population of the Muslim world, when they look at America, they see an America that looks down upon them: that creates and increases that sense of helplessness I pointed to earlier.

QUESTIONS FOR REFLECTION
AND DISCUSSION

1. What major similarities and differences do you see between the Catholic approach to war and the approaches of Judaism and Islam regarding war? How can these similarities and differences help us to better work together for peace?

2. Why do you think, as Rabbi White points out, that peace movements within Judaism don't get a lot of attention?

3. Consider Dr. Sonbol's question: What is war? To understand the contemporary situation and to work for peace, how important is it to consider the differing answers to that question around the world? Once we have examined these answers, what additional strategies must we employ, and what other types of action must we take, in order to work for peace?

PRACTICAL APPLICATION

Personal contact often helps us to deepen our understanding of "different others." Plan to visit a mosque or a synagogue, particularly when educational programs on peacemaking are presented.

Chapter Seven

The Historic Peace Churches

Dialogue Partners

HISTORICAL BEGINNINGS

As Christians struggle these days with issues of war and peace — Was the war in Iraq just? Can a war be just? What does it mean to be a peace-maker? — we would do well to look at how other churches approach these questions. Catholics have a long history of theological reflection in this area, which was detailed in chapter 2. Chapter 6 looked at the role of peace and war in Judaism and Islam. But other Christian churches have their traditions as well, and it would be fruitful to explore them. In fact, certain churches in this country are so associated with peacemaking that they are called "historic peace churches."

This name was given to three churches in the United States that met in Kansas in 1935. The Mennonites, the Religious Society of Friends, or Quakers, and the Church of the Brethren had gathered to discuss how they would respond to the growing unrest in Europe. They decided to make a joint effort to support and develop conscientious objection and alternatives to military service, and also to focus on peace education and peace witness.

These three churches have a long-standing commitment to nonviolence and a stance against war. In particular, in their theology they are opposed to military service; this is the main distinguishing feature of these peace churches. This is not to say that other churches are not committed to non-violence or do not actively work for peace. The Hutterites, the Moravians, and the Amish, for example, also hold these beliefs. The designation of peace church is, as one writer has put it, an accident of history.[1]

Anabaptist Roots

The Mennonites and the Church of the Brethren, along with two other groups, the Hutterites and the Amish, have their roots in the Protestant Reformation of the sixteenth century. For many centuries before this up-heaval, people's lives were ordered in an unchanging hierarchy. Everyone had a place in this hierarchy and a distinct role to play in it: peasants worked the land, the royalty and the nobility ruled, and the clergy mediated God's teaching, as formulated by the church. Life was often violent and insecure, but it was understandable and not to be questioned. People knew what to expect.

The Gospel and those who accept it are not to be protected with the sword, neither should they thus protect themselves.... True, believing Christians are as sheep in the midst of wolves.... They must be baptized in anxiety and trouble, tribulation, persecution, suffering, and death. They must be tried in the fire and must reach the fatherland of eternal rest, not by overcoming bodily enemies with the sword, but by overcoming spiritual foes. They use neither the worldly sword nor engage in war, since among them taking human life has ceased entirely, for we are no longer under the Old Covenant.   —Conrad Grebel, founder, Swiss Brethren Church, 1524

All this changed after Martin Luther nailed his ninety-five theses on the church door of Wittenberg Cathedral. Suddenly, nothing was certain. Luther's action started an earthquake that undermined the very foundations of life as people knew it.

The controversy touched all areas of life, not just religion; the social, economic, and political arenas soon erupted as well, since everything had been so closely interwoven before. Many countries were torn by conflict between warring factions.

The Anabaptist movement, which began in southern Germany and Switzerland, was part of this turmoil, and was actually a breakaway from earlier reforms. "Anabaptist" means "baptize again." The name grew out of this movement's belief that infant baptism was not scripturally based and that people needed to come to faith first, as adults, before being baptized. It began in 1525, when some Protestant students in Zurich, acting on this belief, baptized each other. It is difficult for us today to appreciate the intense controversy that this position caused in the early 1500s. It was not only a theological statement; it spilled over into the political sphere as well.

Historians Donald B. Kraybill and Carl F. Bowman say, "Infant baptism conferred membership into both Catholic and Protestant churches. It also granted automatic citizenship, which gave civil authorities the power to tax and conscript. So the question at hand was not merely the age of baptism, but a much deeper issue of authority in church/state relations."[2] In looking to scripture alone for authority, Anabaptists were declaring themselves independent of both the state and the established churches — which neither was prepared to tolerate. Both the Catholic Church and the new Protestant groups that had gained some power — under Martin

Luther, Ulrich Zwingli, and John Calvin — persecuted the Anabaptists with equal savagery. They were hunted down and drowned, burned, beheaded, starved, and flayed. Most of their leaders met early and violent deaths.

But it was not only in rejecting infant baptism that the Anabaptists set themselves apart from the Catholic Church and the other Protestant churches. They also held strongly to the separation of church and state — a truly new and heretical concept in the eyes of many people at that time. And they also believed that the teaching of the New Testament laid upon all Christians the duty to practice nonviolence.

The Anabaptist movement was not monolithic, however. Like many movements, it had its radical elements. In the 1530s, one group of Anabaptists took control of the Westphalian city of Munster and established a theocracy that was actually anarchy. Private property was eliminated; polygamy was encouraged and sometimes required; those who resisted the regime were punished violently. The state eventually retook the city and the reprisals were brutal.

Yet the great majority of Anabaptists were not violent, and the movement grew and spread across Europe, especially in Germany and the Low Countries. One of its most important leaders was a Dutch Catholic priest, Menno Simons, who embraced the Anabaptist doctrine and way of life and gave his name to one branch of the Anabaptists: the Mennonites. Many Mennonites from Switzerland and Germany, fleeing persecution, came to North America in the eighteenth century, first settling in Pennsylvania and then moving westward. In the late nineteenth century, Mennonites from Russia and Holland emigrated, moving mostly to Canada and to the western United States.

> The regenerated do not go to war nor engage in strife. They are the children of peace who have beaten their swords into plowshares and their spears into pruning hooks and know of no war.... Since we are to be conformed to Christ, how can we then fight our enemies with the sword?   —Menno Simons, 1539

The Mennonites are only one religious group descended from the Anabaptists. The Hutterites trace their origins to some Anabaptists in Moravia in 1528, whose leader was Jakob Hutter. This group, known for sharing their possessions in common, endured many years of persecution in Europe; a small number of them came to North America in the 1870s. Another branch of Anabaptists are the Amish, named for their leader Jakob Ammann. Their roots go back to South Germany and Switzerland in the late 1600s, when they broke off from the Mennonites. In the seventeenth and eighteenth centuries, many of them also came to North

America searching for religious freedom. Finally, we have the Brethren. This group differs from the others in that it was shaped by the German Pietist movement as well by Anabaptism. But, like all the others, it too saw large numbers of its members coming to the United States in search of tolerance and freedom of expression.

The Society of Friends

The Quakers, the third of the historic peace churches (along with the Mennonites and the Brethren), is the only one that is not directly descended from the Anabaptist movement. Its origins go back to seventeenth-century England rather than sixteenth-century Europe. Yet there were marked similarities in these two environments. Both were filled with religious turmoil, turmoil that was linked inextricably with politics. Different religious sects sprang up in England during this time — it was a period of intense religious interest and searching — and many of them had beliefs and practices that disrupted the standing political and economic order. It was in this century, after all, that the English Civil War erupted, a conflict in which politics, utopianism, war, and religion were all intermixed. A group with the interesting name of the Levellers espoused equality for all and took their demands to parliament; another group, the Diggers, believed that the land should belong to everyone and took to digging up common plots to plant gardens. Dissidents called Seekers, Ranters, and the Family of Love also agitated for change.[3]

In the end, most of these groups affiliated themselves with the Quakers, or the Religious Society of Friends, a sect founded by George Fox in 1652. The Friends believed that God speaks to all people, that all people contain within them a spark of the divine, and that therefore all people have inherent worth. Fox spoke of the "Inward Light," which alone guides human beings to God; he held that external elements of religion, such as priests and churches, are not necessary.

Not surprisingly, Fox and his followers met with much opposition and persecution. Their fundamental belief that God has no need of an intermediary to speak to human beings threatened the established religious order. They also engaged in such disturbing practices as refusing to pay tithes, to swear oaths, to show particular honor to people in power, and, like the Anabaptists, to take up arms. And, like the Anabaptists, there were some fringe elements. Neither the Puritan government of Oliver Cromwell nor the restored monarchy of Charles II approved of this new group, whose members were regularly imprisoned, flogged, and branded. Many Quakers left England to go to the colonies in North America, where, initially, they faced an equally hostile reception.

Perhaps the best-known chapter in American Quaker history is the establishment of the state of Pennsylvania under the auspices of William Penn, an English Quaker convert. He called it a "Holy Experiment": a place that would offer sanctuary to Quakers from England and that would demonstrate to the world all that Quakerism could do to change the lives of people for the better.[4] Penn became well known for the manner in which he dealt with the Indians as he was setting up his colony. Alone among Europeans, he maintained that it was possible and morally obligatory to treat these native inhabitants fairly and with respect — a stand that grew out of his Quaker beliefs. His "Great Treaty" in 1682 with the Delaware Indian leaders, in which he acquired land for what would become Pennsylvania and later Delaware — was that rare thing at the time, a peaceful and equitable exchange of land for goods and money. Moreover, his peaceful policies continued for many years afterward.

Our principle is, and our practices have always been, to seek peace and ensue it; to follow after righteousness and the knowledge of God; seeking the good and welfare, and doing that which tends to the peace of all. We know that wars and fightings proceed from the lusts of men.... That the Spirit of Christ, by which we are guided, is not changeable... and we certainly know, and testify to the world, that the Spirit of Christ, which leads us into all truth, will never move us to fight and war against any man with outward weapons, neither for the kingdom of Christ, nor for the kingdoms of this world.   — George Fox and Others, 1660 Declaration Concerning Wars

---

The Friends made many important contributions to the colonies and, later, to the new country, the United States of America. They continued Penn's policy of fair and respectful dealings with Indians. They also were instrumental in the abolition movement, in women's suffrage, and in working for the humane treatment of prisoners and the mentally ill. Additionally, like the groups with Anabaptist roots, they had a staunch policy of refusing to participate in any wars, a policy that went back to their early days in England.

THE NINETEENTH AND EARLY TWENTIETH CENTURIES

Later in their history, all these groups with pacifist roots — the Mennonites, the Quakers, the Brethren — found themselves faced with the challenge of holding on to their nonviolent traditions when America was engaged in a war. They responded to this challenge in different ways, but the churches held on to their beliefs. In the case of the Quakers, this faithfulness led to the loss of a great many of their members during the Revolutionary and Civil Wars. But for all of them, it was the experience of dealing with the demands of the government and popular opinion during wartime that led them to clarify their pacifist beliefs and develop ways of living them out.

During the Civil War, Quakers were able to get Congress to pass legislation that allowed members of peace churches to perform alternative service. It was the first such legislation on the national level. The American Friends Service Committee was founded in 1917. During and after World War I, it worked with refugees in Europe; later, it brought relief to victims of famine and disease there, established orphanages, and worked to rebuild viable agricultural systems. In the 1930s it helped people escape from Hitler's Germany. It was awarded the Nobel Peace Prize in 1947 for its work.

During World War II, members of the Church of the Brethren helped resettle Japanese-Americans who were interned in evacuation camps. Also during that time, the Brethren, the Friends, and the Mennonites formed the Civilian Public Service, a branch of the U.S. Selective Service agency run by the churches without cost to the government. It provided alternative service for people opposed to participating in the military, and its members worked in forestry, soil conservation, and in the mental and public health fields. Their work in mental hospitals led to major advances in mental health care in the United States. By this time, the Brethren and the Mennonites had also set up service committees to work with the government to develop alternative service and to otherwise carry out their peacemaking mission.

RECENT INITIATIVES

In the latter part of the twentieth century, there were some major developments in the work of the peace churches. One such development was the growing realization that a commitment to nonviolence and a refusal to participate in wars must be accompanied by offering some concrete alternatives to violence. This involvement began earlier in some ways, of course, when conscientious objectors performed service during the Second World War, working in mental hospitals, fighting forest fires, and even volunteering to be guinea pigs for medical experiments. Joseph Miller, who served with the Mennonite Central Committee in Hungary, calls it, in the Mennonite Church, "the shift from quiet separation to a theology of active involvement."[5]

Recently, there has been an increased focus on practical peacemaking skills. The peace churches have become leaders in conflict mediation and conciliation and conflict resolution and transformation. Graduate peace studies programs are offered at Eastern Mennonite University and Fresno Pacific University, and the number of undergraduate programs at Mennonite schools is increasing.

Conscientious objectors tending to patients in Cleveland, Ohio, during World War II. Mennonite Central Committee Photograph Collection, Archives of the Mennonite Church, Goshen, Indiana.

In the late 1970s, the Mennonite Church established the Mennonite Conciliation Service (MCS), which offers training in advanced mediation and conciliation skills. People take these skills and use them to mediate conflicts in their families, schools, churches, and communities. MCS itself also provides mediation and consultation services for many different kinds of organizations. By the 1980s, Mennonite groups in Europe were asking the MCS to bring conciliation training there; U.S. Mennonites also traveled to Nicaragua to mediate conflicts. Since then, MCS members have gone to Mozambique, Liberia, and El Salvador to work in conciliation in communities torn apart by war.

Another significant development is the emergence of Christian Peacemaker Teams, a joint program of the Mennonite, Brethren, and Quaker churches, with the support and membership of people from other denominations. Established in 1989, these teams perform nonviolent interventions in areas of conflict around the world; they are currently in Iraq, Colombia, and Hebron on the West Bank. They work to provide a peaceful presence in these places of violence and to support violence-reduction efforts.

Listed below are some key concepts and practices that have gained prominence in recent years. Some members of the historic peace churches have been instrumental in developing them.

- **Conflict Management** generally involves taking action to keep a conflict from escalating further. It implies the ability to control the intensity of a conflict and its effects through negotiation, intervention, institutional mechanisms, and other traditional diplomatic methods. It usually does not address the deep-rooted issues that may be at the cause of the conflict or attempt to bring about a solution (*Search for Common Ground, an organization that works to transform the way the world deals with conflict, emphasizing cooperative solutions pursued on a realistic scale and with practical means*).

- **Conflict Resolution**, by contrast, seeks to resolve the incompatibilities of interests and behaviors that constitute the conflict by recognizing and addressing the underlying issues, finding a mutually acceptable process, and establishing relatively harmonious relationships and outcomes (*Search for Common Ground*).

- **Conflict Transformation** envisions and responds to the ebb and flow of social conflict as life-giving opportunities for creating constructive change processes that reduce violence, increase justice in direct interaction and social structures, and respond to real-life problems in human relationships. . . . It has a positive orientation toward conflict and . . . views peace as centered and rooted in the quality of relationships (*John Paul Lederach, pioneer in conflict transformation work*).

- **Restorative Justice** is concerned with healing victims' wounds, restoring offenders to law-abiding lives, and repairing harm done to interpersonal relationships and the community. It seeks to involve all stakeholders and provide opportunities for those most affected by the crime to be directly involved in the process of responding to the harm caused (*Michelle Maiese, researcher with the Conflict Research Consortium of the University of Colorado. Another leading researcher and writer in restorative justice is Howard Zehr*).

It would be a mistake to assume, however, that these various efforts are equally supported by all the members of these churches. There have always been tensions about how to understand the commitment to nonviolence, how binding it is, and how it is to be carried out. A large proportion of American Quakers, for example, were on the side of the Union in the Civil War; later, many Quakers served in both world wars. And recently, a Quaker scholar commented, "Official statements are often not normative for members. While most Quaker leaders remain committed to what Friends call the 'Peace Testimony,' . . . pacifism and peace activism are contested issues among American Friends. . . . On the other hand, many Friends still put tremendous energy into peacemaking work and are central to numerous efforts to try to create a more peaceful world."[6]

Among the Mennonites, a certain tension has always existed in the church's relationship to the world. This tension is reflected in a concept of Mennonite theology called the *two kingdoms:* the notion that we live in two kingdoms, God's kingdom, represented by the church and its members, and the kingdom of the world, represented by the state and society. The distinction comes from scripture, from Jesus' words about being in the world but not of it. Some people see a historical basis for this thinking, since for many years Mennonites in this country tended to live in rural areas, in Mennonite enclaves. In terms of peacemaking, the two kingdoms perspective often led to a Mennonite habit of withdrawing from the world rather than actively seeking to change it. This is not to say that Mennonites have not contributed a great deal to the world; their history of relief work is a testimony to that. But it was widely recognized as a new direction for the church when it began to focus on "the positive side of helping to resolve conflicts as well as the negative side of refusing to participate in war."[7]

Christian Peacemaker Teams (CPT) have been in the West Bank since 1995 and in Iraq since October 2002. In the West Bank, just south of Hebron, CPT members accompany Palestinian children to school, since often Israeli settlers use violence to try to prevent any travel. Team members also provide documentation of human rights violations of the Palestinian residents by the Israeli army and settlers. In Iraq, during the 2003 war, members placed their bodies near critical infrastructure buildings like hospitals and water treatment plants in an attempt to keep them from being destroyed. After the war, members have, for example, helped Iraqis meet with loved ones who are being detained and worked with Iraqis who want to form Muslim Peacemaking Teams.

Regardless of any tensions, however, the historic peace churches have certainly taken a leading role in active peacemaking efforts around the world.

In recent years, the Mennonite Church and the Catholic Church have engaged in ongoing dialogue. These dialogues have focused on theological and historical issues; some commentators see peace efforts as a fruitful area of interaction.[8] In 2002, a new project, the Catholic Peacebuilding Network, was launched, sponsored by the Joan B. Kroc Institute for International Peace Studies at the University of Notre Dame and Catholic Relief Services (CRS). One of the main participants at the planning meeting for the project was Mennonite John Paul Lederach, who is a pioneer in what is called conflict transformation work. Catholic Relief Services has also sent many people to Eastern Mennonite University's Summer Peacebuilding Program to train them in peacemaking techniques. Lederach himself is currently on the faculty of the Kroc Institute; in this capacity, he has worked with both CRS and with Catholic bishops in different countries across the globe in peacemaking efforts.[9]

In conclusion, let's turn to the words of Gerald Schlabach, professor of theology at the University of St. Thomas and one of the leading scholars in peacemaking today.

> To be a peace church in the 21st century we will have to develop a global, transnational perspective.... We need to institutionalize a widening network of international ties and communication between local churches around the world. But the much-maligned "institutional" churches that sustain global communion through the office and college of bishops already offer an ancient gift from God that we dare not despise or underestimate. We need to stimulate a deepening consciousness of Christian global citizenship and solidarity that penetrates the so-called "pews." But the admittedly-messy "free" churches (Anabaptist, Evangelical, Pentecostal) that have done so much to spread the gospel through grassroots lay movements already offer a lively gift from God that we dare not ignore or dismiss. By God's grace, we already are the global community that we are still becoming. So "let the church be the church" — and it *will* be a peace church.[10]

QUESTIONS FOR REFLECTION AND DISCUSSION

1. How would you yourself define a peace church? Which churches fit your definition? Would you call your church a peace church?

2. One issue that the historic peace churches are heavily involved in is that of conscientious objection. It has become an issue in the

Catholic Church as well. What do you think? Does a person have a right to refuse in engage in combat because he or she thinks all wars are wrong? Suppose the person believes that only a particular war is wrong; should conscientious objector status be granted in that case?

3. Do you see any drawbacks to a stance of total nonviolence in international affairs? What are they? What are the advantages to this stance?

PRACTICAL APPLICATION

Watch one of the following and discuss it. The 2000 PBS documentary *The Good War and Those Who Refused to Fight It* looks at conscientious objectors during World War II: what they did, how they served, and the reactions they faced. It also gives a more general history of conscientious objection in the United States. The 2004 movie *The Conscientious Objector* is the true story of Desmond Doss, who refused to carry a weapon but who served as a medic in World War II and earned a Medal of Honor for his courage. From Heartland Films. Note: It contains language and/or adult situations that may not be suitable for young children.

Chapter Eight

The Power of Forgiveness

WILLIAM BOLE

We have all heard moving stories about the power of forgiveness in people's lives. In her book *The Hiding Place,* Corrie Ten Boom, a survivor of a Nazi concentration camp, tells one such story. After the war, she unexpectedly meets one of the SS guards who tormented her during her time at the camp. At first, she is unable to reach out and shake his outstretched hand; she is frozen, unable to forgive. But she prays and finds herself freed. She can forgive him. More recently, in our own country, a man accused the late Cardinal Joseph Bernardin of molesting him when he was younger. After the allegations were found to be false, the cardinal visited the man, who had become seriously ill, and forgave him. There is even an organization, made up of the relatives of people who have been murdered, whose focus is forgiveness of the murderers and fighting against the death penalty.

But does forgiveness — so awe-inspiring on the individual level — work on the international level? Does it exist as a political force in today's violent intergroup struggles? What exactly *is* forgiveness in political and international affairs? What might it look like in the dangerously complex domain of geopolitics? What are some typical transactions of forgiveness in politics? What are the limitations and ambiguities of such a strategy of international peacemaking?

Some people believe that in certain cases forgiving is not moral, that it trivializes the suffering of the innocent. And when we face the fear and random havoc wrought by terrorists, it would be easy to dismiss forgiveness as something both irrelevant and ineffective. Justice, rather than forgiveness, is what is needed, we may think.

Pope John Paul II confronted these issues. Two months after September 11, 2001, he sent up a heartfelt cry against terrorism, calling it a "true crime against humanity" and "a contradiction of faith in God." He spoke of a post–September 11 world in which "the power of evil seems once again to have taken the upper hand." He called for bringing terrorists to justice, and in this pursuit he saw the use of force as justifiable, within strict moral limits. He spoke of the need to fight social, political, and economic injustices that may serve as recruiting grounds for terrorism.[1]

Justice, however, is not enough, John Paul continued. There is a missing element — forgiveness — which is needed for healing wounds, restoring relationships, and ushering in a deeper reconciliation. "The pillars of true peace are justice and that form of love which is forgiveness," he wrote.[2]

We are saved by the final form of love,
which is forgiveness.   — Reinhold Niebuhr

The title of that statement was *No Peace without Justice, No Justice without Forgiveness,* and with it, Pope John Paul was stretching the tradition of Catholic reflections on war and peace. Arguably, these official reflections had already been stretched in the past generation or two, along with a development of Catholic social teaching. In typical fashion, a discussion of war and peace might center on whether and under what circumstances legitimate authorities have a right and duty to use deadly force, a discussion guided by tenets of the classical just war theory. However, in his 1963 encyclical letter *Pacem in Terris (Peace on Earth),* Pope John XXIII had little to say about war as such, aside from eleven paragraphs under the heading of disarmament. He said nothing about just war criteria. Instead, he drew attention to the conditions or building blocks of peace, particularly human rights and interdependence among nations.[3] Four years later, Pope Paul VI highlighted the importance of human and social development in his encyclical *Populorum Progressio (The Development of Peoples),* declaring that development is "the new name for peace."[4] Arguably, in the decades since, universal church pronouncements touching on war and peace have moved along this track of *peace building,* more than along just war lines. In his post–September 11 statement, Pope John Paul broached a new dimension, which seemed to call for an expanded Catholic slogan: If you want peace, seek justice — and forgiveness.

TRANSLATING FORGIVENESS
INTO POLITICS

Admittedly, forgiveness might seem an unlikely subject of international political discourse. Suicide bombings in the Middle East, fierce clashes between Muslims and Christians in several African countries, the challenge of terrorism: these and other developments might lend an air of implausibility to any discussion of forgiveness and international conflict. Even apart from the current geopolitical context, forgiveness could hardly be considered a traditional value in world affairs. The concept is foreign to most secular political philosophies and peripheral at best to traditional

Christian theories of the common good and a just war. Among twentieth-century philosophers, the German-Jewish refugee Hannah Arendt stood out, writing after the Holocaust that she saw forgiveness as one of two human capacities that make it possible to alter the political future. The other is the ability to enter into covenants.[5]

It is not that forgiveness has been a no-show in the wide world. It surfaced after the nightmare of apartheid in South Africa, when then-president Nelson Mandela awakened many to a reality expressed later in the title of Anglican Archbishop Desmond Tutu's book, *No Future without Forgiveness*. The magnanimous president became an effective symbol of forgiveness and reconciliation; he was a political prisoner for twenty-seven years and made his white jailer an honored guest at his 1994 inauguration. Through the Truth and Reconciliation Commission headed by Tutu, a Nobel Peace Laureate, South Africa formally abstained from revenge. Devised in the wake of elections that transferred power from a white minority regime to the black majority, the commission in effect gave notorious violators of human rights a choice: tell the whole truth or face prosecution. The truth came out — in grisly detail about atrocities during the apartheid era — and many went free. Those two elements helped avert a racial bloodbath forewarned by many.[6]

In Northern Ireland, Catholics and Protestants have been able to imagine a better future through public acts of mutual repentance and forgiveness. In the Balkans, some voices of forgiveness have transcended the obsessive nationalism and ethnocentrism that drove the region to war on several fronts. In Cambodia, Buddhist primate Moha Ghosananda has struggled to release people from a paralyzing past by envisioning a future of forgiveness. He calls for selectively forgiving Khmer Rouge leaders who have repented and renounced violence after perpetrating that nation's unspeakable genocide, but Cambodians need more time.[7]

> He that cannot forgive others breaks the bridge over which he must pass himself; for every man has need to be forgiven.
>
> —Thomas Fuller

These examples aside, there remains a sense of implausibility surrounding this subject. The reason has much to do with conventional notions of forgiveness that do not travel well from the personal to the social and political realms.

To cite one maxim, "forgive and forget" might imply that forgiving means abandoning moral judgment and a clear-eyed understanding of an enemy's crimes. It is a fairly short step from there to conclude that forgiveness is irreconcilable with justice. Indeed, the conventional view has complicated peace efforts in places like Bosnia, where the forgiveness-justice duality "causes really serious blocks in initiating a sincere dialogue on reconciliation, particularly between Christians and Muslims. It also provokes negative attitudes toward outsiders who come to the area vigorously preaching forgiveness as a solution to the people's problems," psychologist Olga Botcharova has observed.[8]

There is, however, a radically different conception in which "remember and forgive" is the more fitting slogan because "forgiveness begins with memory suffused with moral judgment," in the words of Donald W. Shriver Jr.[9] (In a similar vein, Mennonite peace builder John Paul Lederach would replace "forgive and forget" with "remember and change."[10]) Shriver writes, "If your parents died in Auschwitz, your father on Iwo Jima, your sister at Hiroshima, or your grandfather at the end of a lynch-rope in Alabama, you are not going to forget. Ethically speaking, why should you? To be forgotten is the final indignity that one's neighbors can impose on you in your unjust suffering."[11]

This is not to say that remembering is a straight path to forgiveness. As hostilities in places like Northern Ireland and the former Yugoslavia show, memory can move people in exactly the opposite direction. Yet even in settings where memory is lethal, few (upon reflection) would disregard the value of cultivating authentic memories. In other words, few would suggest that forgetting is generally the reliable road to long-lasting forgiveness and reconciliation. "I think that is a myth, about forgiving. Forgiveness is not forgetting; it has more to do with how something is remembered. It's not remembered with bitterness," explains the Rev. Douglas Baker, a Presbyterian who has ministered in both Northern Ireland and the United States.[12]

> Men cannot forgive what they cannot punish.
> —Hannah Arendt

Similarly, there is growing recognition that forgiveness and juridical justice are not mutually exclusive. In Shriver's understanding, forgiveness does not require the abandonment of all versions of punishment of evildoers; what it demands is a turn away from revenge. In like mind, Brian D. Lennon, SJ, has concluded that a person can forgive while deciding that a perpetrator should be punished "for the sake of order and not out of revenge."[13] Saying that forgiveness is compatible in principle with legal justice is not the same as getting it right in every instance and striking the proper balance between these two social goods. Debate continues, for instance, over the amnesty program in South Africa, even though the granting of it was conditional. Likewise, some human rights observers have raised questions about the 2004 act of mercy of East Timor president

Xanana Gusmao, who reduced the prison terms of some pro-Indonesian militiamen who had staged a massacre in 1999. These observers noted that it was a wounded land where the punishment has barely begun.[14]

A DEFINITION

During dialogues on forgiveness sponsored by the Woodstock Theological Center at Georgetown University in Washington, DC, core participants embraced a definition drawn from Shriver's formulation: "Forgiveness in a political context is an act that joins moral truth, forbearance, empathy, and commitment to repair a fractured relationship." Shriver's exact words were "fractured human relation" in *An Ethic for Enemies.* He writes:

> Such a combination calls for a collective turning from the past that neither ignores past evil nor excuses it, that neither overlooks justice nor reduces justice to revenge, that insists on the humanity of enemies even in their commission of dehumanizing deeds, and that values the justice that restores political community above the justice that destroys it.[15]

Each element of Shriver's definition has found expression in the throes of upheaval and confrontation on the global stage.

Moral truth, in particular the social catharsis of truth telling and public confession, is what South Africa pursued in setting up the Tutu commission. Like South Africa, roughly two dozen countries have turned to truth commissions, which are official bodies that investigate atrocities of the near past. These countries have seen the commissions partly as a way of responding to a basic need of victims — to have terrible abuses of human rights acknowledged by society, if not necessarily punished. The idea is that such an airing of truth can promote social healing, and indeed Tutu has written that after hearing their abusers confess to human rights violations, many victims responded by proffering forgiveness on the spot, even though violators often walked away free. His commission, or a quasi-independent committee within it, had the power to grant amnesties to those who made a full disclosure of political crimes during the apartheid era. One key to South Africa's success was this linking of amnesty to full cooperation with the commission. By way of contrast, in at least two other countries, those implicated in rights offenses were granted unconditional amnesty as part of political settlements — which gave them little incentive to confess. For that reason, truth commissions in El Salvador and Chile had far less success in creating a climate of repentance and forgiveness. The element of moral truth was missing.[16]

Forbearance from revenge is what Mandela signaled at his inauguration. Former South Korean dissident Kim Dae Jung did the same at his own presidential inauguration in February 1998, when he vowed, "This

new government will not practice the politics of retaliation."[17] More recently, after a series of payback assassinations by the Israeli military, sixty
Palestinian intellectuals issued a plea for their people not to retaliate. It
was a hint of forgiveness, a gesture of forbearance from revenge.[18]

Empathy is what the late King Hussein of Jordan demonstrated when
he traveled to an Israeli border town where one of his soldiers had gone
berserk, firing at Israeli schoolgirls who were on a class trip. Seven of the
eighth graders were killed. He visited the homes of the Israeli families
and knelt before the parents, begging forgiveness. "I looked in his face
and I saw that he was ashamed, and he had tears in his eyes, and he was
honest," said an Israeli accountant whose thirteen-year-old daughter died
in the 1997 attack. The mother said she could see the truth in his eyes.[19]

The *commitment to repair a fractured relationship* has come through in
many such acts. At Kim's inauguration in South Korea, seated front and
center were four ex-presidents of South Korea, including General Chun
Doo Hwan, who, in 1980, engineered a death sentence for Kim. Shriver,
who was present for the event, points out, "That, it seems to me, in all
of its ambiguity, is what we're talking about. We're talking about the
possibility, after a relationship has been deeply damaged, that it can be
repaired."[20]

To be social is to be forgiving.
— Robert Frost, in "The Star-Splitter"

What the Shriver definition suggests is that forgiveness is a process, not
simply an isolated act. As a *social* process, it goes well beyond the simple
asking or receiving of forgiveness that is characteristic of the interpersonal
encounter (though even between two people, forgiveness is often not so
straightforward or explicit). It is illustrative of the process view that peacemakers could operate on each level of Shriver's definition without uttering
the word "forgiveness." For example, Kim, a Catholic who later received
the Nobel Peace Prize, did not use the word "forgiveness" at his inauguration. Nevertheless, he conducted a transaction of forgiveness: a few words
and a symbolic gesture that expressed forbearance from revenge, together
with the commitment to eventually reconcile.

The above examples are presented here as illustrations of a definition.
To understand this dynamic of social relationships, it is necessary to look
more closely at the transactions of forgiveness. Notable among these have
been public apologies and acknowledgments of wrongdoing, which may
nurture an atmosphere of forgiveness, especially when extended mutually
by conflicting parties.

APOLOGIZING
IN NORTHERN IRELAND

It has been said that the Irish forgive and forget nothing, and yet Northern Ireland has served paradoxically as an international showcase of forgiveness, against a backdrop of bloody conflict between Catholics and Protestants. The road to the 1998 Good Friday peace agreement was paved, in part, by unilateral acts of personal forgiveness offered by victims and their families, as well as corporate acts of repentance extended by leaders.

One of the more memorable exchanges of repentance began with a visit to Dublin by former Archbishop of Canterbury George Carey, in March of 1994. "As an Englishman I am aware of just how much we English need to ask forgiveness for our often brutal domination and crass insensitivity in the 800 years of history of our relationship with Ireland," he declared in a sermon at Christ Church Cathedral.

Early the following year, the Catholic primate of Northern Ireland traveled to Canterbury and responded in kind. "I wish to ask forgiveness from the people of this land for the wrongs and hurts inflicted by Irish people upon the people of this country on many occasions during our shared history, and particularly in the past 25 years. I believe that this reciprocal recognition of the need to forgive and to be forgiven is a necessary condition" of healing between Protestants and Catholics, said Cardinal Cahal B. Daly, now retired as archbishop of Armagh.

At the time, these simple words of forgiveness generated some resentment in Northern Ireland. Both the archbishop of Canterbury and the cardinal of Armagh came under fire for presuming to repent or forgive on behalf of the entire Protestant and Catholic communities. Such representation was probably inescapable in this case: Carey and Daly could not apologize for their own terrible political crimes, because they did not commit any. During a conference at Georgetown University two years later, Cardinal Daly himself acknowledged that the apologies might have been more compelling had they come from people who actually committed the misdeeds. Yet some of those people stepped forward, soon enough. The Protestant paramilitary leader Gusty Spence helped put Northern Ireland in a more forgiving mood when he offered "the loved ones of all innocent victims over the past 25 years abject and true remorse," as Daly related. By the late 1990s, the language of forgiveness was coloring the reconciliation process in Northern Ireland.

These experiences point to questions about agents as well as acts of forgiveness. Who shall forgive? Who shall repent? Strictly speaking, only victims or their families can forgive acts perpetrated against them. Still, leaders of various communities have advanced a social process of reconciliation by engaging in various transactions of forgiveness. Some experts have argued that Daly was less credible in the role of repentant, because he did not share culpability for crimes and misdeeds, which is the point he conceded at Georgetown. Even so, apologies by the culpable have their own pitfalls, especially if the acts of repentance ring hollow (which has been the fate of apologies tendered by the Irish Republican Army). What these illustrations indicate is that apologies, regardless of who is rendering them, are a process in and of themselves. During the Woodstock dialogues, participants identified three steps in such a process: clear acknowledgment, genuine remorse, and a commitment to make restoration.[21]

The Northern Ireland experience also throws light on the limitations of forgiveness as a solution to intractable conflict. Forgiving acts and gestures may have only so much value if not accompanied by social and political reforms. Another way of putting this is that restitution — for example, ending discrimination against Catholics or decommissioning weapons — is necessary to promoting a social climate of forgiveness. Stressing the role of restitution in any scheme of forgiveness, Daly notes,

> I submit that statements of remorse and pleas for pardon and expressions of forgiveness are necessary preludes to and essential concomitants of conflict resolution, but they are not sufficient; they are not effective without cessation of the wrongs and the hurts of conflict, without, in short, the change of behavior and the full purpose of amendment which the Christian tradition has always held to be the defining condition of genuine repentance, and without the just changes and institutions which are necessary for true reconciliation.[22]

ACKNOWLEDGING MISDEEDS IN THE FORMER YUGOSLAVIA

In some highly fractious societies, the most difficult step is to merely acknowledge atrocities and other misdeeds perpetuated by members of one's ethnic or religious group. This has been an ongoing challenge in places such as the former Yugoslavia, where different communities have drastically different perceptions of the reality surrounding their conflicts. Helping aggrieved people to the stage of acknowledgment has been a crucial part of efforts at small-group reconciliation conducted by third parties with an interest in international conflict resolution. One experiment has involved lay people from the Croatian Catholic, Serbian Orthodox, and ethnic Albanian Muslim communities, who came together following brutal ethnic-cleansing campaigns in Bosnia, Herzegovina, and Kosovo, beginning in the mid-1990s.

In this ongoing series of ecumenical and interfaith seminars, facilitators have drawn upon the motif of laments in the Hebrew scriptures, or Old Testament. The Rev. David Steele, a United Church of Christ minister who has led many of the workshops under the auspices of the Washington-based Center for Strategic and International Studies, relates that the purpose of ritualized lamentation in ancient Israel was to "offer up to God all injury and hurt so that God could heal the pain and God could bring justice." This same method of lament creates a bridge between the voicing of grievances and the acknowledgment of wrongdoing by oneself and one's group. The prophet Jeremiah, for example, identifies the suffering of the Jews but also asks his people to examine themselves and their society, as well as to remember the pervasive reality of God's forgiveness.[23]

In other words, this weaving of grief and apology is made possible by theological reflection (Steele's catchall term for reflection upon experiences related to themes ranging from acknowledgment to justice). Through this prism, a more secular language of acknowledgment arises and becomes a centerpiece of these dialogues. It also becomes one of the "most explosive" elements of the seminar process, in Steele's words, emerging suddenly as a challenge to group perceptions and distorted memories.

The past is never dead; it's not even past.
— William Faulkner, *Requiem for a Nun*

At one Serb-Croat seminar, participants were asked to compose a list of wrongful acts committed by their respective groups. That led to an outbreak of acknowledgment acrimony, as one side, the Serbs, failed to acknowledge nearly as much as the Croats.

> And the Croats were extremely offended by that because they felt like they had really been harmed the most, and yet when it came to acknowledging things, they felt that the Serbs were glossing over all kinds of things and not nearly being so honest. And that's the dynamic that became very explosive, extremely explosive in fact within that seminar. It was towards the end of the second day, and the conflict was carried over into suppertime. And even after supper, certain people were going at it, with some Croats just demanding that there be an acknowledgment by the Serbs of the terrible things that had been done. And in this case, the Serbs resisted doing that, and the resistance would kind of grow as they were confronted by angry Croats.

That was part of a forgiveness learning curve. Facilitators knew the Serbs lived in an area that was reverting to Croat control following the 1992–95 war in Bosnia, but they had not fully appreciated the difficulty of moving people to acknowledgment in such insecure surroundings. All the same, Steele and others have found that acknowledgment, though volatile, is necessary. "What people are constantly looking for is acknowledgment of those things that have terribly injured their own community. I hear person after person recounting how they expect an apology from the other side regarding X-Y-Z, particularly a grievance that they have in mind. And I think people need to do that, but I think also that different communities need to be helped in order to do that."[24]

A process of acknowledgment or apology is not without risks, particularly in the most incendiary settings. For example, some observers pointed to fears among many in the former Yugoslavia that public confessions of wrongdoing would backfire, supplying a rationale for retaliatory attacks by enemies. Pitfalls aside, apologies and acknowledgment are but one step, or a sequence of steps, in the overall forgiveness process. Reaching beyond this stage, to actual or explicit forgiveness, carries its own risks, as seen through the small-group dynamics. Steele, who introduces the "choice to forgive" following the acknowledgments during his seminars, explains that the process could backfire if people feel that forgiveness is being foisted upon them. "The biggest problem we face in dealing with forgiveness is the sense or fear among people that someone will force it on them. We need to allow people to approach this sensitive topic at their own speed."[25]

LESSONS LEARNED

Although frequently unheralded, forgiveness is a reality in world political affairs. By speaking of forgiveness as a pillar of peace, Pope John Paul was not just sending up a prayerful intention; he was giving voice to the experiences of many who have begun to see forgiveness as one way of conceiving the task of international peacemaking. This is especially clear if one looks at forgiveness not as a single, instantaneous act, but as a process that includes transactions highlighting truth, forbearance, empathy, and the will to reconcile.

This is not to say that every act of forgiveness will be efficacious. Nor is it to suggest that the process will be immune to the ambiguities of judgment, the possibilities of miscalculation or unintended consequences, which are the risk of any foray into political affairs, as social ethicist John Langan, SJ, has underscored. Conceivably, a determination to forgive could result in further conflict if it is not properly balanced with the requirements of justice — for example, if notorious human rights violators are able to repeat their misdeeds. That said, forgiveness in politics now has a track record, and lessons can be gleaned from the experiences of those who have tried to make it work, especially in the field of international conflict resolution.[26]

Guaranteed remedies are elusive, partly because the elements of forgiveness are largely intangible, its results hard to measure or verify. Yet that elusiveness may also be part of what makes forgiveness a fitting

---

Lessons from the Field
for International Conflict Resolution

- The importance of a serious effort to establish historical truth and disseminate it widely in society cannot be underestimated.

- Political forgiveness should not be confused with general amnesty.

- Victims of political crimes should never feel pressured to forgive.

- Generally speaking, leaders can seek or extend forgiveness on behalf of their constituencies by engaging in a process that may include acknowledgment of historical wrongdoing or symbolic deeds that signal hope of reconciliation.

- One can forgive but also seek to punish for the sake of society, as long as punishment derives from a sense of justice, not from revenge.

- While embracing justice, the concept of political forgiveness rejects the idea that justice is little more than punishment; there must also be the justice that restores relationships.

- Forgiveness in politics takes place — to emphasize — *in politics,* and thus is vulnerable to the limitations and liabilities of any political project.

---

framework for many of today's conflicts, entangled as they are in the intangibles of social identity and the nonmaterial interests of long-aggrieved parties. Forgiveness has its limitations, but so do conventional means of resolving conflicts through war or diplomacy. Humanitarian military intervention may head off a genocidal campaign; a negotiated peace may cease armed hostilities; legal and social remedies might help discourage further fractiousness. But conflicts of the recent past, often deeply carved in social identity, suggest that something more might often be needed, something deeper. Douglas Johnston, a retired nuclear submarine commander, witnessed this reality while working to bridge divisions in the former Yugoslavia. "Certainly no diplomatic or military solution will ever break the cycle of revenge," he remarked. "Unless one can introduce a spiritual component that gets to the business of forgiveness and reconciliation, the same drumbeat is likely to repeat itself for the next few centuries."[27]

*Rabbi Michael Melchior looks on as Pope John Paul II prays at the
Western Wall, the holy site of Judaism, in Jerusalem, March 26, 2000.
Catholic News Service photo/Arturo Mari.*

These geopolitical developments have found a moral and theological
parallel in contemporary Catholic reflections on peace. In his statement
No Peace without Justice, No Justice without Forgiveness, Pope John
Paul II carried forth the message of his predecessors that justice is a pillar
of peace. True peace is the "fruit of justice, that moral virtue and legal
guarantee which ensures full respect for rights and responsibilities, and
the just distribution of benefits and burdens." Yet more is needed. Because human justice is "always fragile and imperfect, subject as it is to
the limitations and egoism of individuals and groups," John Paul said, "it
must include and, as it were, be completed by forgiveness which heals and
rebuilds troubled human relations from their foundations."[28] In this turn
toward forgiveness, John Paul was inviting the church to think of war
and peace in a more theological and even supernatural way, to connect
these discussions more foundationally to Christian faith and the experience of love and reconciliation. Within this invitation, however, is a call
to genuine realism. By their very resistance to conventional solutions,
identity-based conflicts have brought attention to the practical thrust of
social forgiveness.
    From their different perches, John Paul and practitioners like Johnston
arrived at a similar view of contemporary reality. Their conclusion: that

the most intractable conflicts are unlikely to end without the introduction of a radical new factor, such as forgiveness. That is ultimately because human beings have needs that are nonmaterial. They seek things like truth and empathy.

The task ahead is to further parse out the implications of this radical new factor — for Catholic peacemaking, and for the world.

QUESTIONS FOR REFLECTION AND DISCUSSION

1. Talk about "forgive and forget" as compared to "remember and change." What should the role of memory be? Is it better to forget when you're trying to forgive? Or is it important to remember what has happened, in order to prevent it happening again? Which makes more sense to you?

2. Do you think forgiveness has a part to play in international conflicts? Why or why not?

3. What do you think of John Paul II's comment about the connection between peace and justice and forgiveness? He said that peace is not possible without justice. What do you think are his reasons for saying this? He also stated that justice must include forgiveness. Do you agree?

PRACTICAL APPLICATION

While in a Nazi work camp, Holocaust survivor Simon Wiesenthal was once asked by a dying Nazi for forgiveness for all the evil that he, the Nazi, had done to Jews. The dying man was repenting and desperately wanted the peace of mind that forgiveness would bring. But Wiesenthal could not bring himself to grant it. Discuss his dilemma. In instances of egregious abuse, is one obliged to forgive? Does forgiving mean that the victims are dishonored or that justice is not served? What would you have done if you were he? What would you do in a similar situation?

Chapter Nine

Discerning the Future

Signs of Hope

War is, unfortunately, a crucial reality in our world today. We can't escape it. From the beginning, as we have seen, it has been an integral part of human history. It has, therefore, also always been an issue confronting people of all faiths. How do believers look at war? How do we react to it and deal with it? Especially today, with modern warfare seeming to grow ever more lethal, these are key questions to ask.

This book has attempted to give readers some tools with which to answer these questions. It has explored the different traditions in the Christian church's stance on war and peace, both historically and in the present. It has laid out the most pressing issues facing Christians today, bringing together, from the 2003 Woodstock forum, the thinking of some of the most prominent thinkers in this field. It looked at the traditions and current developments in two other major world religions, Judaism and Islam. One chapter analyzed the place of forgiveness in our approach to war; another applied the just war tradition to the phenomenon of terrorism.

At the conclusion of the forum upon which this book is based, some observers were asked to discern what they held to be important questions that the Christian community needs to consider. These observers' comments follow.

MARGARET O'BRIEN STEINFELS

This forum highlighted the fact that there is more than one just war tradition in the church. This is a countertendency to the Catholic propensity for certitude, well-ordered thinking, and definitive statements. There are a lot of new things in the church and in our country. The old categories of the just war theory have to respond to many new realities on the ground, military realities and communication realities. The confusion and ambiguity that has been signaled in this discussion is actually a good thing for the church and for the country.

The presentations also show that some of the best just war thinkers in this country are in the American military; let's have further discussion

120

of this kind. Also, we are all meant to be involved in peacemaking. But there are different words for it: development, education, legal change, rule of law — those are peacemaking efforts, too. It's important to note that we are a democratic society, and there are others around the world. This makes the notion of noncombatant immunity an ambiguous term. We are citizens of a superpower that has started two wars in two years. What is our responsibility? We elected the president.

Position One, the pacifist position, highlighted the need to bring in and listen to people who live in the Middle East. It also raised the idea that our war in Iraq is premised on the security of Israel, a long-standing commitment of ours, but everything we do and they do seems to make the whole Middle East more insecure. What is the future of Israel and the Palestinians? This is a critical issue.

Positions Two and Three, the classical and contemporary just war positions, talked about the difference between preventive and preemptive war, and this is a helpful distinction. George Lopez's analysis leads to the very helpful idea of differing perspectives. We need to understand that people of other countries aren't just wicked and trying to thwart the United States. They have their own logic, their own strategies, their own tactics, and their own national interest. Another point: the presumption against violence does put the burden of proof on just war thinking, and this is helpful. But there is no justice in preserving a false peace. We have to look at history — Munich, for example — and be very thoughtful about how we, the Catholic community, press forward on these issues. Finally, we have the problem of intelligence. We need to continue a rigorous critical examination not only of theories but of facts on the ground.

WILLIAM BOLE

The Catholic position on war and peace has really been moving on two tracks — the just war tradition and the nonviolence tradition. What we have are two conversations. The first track is the just war questions: Is this a just war and is this war being fought morally? The second track is the peace building track: How do we build a durable peace and relationships across ethnic and religious lines? At this forum, the questions have been primarily the just war questions. But over the last four decades, the church has been solidly on the peace building track. The documents have been about human rights and development, international institutions, and the conditions of peace.

Something that hasn't been discussed much here is a contribution that the pope has been making, which is forgiveness. He has been trying to push forgiveness into the war and peace tradition in the church. So questions for another time would be: Are there any openings for forgiveness in the global conflicts of today? Do we have anything to learn from people like Nelson Mandela in South Africa or Kim Dae Jung in South Korea or Corazon Aquino in the Philippines? Is there a strong concept of forgiveness that we could use to analyze global conflicts, especially the ones we've seen since the end of the Cold War (see chapter 8)?

REV. J. BRYAN HEHIR

There are some voices that are not here today. The Catholic tradition on war and peace is a religious tradition that has spawned a moral theory, but it's a moral theory that is no longer ours. Others have learned from us and have moved in different directions. For example, the most well-read book in American academic life on the morality of war, by Michael Walzer, was not mentioned today. Some of his propositions don't fit well into the Catholic framework, but it's significant that most young Americans in academia who think about these issues are reading a book not mentioned here. Another writer, Catholic legal philosopher John Finnis, was also not mentioned. The same is true of some ecumenical voices such as Jean Bethke Elshtain, and some secular theorists like Lawrence Freedman and Hedley Bull. We have to locate our discussion — of the Catholic tradition on war and peace — in a wider world, and not just a wider world of facts and policy, but of how others are thinking about the ethics of war and peace.

In dealing with the morality of war, the search for common ground is fruitful and necessary. But it's also complicated and thus is a little bit like brain surgery: it's important to do it really well. Otherwise, instead of strengthening and disciplining each other, we end up with mush. So let someone committed to absolute nonviolence be committed to absolute nonviolence, and let someone committed to just war be committed to it. Don't try to fudge the difference between the internal logic of these two positions; treat them with their intrinsic significance and start the search for common ground from there. There will be overlap; you'll be able to do some things together — but not everything. Keep the starting positions clear and then try to find the common way that we think about this.

The presumption against the use of force has come late in the tradition. It is an enlightening distinction, but I don't want to root it in the classical authors; it's a contemporary view. Therefore it must be defended in terms of its newness. This presumption places a burden of proof on the use of force that isn't there if you don't invoke it. The argument that the presumption is functionally pacifist is a canard. It's asserted by people who don't recognize that people can use this presumption and endorse the use of force in a number of situations.

You can argue that a significant number of things have changed in the world. So I wouldn't stand comfortably on the notion that you can simply take the tradition as it has been developed, even up to recent times, and that it will be fully adequate to meet the present situation. And I am unenthusiastic about using offensive war as the category that would correct the limitations of the tradition.

Some make the point that the just war tradition provides the moral logic for the UN charter. But there are two different traditions at work here, the moral versus the political/legal. And there's a tension there. Sometimes, as with the nuclear question, the moral tradition raises a whole series of questions that the charter doesn't touch at all. And on humanitarian and military intervention, the moral tradition is more expansive about using force in response to human rights violations than the charter is.

In talking about policy, you can see the influence of the moral tradition over time. Look at the issue of noncombatant immunity, for example, between World War II and today. Nobody paid any attention to it earlier, as witnessed by McGeorge Bundy's statement about the dropping of the atomic bomb. He said, "By the time you go to Hiroshima, no one in the upper reaches of the American government even raised a question about bombing civilians, because that problem had been solved at Dresden and Tokyo." Not so today. It's taken very seriously.

And, in discussing precision warfare, you can run into paradoxical problems, such as you found in the Kosovo bombing. Until the Russians came in and pressured the Serbians, we were running out of targets that would have been acceptable. So to judge the ethics of that war, you had to have not only noncombatant immunity and proportionality, but also reasonable hope of success. You get a very interesting matrix not found very much in the classical authors.

Finally, there's been an evolution going on in U.S. policy; two issues that used to be thought of as diplomatic issues have now become thought of, in some circles, as ones requiring military force. The first is nonproliferation policy. From its inception to the end of the 1960s, it was diplomatic: you could use diplomatic pressure, political means, and economic means. But it was not thought that you could invade a country and make war on it because there was a threat of proliferation. That happened when the early Clinton policy invoked coercive nonproliferation. It was a shift that opens the door to the use of force. The other issue is using force to solve human rights problems — not just genocide, but human rights problems. I take that to be an expansion of just cause in a way that if you simply read the annual reports of Amnesty International, you will have a lot of causes to make war if you have decided that war is an appropriate instrument to solve human rights problems. I think we need to expand the framework for humanitarian military intervention, but not to the level where all human rights problems become just causes for the use of war.

In summary, Margaret O'Brien Steinfels emphasized the significance of the fact that there are several just war positions in the

*church; William Bole reminded us of the importance of each posi-
tion; and Rev. J. Bryan Hehir underlined the importance of historical
consciousness in matters of war and peace.*

LOOKING TO THE FUTURE

Looking at the state of the world, it can be hard to be optimistic. Yet
there have been times in history — some of them quite recent — when
good things happened, when the forces of peace overcame the forces of
injustice and violence. During the Second World War, the whole country
of Denmark refused to comply with the Nazis' demand that all Danish
Jews wear a Star of David to identify them. Instead, all Danes, including
the king, wore the Star of David, and the Nazis were forced to back off.
Mahatma Gandhi worked for social justice in South Africa and India and
is seen as the catalyst for Indian independence from British colonial rule.
Moreover, he insisted upon employing only nonviolent tactics — marches,
boycotts, strikes, fasting, and other methods of peaceful resistance. He in
turn inspired Martin Luther King Jr. in the civil rights movement in the
United States.

In late 1989, the Berlin Wall fell without violence, part of a weakening
of communism all across Europe. A month later, in Czechoslovakia, the
Velvet Revolution took place. It began with student protests demanding
reform of the government; it spread to workers' unions and then through
the populace as a whole. In the end, the communist government of the
country was overthrown — again, without violence.

Peaceful change is possible. We can find examples of it, but we have to
look for it. We are much more familiar with violence and warfare, because
they form such a large part of human history. But the familiar way is not
always the best way, something brought home to us by the events of the
last century. It may be, as some people think, that we cannot afford to
keep doing what we have always done in the past, because that path is too
dangerous.

What *do* we do, then? This is a huge and complicated question, and it
can seem overwhelming. As Catholics, we turn to the church for guidance,
but even there we find differences of opinion and even controversy.

There are, however, some ideas that may help us as we wrestle with
this question. To begin with, we should not rush into anything. It will
do no good, and may do harm, if we hurry the process. This issue is
important enough that it deserves broad and thoughtful consideration.
Second, history tells us and current events tell us, that peace cannot be
separated from issues of human rights and economic justice. Paul VI told
us, "If you want peace, work for justice." If we want a peaceful world, we
must look at and deal with those things that work against peace, things
such as torture, discrimination, oppression, poverty, hunger, and illiteracy.

This gives us a clue as to how to proceed in working to end violence and warfare. We need to focus not on just ending conflict, for this is dealing with symptoms and is only a temporary solution. Rather, we need to go deeper; we need to build a lasting peace. We need to work to create peaceful societies.

Below are descriptions of two efforts in this struggle to create peaceful societies. These stories offer us hope, because they show us that this goal is possible. They also give us valuable information, in that they provide us with some sense of what works.

One story is about the continuing efforts of the *Society of Jesus* in developing nations, and it is basically a good news story. It shows how we can think creatively to develop peaceful societies. For example, in a poor and violent part of Colombia called Magdalena Medio, for the last ten years the Jesuits have led the Middle Magdalena Program of Development and Peace. The program's broad goal is to build up society in the midst of conflict, to improve the lives of the people through economic development work based on human dignity, social justice, and building democracy. This sounds vague, but the ninety-six projects run by the program are anything but abstract, running the gamut from community radio stations to raising

Fr. Francisco de Roux, SJ (center), director of the Middle Magdalena Program of Development and Peace, at a cocoa project he helped start in the mountains west of the Magdalena River Valley. With him are the technicians who run the project.

water buffalo to setting up a coffee cooperative that also develops the economic strengths of women. One of the common threads of many of these
projects is helping the people in the area find ways of earning a living apart
from the lucrative but dangerous, and morally problematic, coca crop.

Violence has plagued the program since it began, with both guerillas
and paramilitary groups active in that part of Colombia, not to mention
powerful multinational corporations interested in the area's rich resources
of lumber, rubber, oil, and gold. The drug trade, too, flourishes. None of
these groups likes what the program is doing. More employment means
fewer young people will join the guerilla movement. Farmers who find
a market for yucca or plantains will not have to grow coca for the drug
traffickers. The consequences have been brutal; a number of the program's
staff members have been murdered; so have more than two thousand of
the region's residents.

Yet many different people and groups have come together to work for
the goal of building a sustainable peace in Magdalena Medio: economists,
lawyers, women's groups, the Catholic Church, the state oil company, the
oil workers union, multinational companies, private entrepreneurs, and,
of course, the people who live there. And the work includes, interestingly,
engaging in dialogue with the very groups who threaten the program's
work, the guerillas and the paramilitary organizations.

Fr. Francisco de Roux, SJ, the program's director, puts it this way: "We
know that justice and peace cannot come from war, despair, and terror. So
our alternative is to go on building an equitable society in which there is
human dignity for everyone, starting with those who have been excluded."

Another group working to build peace is the *Sisters of Mercy of the Americas.* Their Institute Justice Team decided in 2002 to name peacemaking
as an additional issue on which the twelve-country congregation would
focus its justice actions. During the buildup to the war in Iraq, the justice
team, and sisters and associates throughout the Institute, joined anti-war
marches and peace vigils and wrote letters to legislators and newspapers
in an effort to focus on peacemaking and diplomacy instead of war. Before
this time, the focus of Mercy justice advocacy had been on four issues:
poverty, especially among women and children, racism, the environment,
and women's issues.

Based on their study of Catholic social teaching and the involvement of
sisters and associates in advocating for peace, the Institute Justice Team
created a process through which the congregation could take a corporate
stance. By March 17, 2003, nearly three thousand members and associates
affirmed a public stance opposing war against Iraq.

The Sisters of Mercy continue to work for peace. Marilee Howard, RSM,
a member of the Institute Justice Team, serves as an advisor to the Peace
Council, an international gathering of prominent religious people who
work toward peace. Sisters and associates continue to oppose the huge

military budget that consumes funds that otherwise would be spent on social programs, education, health care, and housing. They participate in lobbying, use technology to organize and educate, write letters and make calls to legislators, and join their voices with other groups working for peace.

◆ ◆ ◆

Finally, our work to end war and build peace requires that we *all* become peacemakers. Among other things, this means that we need to make listening and reaching out and forgiveness part of our efforts. It is easy to assume that our perspective is the right one and we need only to convince everyone else of this. But as we noted earlier, in the church there is more than one valid approach to this issue of peace and war, and we need to respect each other's perspective. The truth is that each one of us has only a small piece of the truth. Putting all our pieces together — in community — enables us to see more clearly God's hope for peace on earth and to act on that vision.

QUESTIONS FOR REFLECTION AND DISCUSSION

1. Talk about how it might be possible to have a basic presumption against the use of force but still be willing to use it in certain circumstances. What would those circumstances be? How would you decide?

2. Many people agree that defensive war — going to war when attacked — is permissible. What about preemptive war, where you haven't yet been attacked but an attack is imminent? What about preventive war, where an attack isn't imminent but is very likely in the future? Are these two kinds of war permissible? (See chapter 3 for definitions of these terms.)

3. If you accept the use of force as a way of correcting human rights problems, how do you decide when to use it? What are the criteria, in a world where these problems exist in many different places?

PRACTICAL APPLICATION

What does peace mean to you? Try visualizing what peace would look like. Be as specific as possible; fill in the details. What would peace look like in your school? Your college campus? Your parish? Your neighborhood? Your town? Across the United States? In another country? Describe what you see. What could you do now to help make this happen?

Appendix A

Group Activities and Case Studies

GROUP ACTIVITY I:
THIRTEEN DAYS ACTIVITY

The *Thirteen Days* activity can provide a context for understanding how the contemporary just war tradition developed. It also can lead to a discussion of the difficulty of adhering to just war principles in times of crisis.

Background

The Cuban Missile Crisis took place over thirteen days in October 1962 and brought the world to the brink of global nuclear war. The crisis, and the arms race that preceded it, provided an impetus for the shift in the Catholic Church's teaching on war and peace. This shift was demonstrated in Pope John XXIII's encyclical *Pacem in Terris* (*Peace on Earth*) in 1963, and later in the documents of the Second Vatican Council. *Peace on Earth* was the first papal encyclical not addressed exclusively to Catholics, but rather to the entire world. It challenged all people of the world, "based on the terrible destructive force of modern weapons," to consider that "it is contrary to reason to hold that war is now a suitable way to restore rights which have been violated." The film *Thirteen Days* dramatically chronicles the people and events that made up the Cuban Missile Crisis, providing post–Cold War viewers with a chance to witness the kind of anxiety that led the late twentieth-century church and world to rethink its attitude toward war. The movie also reminds us that though the Cold War may have passed, the age of its weapons has not. The moral challenges that the main characters — John F. Kennedy, Robert Kennedy, and Kenny O'Donnell — face and the way they meet those challenges provide a good example of just war thinking in action. At the risk of being seen as "morally weak," the Kennedys forego the advice of their military advisers and manage to avert global war with a minimum of bloodshed.

129

Preparation

The DVD of *Thirteen Days* includes a forty-eight minute documentary, "The Roots of the Cuban Missile Crisis," which the discussion leader may want to watch ahead of time to get additional historical background. The DVD also features biographical sketches of some of the historical persons involved. The leader might also want to review (and perhaps even prepare a summary handout that lists) the pertinent statements in *Pacem in Terris*, *Gaudium et Spes*, and the letter of the American bishops, *The Challenge of Peace*, which provides one of the best descriptions of the church's "new attitude" toward war that began around the time of the Cuban Missile Crisis.

Carrying Out the Activity

This activity will require a minimum of three hours. Ideally, it would be carried out all at once, but it could be spread out over a period of two or three meetings.

The discussion leader might begin by giving a brief historical introduction and some questions to guide the viewing. Some possible questions are: What is the decision-making process like? What motivates it? What is the atmosphere or the feeling of the film? What bits of dialogue are particularly striking? Then show the film in its entirety. If the activity is to be extended, show the film up through the president's press conference announcing the quarantine.

Discussion Questions

1. Why is President Kennedy reluctant to go forward with the invasion plan?

2. What is the significance of President Kennedy's reference to *The Guns of August?*

3. How is Robert Kennedy's insistence upon coming up with an alternate plan, "no matter how crazy," connected with the requirements for a just war?

4. How does the quarantine plan compare to the original proposals by the president's military advisers?

5. What risks come with the quarantine plan, and what obstacles come with their attempts to put it into effect?

6. Why do you think the events surrounding the Cuban Missile Crisis led to a new attitude more opposed to war in the world and in the church?

7. How does the film demonstrate the care we must take in making decisions about war?

8. Do you agree that the destructive power of modern weapons should make us more reluctant to go to war, or do you think it demands that we be more aggressive?

9. Does the end of the Cold War mean we no longer have to be so concerned about the destructive power of modern weapons?

10. What insights might we glean from *Thirteen Days* about the current situation in the world?

11. What changes in our attitude toward war are demanded by world events in the twenty-first century?

12. Must leaders risk "crazy ideas," as the Kennedys did, or can we no longer afford such risks?

GROUP ACTIVITY II:
THREE KINGS ACTIVITY

Warning: *This movie contains violent images and language which, though not gratuitous, might make it unsuitable for anyone younger than eighteen years old.*

This activity provides an opportunity to discuss issues surrounding the recent war in Iraq and the fight against terrorism from the historical perspective of the First Gulf War.

Background

It's the end of the First Gulf War (1990–91) and U.S. forces are getting ready to pull out of Iraq. It's a time of celebration and confusion. In Iraq, reporters are on the scene, wanting the story of victory and of the liberation of Kuwait. Some soldiers are asking the question: What did we do here? In the background, we see the rounding up of Iraqi prisoners and we learn that the U.S. government is abandoning Iraqi insurgents who were promised military support if they rose up against Saddam Hussein.

Against this backdrop, soldiers Troy Barlow, Conrad Vig, and Chief discover a map being hidden by an Iraqi prisoner. The map appears to show the location of stolen Kuwaiti gold. Hearing of the discovery, disgruntled Special Forces officer Archie Gates intrudes himself into the group. After some negotiation, the four soldiers, the "Three Kings" of the title, set off secretly in pursuit of the gold.

They find the gold, but in the same village they also find themselves in the middle of a standoff between Saddam's army and Iraqi insurgents. Tension mounts, and the soldiers are forced to make a decision. Should they stick with the plan, just take the gold and leave (as the Iraqi soldiers are encouraging them to do)? Or should they help the insurgents escape, thus putting themselves and the gold at risk? When a woman who is begging them to stay is shot, Archie feels they have no choice but to respond, and chaos ensues. Many aspects of the moral situation are explored as they try to escape with the insurgents and the gold, only to have a new conflict break out.

Preparation

Discussion topics for this film could include: American perceptions of Muslims and the Middle East, and Muslim perceptions of Americans; whether the First Gulf War met the just war requirements; what is required outside of a formal war situation when faced with injustice — should force be used or not? what effect does the media have on such situations?

It might help to review the sections on the just war tradition and Islam in this book. You might also want to include news stories or analyses of the recent Iraq conflict so you can compare the two situations. If you wish, try reading the *America* magazine (March 4, 2002) article "Turning to the Islamic Faith" by Karima Diane Alavi, which could also provide some helpful context and perspective for a discussion (available at *www.americamagazine.org*).

Carrying Out the Activity

This activity requires at least two and a half hours to complete, though it could be cut down if you were to show just a few scenes from the film and fill in the rest before and after showing them. Crucial scenes are the one in which Archie decides they have to do something to help the insurgents, and the one in which Troy is being questioned by the Iraqi soldier. You could also spread the activity over two meetings. At the first meeting, show the movie up to the point where they go into hiding and Troy is captured, and follow with discussion. At the next meeting, show the rest of the film, and finish the discussion.

Before showing the film, you could introduce some or all of the issues listed above as things for people to think about as they watch it. Your approach will depend on whether you show just some scenes, show the whole film over two meetings, or watch it all at once.

Discussion Questions

1. What do you think about the frequent references to Iraqis as "ragheads" or "towelheads"? Is there a reason for it?
2. What do you think they mean when they say "this is a media war"?

3. What is Archie frustrated with when he says, "I don't even know what we did here"?

4. Should U.S. forces have stayed to help the people fight Saddam, or was it right to pull out once Kuwait was liberated?

5. Does the First Gulf War meet the criteria for a just war? Does the most recent conflict in Iraq?

6. What does Archie mean when he says the most important thing is necessity?

7. Why does necessity change? What made the difference in the group's decision to help the people?

8. How does Chief defend their decision to help the people before leaving?

9. Is the portrayal of the Iraqi people different than you expected? Is it just because this is a movie, or do you think the portrayal of Iraqis is more realistic than what we sometimes imagine them to be?

10. Is the Iraqi soldier who tortures Troy more like what you expect an Iraqi person to be like?

11. What's the significance of the question about Michael Jackson? What does it say about how some people in the Middle East might perceive the United States?

12. Even though the story takes place after the war is officially over, what do you think it is saying about war in general, and this war in particular?

13. How are the soldiers changed by their experience? How are they not changed?

14. Can bad intentions lead to good results? Does that say anything about how we understand war?

15. Do you see roots of the most recent Iraq conflict in this film? What lessons can we learn from both this and the more recent Iraq conflicts?

CASE STUDIES

The recent conflicts in Afghanistan and Iraq, and the earlier genocide in Rwanda, give us an opportunity to explore the current understanding of what constitutes a just war. The following chronologies and analyses are meant to provide background on these events to help readers understand how they happened.

Afghanistan

Chronology. The war in Afghanistan was based on the U.S. government's belief that Afghanistan's government — the Taliban — was complicit in the September 11, 2001, terrorist attacks on the United States. The United States suspected Afghanistan of harboring al Qaeda terrorists, including Osama bin Laden. The United States demanded that Afghanistan turn over bin Laden to the United States or face military attack. The Taliban refused to comply with this request, though it did suggest a willingness to negotiate. The United States repeated its demands and refused any negotiation. This eventually led to a U.S. invasion of Afghanistan, which deposed the Taliban government. After that, the U.S. military set about tracking down and capturing or killing terrorists within Afghanistan's borders. This included a search for Osama bin Laden, whom they did not find.

Analysis. The United States considered the invasion justified insofar as it served as retaliation for the terrorist attacks of September 11, 2001. The United States did not seek United Nations approval for its action because it believed it to be an instance of legitimate defense, justified according to contemporary just war theory. Indeed, as Professor Sonbol suggests (see her remarks in chapter 6, page 92), even Islamic nations in the Middle East might be inclined to see the United States as justified in this instance.

Iraq

Chronology. The war with Iraq was based on the perceived threat of Iraq to the United States and the world, based largely on the suspicion that Iraq was developing nuclear and/or chemical weapons. There was also the suggestion of a connection between Iraq and the terrorist attacks of September 11. In this case, the United States decided it could not act unilaterally or without appealing to the authority of the United Nations. Insisting that Iraq was engaged in a weapons program right under the nose of United Nations inspectors, the United States sought a UN resolution to authorize force to compel Iraq to comply with UN resolutions. Not receiving the support it needed in the UN for such a resolution, the United States made a decision to assemble a coalition and attack Iraq, citing the authority of a previous UN resolution authorizing force should Iraq fail to comply with its demands. Eventually, the United States and its coalition partners invaded and occupied Iraq, deposing Iraqi dictator Saddam Hussein. They did not find the evidence of nuclear or chemical weapons that they expected to find.

Analysis. This case demonstrates the way in which other justifications for war beyond legitimate defense have been transferred to the authority of an international body, in this case the United Nations. Thus, as in this case, if a nation wants to justify in the court of world opinion a preemptive attack on another nation (prohibited by the United Nations charter), it is necessary to engage in the process of seeking approval from the United Nations. The eventual U.S. justification for the invasion of Iraq was based on the premise that it was acting on the authority of a previous UN resolution, which could be seen as demanding redress or punishment for Iraq's failure to cooperate fully with inspectors and its unjust withholding of information and/or weapons. By means of this analysis one can see that even if it acted without UN approval, the United States did recognize that the authority to authorize military action in a situation where one has neither been attacked nor is under immediate threat belongs to the UN, which can authorize wars waged for reasons allowed by the classical just war tradition — restitution, redress, and punishment.

Rwanda

Chronology. On April 6, 1994, the president of Rwanda, Juvenal Habyarimana, was killed when his plane was shot down. That incident set off one of the worst genocides of the twentieth century, in which some members of the majority Hutu group, which was in power, targeted the minority Tutsis (and moderate Hutus) for slaughter. The presidential guard, some members of the armed forces, and extremist militias started the systematic killings, beginning with the people considered likely to oppose the campaign, such as opposition leaders. It soon spread. Hutus all over the country were encouraged to take part in the campaign, and many did. Those who tried to resist were often killed themselves. When it was over, three months later, nearly a million people were dead.

When the slaughter began, UN peacekeeping troops were in the country, but their mandate forbade them to engage in armed intervention.[1]

Some Western countries sent in troops to evacuate their citizens and then left. The United Nations mission stationed there briefly tried to mediate between the warring parties; then, on April 21, the UN Security Council, at the urging of the United States, voted to withdraw the mission, removing most of its troops from the country. In May, when the extent of the killings became more widely known, the UN voted to send in forces — but first the vote was delayed by U.S. Secretary of State Madeleine Albright, and then actual deployment of troops was hamstrung because arguments ensued about who would pay for them.[2]

On June 22, French troops — with the approval of the UN Security Council — entered Rwanda. They established a humanitarian zone, thus saving, by one estimate, tens of thousands of lives.[3]

When the genocide began, the rebel Rwandan Patriotic Front had attempted to stop it by suggesting a joint effort with the Rwandan government and the UN mission. When this was rejected, it launched its own campaign, moving throughout the country and driving off the extremists, often themselves engaging in killing. On July 4, the RPF took over the capital, Kigali. Two weeks later, it established a new government.

On balance, the judgment seems to be that the rest of the world stood by and did nothing to help during this genocide. In March 1998, President Clinton apologized to the victims of the genocide. Later that year, UN Secretary General Kofi Annan apologized as well. In 1999, the International Federation of Human Rights Leagues and Human Rights Watch USA assigned blame to the UN, the U.S., France, and Belgium for their inaction. The independent Carlsson Report of 2000 also pointed the finger at the United Nations, saying "the Security Council bears a responsibility for its lack of political will to do more to stop the killing."

Analysis. In the contemporary just war tradition, only an international body — the United Nations — can authorize the use of force by one nation against another, except in cases of self-defense. The United Nations, then, would be the deciding authority in all other instances, such as humanitarian intervention, which has become an increasingly urgent issue in today's world. But the events that occurred in Rwanda in 1994 reveal the problems that can develop in working within this framework.

To begin with, the issue of information is crucial. Any action must be based on solid data and analysis. With Rwanda, it appears that the United Nations did have this information. An official of Physicians for Human Rights has stated that the organization Human Rights Watch alerted the UN of serious trouble brewing in Rwanda as early as 1993. In January of 1994, the commander of the UN Mission in Rwanda informed the UN of the existence of arms caches and lists of Tutsis to be killed. He asked for permission to take action, but it was denied.[4] In fact, in 2000, the Carlsson Report on Rwanda found that the UN ignored the evidence it was given of the planned genocide and then refused to act after it began.

Another issue lies in the fact that the United Nations is greatly subject to influence by its member nations. The Carlsson Report also found that the United States effectively prevented the Security Council from authorizing significant action in Rwanda, both before and during the genocide. On April 15, the State Department told the US Mission to the UN that it opposed any effort to keep the UN mission in Rwanda, which would have helped lessen the killing. Recently obtained documents show that the United States even resisted labeling the events in Rwanda as genocide because, in the words of one defense official: "Be careful. Legal at State was worried about this yesterday — Genocide finding could commit U.S. government to 'do something.'"[5] It took weeks for the term to be applied.

Related to the issue of influence, the United Nations is limited in what it can do, practically, by the support of its members — or the lack of it. In April, after ten Belgian soldiers were killed, Belgium took its troops out of the country, and they were recognized as the most experienced in the mission. In May, when much of the killing was over, the United Nations proposed a strong plan to go into Rwanda to protect people who were left and offer assistance. The United States opposed the plan, saying it was not ready to bring equipment and troops into the country.

The United Nations charter does give it a mandate to respond to instances of genocide. The question is why it does not consistently and effectively do so.

IDEAS FOR SHORTER MEETINGS

Youth ministers and religious educators often don't have time to show an entire film. So here are some suggestions for how to use various resources in a shorter period of time.

- Use just one or two particularly poignant or applicable scenes from a film.

- Complement with a song or poem on a related theme.

- Include a handout that features the song lyrics and perhaps a relevant quote from the *Catechism,* one of the papal encyclicals, or even a famous person or saint.

Here are some examples, grouped by discussion topic:

Making Choices about War

- Show the scene from *Thirteen Days* when President Kennedy meets with his advisors to ask them what to do about the Cuban Missile Crisis.

- Song: "Ride Across the River" by Dire Straits.

- Excerpt the *Catechism*'s section on "Peace" and "Avoiding War" (2309).

Presumption against War?

- Show the scenes of the Battle of Stalingrad from *Enemy at the Gates.*

- Song: "War" by Bruce Springsteen.

- Quote John Paul II from *Centesimus Annus* (52): "Never Again War!"

Nonviolence

- Show the scene of the Dharasana Saltworks protest from *Gandhi.*

- Song: "Peace on Earth" by U2.

- Quote John Paul II from *Centesimus Annus* (23): "May people learn to fight for justice without violence...."

The Effects of War/Coming Home

- Show a scene from *Born on the Fourth of July* or *Last Letters Home*.
- Song: "Born in the USA" by Bruce Springsteen.
- Read together Ernest Hemingway's short story "Soldier's Home."

Losing Loved Ones

- Show a scene from *Last Letters Home*.
- Read James Dickey's poem "The Performance."

The Excesses of War

- Show the scene of General Dyer's massacre in *Gandhi*.
- Song: "Sunday Bloody Sunday" by U2.
- Look at Kurt Vonnegut's description of the bombing of Dresden in *Slaughterhouse-Five*.

Should We Meet Injustice with Violence?

- Show a scene from *Braveheart* calling the people to battle against oppression.
- Show the scene from *The Mission* in which Father Gabriel and Rodrigo are discussing how to respond to the coming troops.

Who Is My Enemy?

- Show the opening scenes from *Three Kings:* "Are we shooting people?"
- Show the scene from *All Quiet on the Western Front* when the young German soldier sits in the trench with the French soldier he's just killed.

Appendix B

Cultural Resources

FICTION, POETRY, PLAYS

Note: The text in italics at the end of an entry is a quote from that work.

All Quiet on the Western Front

World War I produced this powerful 1929 novel by Erich Maria Remarque, a German who served as an infantryman on the French front. He clearly states his intent in writing it: it is for "a generation of men who, even though they may have escaped the shells, were destroyed by the war." Destruction, in fact, runs through the book; Remarque explores all the horrors of this war. Some were new, such as poison gas, trench warfare, and barbed wire; others were age-old, like rats and lice. The effect of war on the ordinary soldier is a main theme; the narrator talks of men discussing who will get a dying comrade's boots and also of the gut instinct to kill that turns men into animals. It is an explicit condemnation of nationalism and patriotism, what he sees as lies that support and encourage war.

Discussion Question: In light of the novel's condemnation of nationalism and patriotism, how do you think the notion of patriotism affected the U.S. entry into war with Iraq?

Here hang bits of uniform, and somewhere else is plastered a bloody mess that was once a human limb. Over there lies a body with nothing but a piece of the underpants on one leg and the collar of the tunic around its neck. Otherwise it is naked and the clothes are hanging up in the tree.

You still think it's beautiful to die for your country. The first bombardment taught us better. When it comes to dying for country, it's better not to die at all.

Catch-22

Although this novel by Joseph Heller, published in 1961, has a World War II setting, it belongs more to the Vietnam War genre in theme and tone. Like *All Quiet on the Western Front*, it is completely unsentimental about war; there is no heroism or glory here. It differs, however, in that it does not dwell on war's carnage and brutality; rather, it adopts an ironic, even comedic, tone to show its meaninglessness and absurdity. The main character, Yossarian, spends his time trying to stay alive and battling a military bureaucracy primarily interested in enhancing its status and indifferent to the men's safety or lives. All the characters reflect absurdity in some way: a chaplain who flees his duties because he cannot fight against a false — and unknown, even to his accusers — crime; an airman who bombs his own squadron because it will make him profit in a business deal with the Germans; a colonel who sends men to their death in order to get a promotion.

Discussion Question: Where do sanity and morality lie? In following the rules? When is it moral to disobey the rules?

> *There was only one catch and that was Catch-22, which specified that a concern for one's own safety in the face of dangers that were real and immediate was the process of a rational mind. Orr was crazy and could be grounded. All he had to do was ask; and as soon as he did, he would no longer be crazy and would have to fly more missions. Orr would be crazy to fly more missions and sane if he didn't, but if he was sane he would have to fly them. If he flew them he was crazy and didn't have to; but if he didn't want to he was sane and had to.*

"The Charge of the Light Brigade"

This poem by Alfred Lord Tennyson is all that many people know of the Crimean War (1853–54), which pitted Britain, France, the Ottoman Empire, and Sardinia against Russia. The poem tells the story of the ill-fated attack of a British cavalry brigade, an attack that resulted in the death of most of its members. It celebrates bravery and heroism — but in the face of misunderstandings, petty rivalries, and ultimately fatal errors in judgment. One man gave an order not realizing that others could not see what he could see. Another relayed that order in ambiguous terms. Yet another failed to make sure he understood that order. No one in leadership comes off in a good light.

Discussion Question: What truly constitutes bravery?

> *"Forward, the Light Brigade!"*
> *Was there a man dismay'd?*
> *Not tho' the soldier knew*
>   *Some one had blunder'd:*
> *Their's not to make reply,*
> *Their's not to reason why,*
> *Their's but to do and die:*
> *Into the valley of Death*
>   *Rode the six hundred.*

"Does it Matter?"

Siegfried Sassoon, author of this poem, was a decorated hero in World War I, whose early poetry portrayed war as a noble enterprise (in his collection *The Old Huntsman*). He gradually came to see war as nothing but brutality and waste, and wrote poetry that expressed this (in his collection *Counter-Attack*). This poem, from that later work, reflects a grim reality of that particular war: the great number of soldiers who were left maimed. It asks satirically: Does it matter if you're missing a leg or your sight? People are kind, and besides, they know you fought for your country.

Discussion Question: Do the goals of war ever justify its costs to individuals? Consider the kinds and extent of injuries suffered by both soldiers and civilians in the current Iraq conflict.

Drum Taps and *Sequel to Drum Taps* (integrated into *Leaves of Grass*)

These volumes of poetry by one of America's greatest poets, Walt Whitman, reflect the journey the writer took in his attitude to war. It begins with stirring accounts of young men marching off to fight for the Union, for the cause that Whitman fiercely supported. The prelude speaks of "the young men falling in and arming.... The blood of the city up — arm'd! arm'd! the cry everywhere.... War! an arm'd race is advancing! — the welcome for battle — no turning away." This describes what he saw in Manhattan, at the start of the war. Yet later, Whitman spent several years in Washington nursing wounded soldiers in military hospitals, and the experience affected him profoundly. From his patients — he himself never fought — he learned of the war's reality for the ordinary soldier: the dirt, the loneliness, the pain, the fear, and the loss. This, rather than the politics of war, is what informs his later poems, such as "The Wound Dresser," "To One Who Is About to Die," "A March in the Ranks Hard Press'd," and others.

Discussion Questions: Talk about the tone of these later poems of Whitman. Despite the suffering and death they show, what is his attitude toward the war? Does he see it as a waste?

> *Aroused and angry,*
> *I thought to beat the alarum, and urge relentless war;*
> *But soon my fingers fail'd me, my face droop'd, and I resign'd myself,*
> *To sit by the wounded and soothe them, or silently watch the dead.*

"Dulce et Decorum Est"

Perhaps the most famous poem to come out of the First World War, this work by Englishman Wilfred Owen gains some of its power from the fact that he himself died, very young, in that war. In it, he speaks of marching through sludge, of barefoot men with bloody feet, a gas attack — and one man who dies from it, drowning in its green light. He ends by quoting, with scorn, that "old lie": Homer's dictum that it is sweet and proper to die for one's country.

Discussion Question: Compare this poem to another World War I poem, one by Owen Seaman titled *Pro Patria*. The title is also taken from Homer's adage. But Seaman takes a different perspective, seeing the war as England's great fight and a "high test" for her "warrior sons."

A Farewell to Arms

Ernest Hemingway based *A Farewell to Arms*, often called the best American novel to come out of World War I, on his own experience as an ambulance driver in Europe during the war. Published in 1929, the book tells the story of the love between Frederic Henry, an American ambulance driver, and Catherine Barkley, a nurse's aide, in the midst of suffering and death, primarily on the Italian front. It relates, in grim detail, the cruelty and the carnage of war, despite the couple's attempt to use love to escape from it. Disillusionment with war is a strong theme — although this is interesting, given Hemingway's often-stated scorn for men without experience of war.

Discussion Question: Did Hemingway see war, despite its evils, as something that could help strengthen and shape a man?

> *If people bring so much courage to this world the world has to kill them to break them, so of course it kills them. The world breaks every one and afterward many are strong at the broken places. But those that will not break it kills. It kills the very good and the very gentle and the very brave impartially. If you are none of these you can be sure it will kill you too but there will be no special hurry.*

Going after Cacciotto

This novel by Tim O'Brien follows a young soldier who leaves the war in Vietnam to walk the eight thousand miles to Paris, and his squad, which is sent to find and capture him. It alternates between reality and fantasy, between Vietnam and Europe, between civilization and chaos. Moral issues of the war play a central role: What are the soldiers fighting for? What about the atrocities? What's the right thing to do? *Is* there even a right thing to do?

Discussion Question: How do you decide what's right when you're in a situation that's inherently violent and cruel?

> *The point is that war is war no matter how it is perceived. War has its own reality. War kills and maims and rips up the land and makes*

*orphans and widows. These are the things of war. Any war. So when
I say there's nothing new to tell about Nam, I'm saying it was just a
war like every war.*

"Gunga Din" and "Fuzzy-Wuzzy"

These are poems by Rudyard Kipling, winner of the Nobel Prize for literature in 1907. Born in 1865, he is sometimes called the bard of British Imperialism; he accepted uncritically the notion of the inherent superiority of Western and British culture, and his works celebrate the British Empire. He saw the empire as the West fulfilling its duty to bring its civilization to the primitive cultures of Africa and Asia. While his attitude was typical of his time, it appears misguided and racist today. Yet his war poems paint a powerful picture of the conflict of his era, especially in their portrayal of the British enlisted man. They also reveal that Kipling could see courage and nobility in people of all races and cultures. The narrator in "Gunga Din," a British soldier in India, describes the bravery and self-sacrifice of an Indian water bearer. "Fuzzy-Wuzzy" praises the courage of Sudanese fighters; they were the only force ever to break through a famous British battle formation called the square.

Discussion Questions: How do the narrators of these poems perceive the people that the British colonized (Indians and Sudanese, in these cases)? How do you think these perceptions affect a culture's propensity to engage in conflict? Is it ever all right to forcibly impose one's own culture on another culture?

> *Din! Din! Din!*
> *You Lazarushian-leather Gunga Din!*
> *Tho' I've belted you an' flayed you,*
> *By the livin' Gawd that made you,*
> *You're a better man than I am, Gunga Din!*

Henry V and *Troilus and Cressida*

These two plays by Shakespeare both focus on war. The first relates the story of King Henry V of England and his victory at the Battle of Agincourt, part of the Hundred Years' War between the English and the French. Henry's speech before the battle is famous, especially his words "we band of brothers"; the theme of courage and the glory found in war runs throughout the play. Yet other elements show the less noble aspects of war: the horrific reprisals with which Henry threatens a town under siege if it does not surrender, and his order to kill all the French prisoners. *Troilus and Cressida*, set during the siege of Troy by the Greeks, paints war in a starkly grim light. The characters are generally unlikable, even the so-called heroes, unsavory plots abound, and the supposed love between

Troilus and Cressida is betrayed. The play concludes after a battle, with the slaughter of an unarmed Hector by Achilles and some other Greeks.

Discussion Questions: Compare the portrayal of war in the two plays. How are they different? Are there any similarities?

> *We few, we happy few, we band of brothers.*
> *For he to-day that sheds his blood with me*
> *Shall be my brother; be he ne'er so vile,*
> *This day shall gentle his condition;*
> *And gentlemen in England now a-bed*
> *Shall think themselves accurs'd they were not here,*
> *And hold their manhoods cheap whiles any speaks,*
> *That fought with us upon Saint Crispin's day.*
> —*Henry V*

> *Here is such patchery, such juggling, and such knavery. All the ar-*
> *gument is a whore and a cuckold—a good quarrel to draw emulous*
> *factions and bleed to death upon. Now the dry serpigo on the subject,*
> *and war and lechery confound all!*   —*Troilus and Cressida*

Leo Africanus

Amin Maalouf has written a fictional piece about a real person, a Muslim man who lived in the fifteenth and sixteenth centuries. Born Hasan al-Wazzan, he starts his life in Granada, Spain, during the Moorish occupation there; later he travels to North Africa, to Italy, and to Byzantium. He meets people of all races and religions. The book paints a broad picture of the known world at the time; we see wars and invasions, inventions and religious turmoil. In particular, it offers a good study of the Muslim world. Readers will find it a good way to start learning about Islam.

Discussion Question: What things about Islam did you learn from this book that surprised you?

Night

This book relates Elie Wiesel's shattering childhood during the Holocaust. A Hungarian Jew, he spent time at both Auschwitz and Buchenwald and lost his whole family in the camps. The story seems one of unrelieved horror — starvation, forced labor, inadequate clothing, beatings, torture — yet he refuses to succumb to the brutality that seems to pull at everyone there. As he and the other prisoners are forced to watch a child being hanged, he hears someone wonder where God is, and something in him answers, "He is here, hanging on this gallows." Wiesel's experience led him to a life of making sure that the Holocaust is remembered, and of speaking out against any hatred and cruelty. He has said, "To remain silent and indifferent is the greatest sin of all."

Discussion Questions: How should we react today to situations of widespread evil and of genocide? Is our obligation to resist evil stronger than our obligation to stay at peace?

Occupied Voices: Stories of Everyday Life from the Second Intifada

Published in 2003, this book is written by a Jewish woman from the American Midwest who spent some time living with Palestinian families. It opens a window onto the lives of these people, many of whom have experienced only war, not peace. Wendy Pearlman relates her own spiritual journey as she describes people about whom so little is known; she uses their stories as a lens to tell the larger story of the Second Intifada.

The Price of Courage: A Korean War Novel

Published in 1999, this novel by Curt Anders is set during what some have called "The Forgotten War." It tells the story of one man's transformation from raw soldier to seasoned battle veteran, and it's a journey filled with fear and courage, fatal errors and grim perseverance. It describes the reality of combat, showing the devastation and the waste of a war that seemed to center on gaining a few feet of land at the cost of many lives. Yet it also highlights the bravery and sacrifices of the ordinary soldier caught in a confusing and terrifying place.

Discussion Questions: Talk about the various decisions the main character, Eric Holloway, has to make. What is his moral yardstick? How does he decide? What are the moral implications of his decisions?

The Red Badge of Courage

This 1895 Civil War novel by Stephen Crane made quite an impact when it was published because of its realistic portrayal of warfare and its refusal to see war as an epic struggle. Crane describes the war through the eyes of Henry Fleming, a young Union soldier who starts out with a romantic and egotistic view of war but who quickly runs up against its harsh reality and his own flawed character. The language is terse, almost journalistic, which adds to the power of the description of war — a power that contrasts ironically with Crane's view that the war has no real meaning.

Discussion Questions: Could Fleming have come to the maturity he does in the course of the novel if he had never seen battle? Does war, indeed, ever have meaning?

The men dropped here and there like bundles. The captain of the youth's company had been killed in an early part of the action. His body lay stretched out in the position of a tired man resting, but

*upon his face there was an astonished and sorrowful look, as if he
thought some friend had done him an ill turn. The babbling man was
grazed by a shot that made the blood stream widely down his face.
He clapped both hands to his head. "Oh!" he said, and ran. Another
grunted suddenly as if a club had struck him in the stomach. He
sat down and gazed ruefully. In his eyes there was mute, indefinite
reproach. Farther up the line a man, standing behind a tree, had
had his knee joint splintered by a ball. Immediately he had dropped
his rifle and gripped the tree with both arms. And there he remained,
clinging desperately and crying for assistance that he might withdraw
his hold upon the tree.*

A Rumor of War

Philip Caputo's account of his time in Vietnam, published in 1977, chronicles his transformation from an idealistic and gung-ho new recruit to a
stunned and demoralized survivor. He describes in detail the intensity and
the boredom of guerilla conflict and the toll it takes on those who must
fight it. This is the book's focus, rather than bravery or heroism, and he
does not spare us the atrocities he witnessed and took part in. War, he
shows us, is strictly survival, nothing else.

Discussion Questions: How would I behave in combat? What would I
do in order to survive?

*In those weeks we did not see heavy fighting . . . but we saw enough to
learn those lessons which cannot be taught in training camps; what
fear feels like and what death looks like, and the smell of death, the
experience of killing, of enduring pain and inflicting it, the loss of
friends and the sight of wounds. We learned what war was about,
"the cares of it, and the forms of it." We began to change, to lose the
boyish awkwardness we had brought to Vietnam. We became more
professional, leaner and tougher, and a callus began to grow around
our hearts, the kind of emotional flak jacket that blunted the blows
and stings of pity. . . .*

Slaughterhouse-Five, or, The Children's Crusade

The core of this novel by Kurt Vonnegut is the Allied firebombing of the
German city of Dresden in World War II. Vonnegut, a POW in Dresden
at the time, witnessed the massive destruction it caused; the book is his
attempt to come to terms with its horrors. More than 130,000 people —
civilians — died, either caught in one of the thousands of fires that raged
or suffocated because the fires sucked all the oxygen out of the air. This
is clearly an antiwar book. Its very structure reflects Vonnegut's vision of
the chaos and meaninglessness of war. The protagonist, Billy Pilgrim, is

unstuck in time and the book jumps back and forth in time as well, as he tries to cope with his memories.

Discussion Questions: Talk about civilian casualties during wartime. How do we limit them? Direct targeting of civilians is forbidden, but what about actions that indirectly affect them? What do you do when allowing the deaths of civilians will preserve something very important militarily (as happened with Churchill and the bombing of Coventry in World War II)?

> *You know we've had to imagine the war here, and we have imagined that it was being fought by aging men like ourselves. We had forgotten that wars were fought by babies. When I saw those freshly shaved faces, it was a shock. "My God, my God!" I said to myself. "It's the Children's Crusade."*

"Spain 1937"

W. H. Auden wrote this poem after a trip to Spain during the Spanish Civil War. It reflects his support for the Republican forces that were fighting against General Franco and his fascist allies. The poem calls for a commitment and for action, asserting that at certain times it is crucial for people to step forward and fight for a cause. "Yesterday the belief in the absolute value of Greek . . . but today the struggle."

Discussion Question: Are some causes worth fighting for? Some commentators have suggested that if the Republicans had won in Spain, the Nazi takeover of Europe might have been delayed or weakened, with a resulting lessening of casualties. How does one decide?

When Heaven and Earth Changed Places: A Vietnamese Woman's Journey from War to Peace

A memoir by Le Ly Hayslip, this book recounts her life, first in Vietnam and then in America. Yet the deeper theme is the impact of war on an entire people. Hayslip's experiences are horrific; she is tortured, raped, and exiled from her village; she is thrown out on the street after bearing her employer's baby; for a while, she works as a bar girl to take care of her son. We see the actions of the French, the Viet Cong, the South Vietnamese, and the Americans, and we learn that, in war, no side is totally innocent. Yet, most memorably, we also see the power of forgiveness, which is a thread that runs through Hayslip's life. Hayslip says that her book tries to sound "the bell that breaks the pattern of hateful feelings."

Discussion Question: Talk about the role of forgiveness in war time. Is it effective, or even necessary?

FILMS

Note: Many of these films, because of the subject matter, contain graphic and violent material.

Band of Brothers (2001)

This HBO miniseries — ten episodes — tells the true story of Easy Company, an elite rifle unit that fought in World War II. Based on interviews with survivors and soldiers' letters and diaries, the series follows the company from boot camp through some of the European front's major battles, showing all the chaos, brutality, and bravery of war.

Discussion Questions: Talk about the sacrifices made by the members of Easy Company. Why did they do what they did? Did all the people react the same way to the experience of war, or was there a range of reactions? Do you think the context of World War II — fighting Hitler — affected soldiers' attitudes and actions?

Black Hawk Down (2001)

This film might appeal to young adults, because it depicts a conflict that took place during their lifetime. It relates the story of the ill-conceived "extraction" mission by U.S. forces in Somalia in 1993, when two downed helicopters leave soldiers pinned down in an urban battlefield where there is no clear distinction between friend and enemy. Gritty, realistic, and disturbing, it is sure to spark strong emotions and a sense of disorientation, not unlike that of the main characters in the film.

Discussion Questions: What does one do when, as happens all over the world (in Congo, for one), complex conflicts rage, with no clear understanding of who is "good" or "bad"? What responsibilities do countries like the United States have? Especially if there is evidence of genocide, is there a moral obligation to intervene? (Film with related theme: *Hotel Rwanda*, 2005)

Braveheart (1995)

This epic tells the story of William Wallace, the hero who led the struggle for Scottish freedom from England. It is a stirring tale; Wallace leads the Scots into battle with the words, "You can take our lives, but you can't take our freedom!" It's hard not to sympathize with his cause. Yet we see the heavy cost in the brutally realistic battle scenes and Wallace dies a martyr's death at the end.

Discussion Questions: Was Wallace blinded by his ideals and leading his countrymen into a hopeless battle? Or was the fight necessary to shake off oppression? Even if the intention is pure and the cause worthwhile, does it justify the cost in lives and brutality? This film runs for nearly three hours, so it might be more practical to show particular scenes, like some of Wallace's speeches and subsequent battles, for a more focused discussion. (Film with similar themes: *Rob Roy*, 1995)

Bridge on the River Kwai (1957)

This classic film of the Second World War takes place in Southeast Asia, where British prisoners of war are forced by their Japanese captors to build a bridge to help the Japanese war effort. Colonel Nicholson, the chief British officer, is a by-the-book soldier, totally loyal to the British Army. Yet he ends up agreeing to do the work, seeing it as a way of proving the superiority of all things British. Meanwhile, the Allied command has plans to blow up the bridge. At the end, Nicholson confronts the destruction of what has become for him a symbol of everything he stands for. The film's conclusion is ambiguous, so we don't really know what lies behind Nicholson's final action.

   Discussion Questions: Colonel Nicholson has his particular concept of honor. What do you think of it? How would you define honor? How does the experience of warfare impact people's moral decisions?

Cold Mountain (2003)

This movie explores the effects of the American Civil War on both soldiers and civilians. It relates the story of Inman, a Confederate soldier, on his long journey back to his beloved, Ada. She, meanwhile, is struggling to survive on her farm. As well as horrific battles, the movie depicts the treachery and brutality that occur on the home front. One particularly searing scene shows two Home Guardsmen torturing a woman in order to flush out her two sons, who have deserted their regiment. *Cold Mountain* shows how the cruelty of war touches everyone.

   Discussion Questions: What are the parameters for civilian rights in time of war? Can anything be justified in the name of security?

Courage under Fire (1996)

In this military mystery-drama, Lt. Col. Sterling is charged with determining whether the deceased Captain Walden should receive the Medal of Honor for her service in the Gulf War — which would make her the first woman so honored. The war scenes are offered in flashback, each telling the story according to the testimony of Walden's fellow soldiers. Unsurprisingly, each has a different story. The confusion of battle and the workings of prejudice both conspire against Sterling's coming to a clear conclusion.

Discussion Questions: What is courage? Do men make better soldiers? Should women be soldiers at all? How can one ever know what actually happens in a war? (Tim O'Brien has also explored this theme; see his *The Things They Carried*.)

Crimson Tide (1995)

This is a post–Cold War nuclear thriller. The USS *Alabama*, a nuclear submarine, goes to Russian waters when rebels take over a Russian nuclear base. If the rebels launch nuclear missiles, the *Alabama* is instructed to launch its own. Tension arises between the sub's young executive officer, Hunter, and its seasoned captain, Ramsey. They must rely on radio transmissions to update them on the situation, but when they receive an "emergency action message" it is incomplete. Ramsey thinks it is an order to fire missiles; Hunter is not sure and does not want to start a nuclear war by mistake.

Discussion Questions: Use this film to talk about the post–Cold War nuclear situation. Are we really safe from the threat of nuclear war? Many different groups and nations now have access to such weapons; does this make things even more dangerous? When it comes to nuclear war, must we, like Hunter, err on the side of caution? Does the existence of such weapons really require a presumption against war? (Film with similar themes: *The Hunt for Red October*, 1990)

Gandhi (1982)

Showing this entire three-hour-plus film will probably be impractical, but numerous powerful scenes could be used to great effect. It traces the life of Gandhi, from his early days encountering apartheid in South Africa, through his efforts for Indian independence, up to his assassination. No other film chronicles the tragedy and triumph of nonviolent resistance as well as this one. We see the massacre of nonviolent protesters and the unforgettable account of the Dharasana Saltworks protest, where one by one protestors step forward, not resisting as they are beaten down. The film shows the possibility of successful nonviolent resistance, but also its cost.

Discussion Questions: Is resisting nonviolently worth it, or even practical, in the face of such violence? Could India have achieved independence by violent conflict, rather than by the nonviolent revolution led by Gandhi? Which achieves more, nonviolent witness or war? Using the latest DVD version of the film, one can also take advantage of newsreel footage of Gandhi himself, as well as a montage of several of his most famous quotes.

Good Morning, Vietnam (1987)

This comedy offers a lighter look at the Vietnam conflict. Robin Williams plays radio DJ Adrian Cronauer, brought in to bring a bit of humor to Armed Forces Radio. It provides a less serious way of discussing many of the issues involved with the war and might work well with younger audiences. It does have a serious side, however. Adrian discovers that he is being used to promote propaganda and must decide whether to toe the line or speak up for the truth. Some of his experiences also bring him closer to the reality of the war than his usual DJ duties.

Discussion Questions: *Good Morning, Vietnam* provides a good vehicle to discuss issues still relevant today. How much freedom should the press have during a time of war? What information does the government have a responsibility to divulge to the public, not to mention to its soldiers? How does a soldier choose between obeying his or her conscience and obeying the orders of superior officers? (Films with related themes: *Catch-22*, 1970, and *M*A*S*H*, 1970)

The Guns of August (1964)

This documentary uses rare archival footage to recount the historical background and experience of the First World War. It allows viewers to delve directly into this "war to end all wars," with which many young people may have only a passing familiarity. It can promote perspective on and discussion of the beginnings of modern warfare. There is also the potential for connecting this with a discussion of *Thirteen Days*, in which Barbara Tuchman's book about World War I, *The Guns of August*, is mentioned. The suggestion is that President Kennedy had just read the book, which was published the same year as the Cuban Missile Crisis.

Discussion Questions: In what ways did we step over the line in World War I, and how did we get to where we are now? How much have we learned from the past? Are we doing better in avoiding some of the atrocities we can see going back to the beginning of the twentieth century?

The Guns of Navarone (1961)

A classic World War II film, *The Guns of Navarone* tells the story of people assigned a seemingly impossible mission: to destroy two huge German guns that are trapping British soldiers on an island off Greece. The guns cannot be reached by sea or air; a sheer cliff must be scaled. A small group of commandoes sets out to do this, facing natural obstacles, enemy attack, and betrayal from within. The morality of war does come up in some of the dialogue, but the movie's focus is adventure and suspense.

Discussion Questions: Can you imagine enduring torture for a cause you support, as Anna does? Would you be willing to sacrifice your own life and those of other people for a cause, or for duty, as Mallory is? Talk about the dilemma Mallory faces when he confronts the traitor.

Hart's War (2002)

This film is set in a German prisoner of war camp during World War II. Two American prisoners are found murdered, and the Americans are allowed to hold a trial. A young officer, Hart, is charged with defending the accused, an African American soldier, although in the racist climate there it seems the verdict has already been decided. Meanwhile, the ranking American officer, McNamara, has his own plans, which may subvert justice.

Discussion Questions: Hart, who has never seen battle, gave up information to the Nazis under torture and now wrestles with feelings of shame. The film raises the question of how we define courage and honor, especially in the horrific conditions of war. It also explores the issue of whether the means justify the end. Is it right to sacrifice one person to do something that will save the lives of many others?

Hotel Rwanda (2004)

This gripping movie tells the true story of Paul Rusesabagina, a Rwandan man caught in the middle of the genocide that ravaged his country in 1994 and left almost 1 million people dead. Rusesabagina manages a luxury hotel and at first does not think the growing unrest will touch him or his family. But he comes to see that no one will do anything to stop it. He uses the hotel to protect his family and the hotel staff, and then opens it to anyone who seeks refuge there. At the same time, he is frantically trying to persuade people and groups outside the country to intervene, while also negotiating with brutal militia leaders to keep them from storming the hotel and killing everyone. When it was over, he has saved not only his family but more than a thousand other people as well. Note: Amnesty International has a downloadable organizing kit on human rights based on *Hotel Rwanda*. *amnestyonline@takeaction.amnestyusa.org.*

Discussion Questions: Why do you think no outside groups or countries did anything to help for so long? Should they have intervened? Would it have been right for the UN commander to use force to help the victims, even though his mandate forbade it? Did Paul Rusesabagina do the right thing?

Joan of Arc: Child of War, Soldier of God (2005)

This made-for-television drama from Faith and Values Media tells the story of the fifteenth-century saint in her own words, using her testimony from her trial. Joan speaks of the voices she heard that she believed came from God, voices that called her to drive the English from France and bring peace to her land. We see the consequences of her decision to obey the voices. She led the French in battle against the English and caused the heir to the French throne to be crowned king. But eventually things went against her, and Joan was tried for heresy and burned.

Discussion Questions: Joan's faith led her to take stances that opposed what everyone around her believed to be right. Talk about how to follow God in difficult situations. How do we know we're really doing what God wants? What about possible consequences?

The Mission (1986)

In sixteenth- and seventeenth-century South America, Jesuit Father Gabriel works with the Guaraní people with the unlikely help of Rodrigo, a reformed slave trader. Then they are told they must abandon the mission, but the Guaraní insist they will not leave their home. Father Gabriel and Rodrigo decide to stay with the people, but disagree about what to do. As troops descend upon the mission, Rodrigo leads some of the Guaraní in battle, while Father Gabriel prays with others. Both are killed, along with many of the Guaraní, but a few of the Guaraní make their way back into the jungle to start anew.

Discussion Questions: What is the right course of action in such a situation — to fight, to not resist, or to resist nonviolently? Were both Father Gabriel and Rodrigo justified and right in what they did? If so, why?

Patton (1970)

World War II General George Patton personifies our mixed feelings about war and soldiering: few will claim war as a desirable pursuit, yet we tend to hold up as heroes those who excel at battle. Patton, a brilliant strategist, was such a person. He saw himself cast in the mold of ancient military heroes; he was a philosopher, a poet, and a man who could show great care for those under his command. Yet he could also be ruthless in pursuit of success in battle. At one point, he accuses a soldier suffering from battle fatigue of cowardice and strikes him. *Patton* is nearly three hours long, but many of the scenes hold together so well that a discussion could focus on just one or a few of them.

Discussion Questions: What does it mean to be a hero, especially a military hero? Can we hold soldiers up as heroes even if we are uncomfortable with their purpose? What are differences between the archetypal ancient soldier-hero and the soldier of today? In the movie, General Omar Bradley tells Patton: "I do this job because I've been trained to do it. You do it because you love it." Which is better suited for the conflicts of today? Is it possible to oppose a war and still support our troops? (Film with related themes: *We Were Soldiers*, 2002, and *The Great Santini*, 1979).

The Pianist (2002)

The film tells the true story of Wladyslaw Szpilman, a Jewish Polish pianist who escaped the Warsaw ghetto and hid for months in ruined apartments, living on scraps of food found in abandoned kitchens. Along the way, he finds both evil people and good people. Many Poles help him, risking their lives to do so; a German soldier finds an attic for him to stay in and brings him food. The film is, in the words of its director, a testimony to the power of music, the will to live, and the courage to stand against evil.

Discussion Questions: Why do you think some people helped Szpilman and others didn't? What does it mean to stand against evil? Does it always mean actual combat? Are there situations today that call for such a stand?

Platoon (1986)

This movie about the Vietnam War gives the viewer an experience of war from the perspective of the soldier in the field. The main character, Chris, is a newcomer in Vietnam trying to find a place in a group of hardened soldiers. Chris comes from an upper-middle-class background and has dropped out of college to join the army, in part to demonstrate his belief that not only the poor should go to war. What he finds is a constant challenge to maintain his humanity when faced with horrific acts perpetrated both by the enemy and his own fellow soldiers.

Discussion Questions: How can soldiers hold on to their moral values in a war where passions run high? In what ways might the experience of soldiers in Vietnam be similar to that of soldiers in the recent Iraq conflict? Are most of them like Chris, or are they poor men and women with fewer educational and career options, or reservists who were called up? (Film with related themes: *Casualties of War*, 1989)

Romero (1989)

This film tells the story of Oscar Romero, archbishop of San Salvador. When he is appointed, he is considered a moderate and unlikely to stir things up. But after his friend, the Jesuit priest Rutilio Grande, is murdered, the new archbishop is awakened to the oppression suffered by the poor of his diocese. He chastises those who promote violent resistance, but speaks out publicly against the injustices endemic in El Salvador. But in doing so, he challenges the ruling elite of the country. Eventually, his calls for justice enrage them so much they have him assassinated.

Discussion Questions: Romero is a Catholic hero; some consider him a saint. His life and death raise questions about how to best resist oppression and injustice. Is the only option a resort to violence? Or can we, like Romero, choose to resist nonviolently, even if it puts our own lives at risk? (Films with similar themes: *Salvador,* 1986, *Men with Guns,* 1997)

Saving Private Ryan (1998)

Early on, this film starkly juxtaposes the horror and heroism of war in its brutally realistic portrayal of the D-Day invasion that turned the tide of World War II in favor of the Allies. Then the movie's focus narrows. Army higher-ups, realizing that a mother is about to learn of the deaths of three of her sons, dispatch a small group of D-Day survivors to the French countryside to find and bring back the fourth son, Private Ryan, if he is still alive. Suddenly, for these men, the war isn't about beating the Germans, but finding one man. This search is a dangerous one; some of them are injured and some lose their lives.

Discussion Questions: Is it right to risk the lives of a number of people to save one, even given the movie's circumstances? Who has priority? How do you decide? As an activity, try examining the point of view of the various characters. Since this film is almost three hours long, discussion could center on some of its scenes. The DVD includes interviews with some soldiers who survived the D-Day invasion; this would make a valuable contribution to discussion. (Film with related themes: *Enemy at the Gates,* 2001)

Schindler's List (1993)

This film is based on the life of Oskar Schindler, a German businessman who lived in Europe during World War II. Schindler profits from the Nazi takeover by using free Jewish labor in his factory. He ingratiates himself with the Nazis, becomes part of their circle, and enjoys the benefits of this association. But as the film progresses, he finds himself moved by the savage persecution of the Jews who work for him; eventually, he uses his gifts as a wheeler-dealer to save more than one thousand of them from the death camp.

Discussion Questions: What do you think changed Schindler? Why does he make the choices he does? What guides him? What guides the choices we make?

The Thin Red Line (1998)

The Thin Red Line tells the story of the World War II Battle of Guadalcanal. It gives us a sense of the state of mind and the history of a group of soldiers engaged in attacking a highly defensible position. There is a sense of hopelessness and uncertainty, highlighted by the intense argument caused by Captain Staros when he questions an order by Lt. Col. Tall, an order he believes entails a suicide mission.

Discussion Questions: Should a commanding officer issue an order that he or she believes to be wrong or not in the best interest of his soldiers or the battle? Is a soldier required to follow orders blindly or is there room for practical moral judgment? (Film with related theme: *Gallipoli*, 1981)

Thirteen Days (2000)

For an extended discussion and suggested activity for this film, see page 129.

Three Kings (1999)

For an extended discussion and suggested activity for this film, see page 131.

Windtalkers (2002)

Windtalkers looks at the Navajo Indians who were recruited in the Second World War because their language became a new secret code. Joe Enders is assigned to one of these "codetalkers," with orders to make sure that he — and the code — do not fall into enemy hands. This picture certainly shows the brutality of war but is also concerned with questions of racism (the Navajo soldiers are not accepted by their white counterparts) and the moral decisions peculiar to war, like whether or not to sacrifice the soldier and perhaps friend next to you for the sake of some future victory.

Discussion Questions: Enders is ordered to "protect the code" at all costs, even if it means killing the codetalker rather than let him be captured. What do you think of this? Would such a killing be justified, since losing the code to the enemy would mean many other people would die?

The World at War (1974)

This twenty-six-part documentary series has been called the definitive visual history of World War II. It contains original material made by both the Allies and the Axis powers and covers the war from its origins in the 1920s to the Cold War aftermath. Among other things, it looks at the Hitler Youth Movement, the Holocaust, the air battle over Britain, Germany's defeat at Stalingrad, wartime Japan, and the development of the bomb. Also included are songs, maps, speeches, photos, and interviews with survivors of the war.

Discussion Questions: This documentary is obviously too long for many groups to watch in its entirety. One possibility is to watch selected parts and then discuss the issues involved. For example, view the parts that explain the background to the war and talk about its causes. Could it have been avoided? What could have been done differently? Should the United States have been more involved internationally after World War I? Or watch the part dealing with the atomic bomb. Afterward, talk about questions such as: Did the United States have an obligation to develop the bomb, since Germany was also working on it? Did dropping bombs in Japan save Allied lives? Was the second bomb necessary?

Notes

Introduction

1. Experts do not agree about the use of this terminology. Some do not believe that what is currently labeled by some as the "classical" position accurately reflects the church's ages-old just war position. Drew Christiansen, SJ, for example, prefers the term "permissive" just war position, rather than "classical" just war position.

Chapter One / A Sketch: The World and War

1. Steven A. LeBlanc with Katherine E. Register, *Constant Battles: The Myth of the Peaceful, Noble Savage* (New York: St. Martin's Press, 2003), 6–9.

2. R. Brian Ferguson, "The Birth of War," *Natural History Magazine* (July–August 2003), 28–35.

3. John Keegan, *A History of Warfare* (New York: Alfred A. Knopf, 1993), 11, xvi.

4. Ibid., 108.

5. Ibid., 4–6.

6. John Keegan, ed., *The Book of War* (New York: Viking Penguin, 1999), ix–x.

7. James O'Gara, *The Church and War* (Washington, DC: National Council of Catholic Men, 1967), 11–14.

8. Philippe Contamine, *War in the Middle Ages,* trans. Michael Jones (Oxford and New York: Basil Blackwell, 1984), 263–64.

9. Ibid., 266–67.

10. Thomas Head and Richard Landes, eds., *The Peace of God: Social Violence and Religious Response in France around the Year 1000* (Ithaca: Cornell University Press, 1992), 2, 109.

11. Ibid., 6.

12. Ibid., 7–8.

13. George T. Dennis, "Defenders of the Christian People: Holy War in Byzantium," an offprint from *The Crusades from the Perspective of Byzantium and the Muslim World,* ed. Angeliki E. Laiou and Roy Parviz Mottahedeh (Washington, DC: Dumbarton Oaks Publications Office, 2001), 31.

14. Ibid., 32, 35–36.

15. Steven Runciman, "The Penetration of the Crusading Ideal," in *The History of Popular Culture to 1815*, ed. Norman F. Cantor and Michael S. Werthman (New York: Macmillan, 1968), 122–23.

16. William J. Bausch, *Pilgrim Church: A Popular History of Catholic Christianity* (Notre Dame: Fides/Claretian, 1977), 202–7.

17. Keegan, *A History of Warfare*, 296–97, and Bausch, *Pilgrim Church*, 272.

18. The rise of the modern nation-state was a major development in the evolution of warfare. For more information, consult works on the history of early modern Europe.

19. Bausch, *Pilgrim Church*, 345–46.

20. Geoffrey Parker, ed., *Cambridge Illustrated History of Warfare* (Cambridge: Cambridge University Press, 1995), 2.

21. Ibid., 9.

22. Keegan, *A History of Warfare*, 50.

23. Keegan, *The Book of War*, xvii.

24. Ibid., xvi.

25. *Cambridge History of Warfare*, 368–69.

Chapter Two / War and Peace: Parallel Traditions

1. James Childress, "Moral Discourse about War in the Early Church," *Journal of Religious Ethics* 12, no. 1 (Spring 1984): 2.

2. Ibid., 3.

3. Ibid., 1.

4. Augustine, *The City of God*, trans. M. Dods, in *A Select Library of the Nicene and Post-Nicene Fathers of the Christian Church*, ed. Philip Schaff (Grand Rapids: Eerdmans, 1993), 2:407.

5. Thomas Aquinas, *Summa Theologica*, in *Saint Thomas Aquinas: Philosophical Texts*, ed. Thomas Gilby (New York: Oxford University Press, 1960), II–II, question 40, article 1.

6. Ibid.

7. Ibid.

8. Editorial, *La Civiltà Cattolica*, July 6, 1991.

9. John Paul II, "Address to the International Conference on Nutrition," *Origins* 22, no. 28 (December 24, 1992): 475, cited in "The Harvest of Justice Is Sown in Peace," n. 36. There is also a more extensive treatment in *Compendium of the Social Doctrine of the Church* (Pontifical Council for Justice and Peace, 2004).

Chapter Four / The Current Situation

1. "Technology of War," *science.howstuffworks.com.*, 1998–2005.

2. Ibid.

3. Lt. Col. Thomas X. Hammes, "The Evolution of War: The Fourth Generation," in the *Marine Corps Gazette* (September 1994).

4. John J. Arquilla and David F. Ronfeldt, "Cyber War Is Coming," in *Comparative Strategy* 12 (1993): 141–65.

5. Mary Kaldor, *Old and New Wars* (Palo Alto, CA: Stanford University Press, 1999).

6. Thomas X. Hammes, *The Sling and the Stone: On War in the 21st Century* (St. Paul, MN: Zenith Press, 2004), 2.

Chapter Five / Effective Ways to Fight Terrorism While Retaining Our Values

1. Stephen E. Flynn, *America the Vulnerable: How the U.S. Has Failed to Secure the Homeland and Protect Its People from Terrorism* (New York: HarperCollins, 2004).

2. Much of this article is drawn from Maryann Cusimano Love, *Morality Matters: Ethics and the War on Terrorism*, forthcoming from Cornell University Press.

3. See St. Augustine, *City of God*, trans. Thomas Merton (New York: Modern Library Paperback Classics, 2000).

4. Maryann Cusimano Love and Martha Crenshaw, "Networked Terror," in *Beyond Sovereignty: Issues for a Global Agenda*, 2nd ed. (New York: Thomson/ Wadsworth, 2003).

5. Martha Crenshaw, "Organized Disorder: Terrorism, Politics, and Society," in *The Democratic Imagination*, ed. Ray C. Rist (New Brunswick, NJ: Transaction Publishers, 1994), 143–44.

6. Maryann Cusimano Love, "Globalization, Ethics and the War on Terrorism," *Notre Dame Journal of Law, Ethics, and Public Policy*, "Violence in America" Issue (2002); Maryann Cusimano Love, "Morality Matters: Ethics and Power Politics in the War on Terrorism," *Georgetown Journal of International Affairs*, Ethics in Conflict issue (Summer/Fall 2002).

7. Love and Crenshaw, "Networked Terror."

8. "Improving Our Image," *Montreal Gazette*, March 4, 2002, B2.

9. Mike Allen and Amy Goldstein, "Security Funding Tops New Budget," *Washington Post*, January 20, 2002, A01.

10. Jonathan Weisman, "Iraq Cost Could Mount to $100 Billion, Impact on Other Programs Feared," *Washington Post*, July 13, 2003, A22.

11. Alexander T. J. Lennon, *The Battle for Hearts and Minds: Using Soft Power to Undermine Terrorist Networks* (Cambridge, MA: MIT Press, 2003).

12. Peter Baker, "Karen Hughes to Work on the World's View of the U.S.," *Washington Post*, March 12, 2005, A3.

13. The 9/11 Commission, *The 9/11 Commission Report: Final Report of the National Commission on Terrorist Attacks upon the United States* (New York: W. W. Norton, 2004), 375.

14. Ibid., 375–77.

15. Edward S. Walker quoted in Robert G. Kaiser, "U.S. Message Lost Overseas: Officials See Immediate Need for Public Diplomacy," *Washington Post*, October 15, 2001, A1.

16. Senator Jesse Helms quoted in Kaiser, "U.S. Message Lost Overseas," A1.

17. Kaiser, "U.S. Message Lost Overseas,"A1.

18. The 9/11 Commission, *The 9/11 Commission Report*, 377.

19. An earlier version of this argument was first published as "Morality Matters: Ethics and Power Politics in the War on Terrorism," *Georgetown Journal of International Affairs* (Fall 2002); Thomas Friedman, "World War III," *New York Times*, September 13, 2001; Roger Barnett, *Asymmetrical Warfare: Today's Challenges to U.S. Military Power* (Washington, DC: Brassey's, 2003).

20. Robert D. Kaplan, *Warrior Politics: Why Leadership Demands a Pagan Ethos* (New York: Random House, 2001).

21. Prime Minister Tony Blair, "Prime Minister's Statement, Bloody Sunday Inquiry," January 29, 1998, House of Commons Official Report, Parliamentary Debates (Hansard), *www.bloody-sunday-inquiry.org.uk/index2.asp?p=7*.

22. Paul Wilkinson, "The Orange and the Green," in *Terrorism, Legitimacy and Power*, ed. Martha Crenshaw (Middletown, CT: Wesleyan University Press 1983), 117.

23. Irving Louis Horowitz, "Political Terrorism and State Power," *Journal of Political and Military Sociology* (Spring 1973): 145–57.

24. Love, "Globalization, Ethics and the War on Terrorism."

25. The exception is Palestinian nationalist terror groups, which really ought to be considered separately from al Qaeda. Palestinian nationalist terror groups receive significant aid from Arab states for a number of reasons. Governments in the region want to aid Palestinians at the expense of Israel, but not at the expense of their own land or pocketbooks. They do not want to house large Palestinian populations that may change local political balances and lead to unrest (as happened to Jordan in its civil war). Sponsoring Palestinian nationalist terror groups is a way to support the Palestinian cause while directing its locus, and any attendant political disruptions and costs, elsewhere. Supporting Palestinian nationalism is a way to prove a regime's pan-Arab credentials, while simultaneously taking a deniable and indirect shot at Israel. Also, Palestinian nationalist groups undertake many functions, including charitable social services for Palestinian civilians as well as violence against Israel and its allies. Governments donate money to aid Palestinian civilians, turning a blind eye to financial diversions to Palestinian violence.

26. Flynn, *America the Vulnerable*.

27. Sam Nunn, "Are We Doing All We Can to Prevent a Nuclear Attack? The Simple Answer Is No, We Are Not," speech to the National Press Club, Washington, DC, March 9, 2005, *www.nti.org*.

28. Testimony of John R. Bolton to the Committee on International Relations, U.S. House of Representatives, June 4, 2003; see *www.house.gov/international_relations/108/*; The White House, Office of the Press Secretary, "Proliferation Security Initiative: Statement of Interdiction Principles," September 4, 2003, *www.whitehouse.gov*.

29. Reuters, "Nuclear-Related Shipment to Libya Said Blocked," December 31, 2003; "Uranium Kit Seizure Pushed Libya to Come Clean," *The Guardian*, January 1, 2004.

30. Colin Powell, "Perspectives: Powell Defends a First Strike as Iraq Option," interview, *New York Times*, September 8, 2002, sec. 1, 18.

31. R. Scott Appleby, "Catholic Peacebuilding," *America* 189, no. 6 (September 8, 2003).

Chapter Six / The Interreligious Dimension

1. Fred James Hill and Nicholas Awde, *A History of the Islamic World* (New York: Hippocrene Books, 2003), 198–99.

2. David R. Smock, ed., *Perspectives on Pacifism: Christian, Jewish, and Muslim Views on Nonviolence and International Conflict* (Washington, DC: United States Institute of Peace Press, 1995), 26.

3. *Judaism: Power and Interpretation: In the Name of God: Religion and Violence*, report on a Carnegie-Georgetown Forum, September 19, 2002, cosponsored by Georgetown University.

4. From a talk given at "The Ethics of Warfare: Muslim, Jewish, and Christian Religious Traditions," a conference at Washington University, St. Louis, January 22–23, 1991. A summary by J. Patout Burns was published in *Journal of Religious Pluralism* 2 (1993): 83–96.

5. Yehudah Mirsky, "The Political Morality of Pacifism and Nonviolence: One Jewish View," in *War and Its Discontents: Pacifism and Quietism in the Abrahamic Traditions*, ed. J. Patout Burns (Washington, DC: Georgetown University Press, 1996), 51.

6. From the conference "The Ethics of Warfare: Muslim, Jewish, and Christian Religious Traditions."

7. Cited in Smock, *Perspectives on Pacifism*, 21.

8. Cited in ibid., 25.

9. Ibid., viii.

10. Philip K. Hitti, *Islam: A Way of Life* (Washington, DC: Regnery Gateway, 1970), 26.

11. Hill and Awde, *A History of the Islamic World*, 47.

12. Ibid., 47–48.

13. Kirk H. Sowell, *The Arab World: An Illustrated History* (New York: Hippocrene Books, 2004), 82–83.

14. Sohail H. Hashmi, "Interpreting the Islamic Ethics of War and Peace," in *The Ethics of War and Peace: Religious and Secular Perspectives*, ed. Terry Nardin (Princeton, NJ: Princeton University Press, 1996), 146.

15. Bassam Tibi, "War and Peace in Islam," in *The Ethics of War and Peace*, 128–29.

16. Cited in Teresa Watanabe, "Interpreting Islam: War and Peace," in the *Los Angeles Times*, October 5, 2001.

17. Imam Dr. Abdul Jalil Sajid, "Islam and Ethics of War and Peace," a paper written for a lecture series of the Westmoreland General Meeting of the Society of Friends (in Britain), 2000–2003, 9–10.

18. Hashmi, "Interpreting the Islamic Ethics of War and Peace," 165.

19. Tibi, "War and Peace in Islam," 133.

20. Ibid., 135.

21. Hashmi, "Interpreting the Islamic Ethics of War and Peace," 158.

22. Ibid., 148–49.

23. Sajid, "Islam and Ethics of War and Peace," 13–16.

24. Cited in Smock, *Perspectives on Pacifism*, 30.

25. Hashmi, "Interpreting the Islamic Ethics of War and Peace," 161.

26. Ibid., 153.

27. Cited in Smock, *Perspectives on Pacifism*, 35.

28. Cited in ibid., 32.

Chapter Seven / The Historic Peace Churches: Dialogue Partners

1. Gerald W. Schlabach, "Meeting in Exile: Historic Peace Churches and the Emerging Peace Church Catholic," a lecture for Presentation Sisters' Peace Studies Forum, January 23, 2004, Fargo, North Dakota.

2. Donald B. Kraybill and Carl F. Bowman, *On the Backroad to Heaven: Old Order Hutterites, Mennonites, Amish, and Brethren* (Baltimore: Johns Hopkins University Press, 2001), 2.

3. Margaret H. Bacon, *The Quiet Rebels: The Story of the Quakers in America* (New York: Basic Books, 1969), 9–10.

4. Ibid., 50.

5. Cited in Cynthia Sampson and John Paul Lederach, eds., *From the Ground Up: Mennonite Contributions to International Peacebuilding* (New York: Oxford University Press, 2000), 6.

6. Thomas D. Hamm, *The Quakers in America* (New York: Columbia University Press, 2003), 162.

7. Sampson and Lederach, *From the Ground Up*, 14.

8. Drew Christiansen, "An Exchange of Gifts," *America* 188, no. 7 (March 3, 2003), 19–22.

9. Ibid.

10. Schlabach, "Meeting in Exile," 2, 10.

Chapter Eight / The Power of Forgiveness

1. Pope John Paul II, *No Peace without Justice, No Justice without Forgiveness*, Zenit News Agency (*www.zenit.org/english/war/visualizza.phtml?sid=13939*). The quotes in this paragraph appear, respectively, in numbers 4, 71, and 1, in the document's ordering.

2. Ibid., no. 2.

3. David J. O'Brien and Thomas A. Shannon, eds., *Catholic Social Thought: The Documentary Heritage* (Maryknoll, NY: Orbis Books, 1992), 131–62. The

discussion of disarmament appears in paragraphs 109 through 119 of *Pacem in Terris.*

4. Ibid., 258. The words "Development is the New Name for Peace" come from the heading of section 4 of *Populorum Progressio,* which runs from pages 240 through 262 of the O'Brien-Shannon collection.

5. Arendt cited in Donald W. Shriver Jr., *An Ethic for Enemies: Forgiveness in Politics* (New York, Oxford: Oxford University Press, 1995), 6.

6. Desmond Tutu, *No Future without Forgiveness* (New York: Doubleday, 2000). On page 23, Tutu explains that if black leaders had insisted on bringing white abusers to trial, they would have had justice — and a South Africa "lying in ashes."

7. Related in Marc Gopin, *Between Eden and Armageddon: The Future of World Religions, Violence, and Peacemaking* (New York, Oxford: Oxford University Press, 2000), 44–47; and in R. Scott Appleby, *The Ambivalence of the Sacred: Religion, Violence, and Reconciliation* (Lanham, MD: Rowman & Littlefield, 2000), 123–40.

8. Botcharova in Woodstock Colloquium *Forgiveness in Conflict Resolution: Reality and Utility — The Bosnian Experience* (Washington, DC: Woodstock Theological Center, 1997); quote appears on 89–90.

9. Shriver, *An Ethic for Enemies,* 7.

10. John Paul Lederach, "Five Qualities of Practice in Support of Reconciliation Processes," in *Forgiveness and Reconciliation: Religion, Public Policy, and Conflict Transformation,* ed. Raymond J. Helmick, SJ, and Rodney L. Petersen (Philadelphia: Templeton Foundation Press, 2001), 201.

11. Shriver in Woodstock Theological Center Forum entitled "An Ethic for Enemies: Forgiveness in Politics" (November 15, 1995), *Woodstock Report* (March 1996), *www.georgetown.edu/centers/woodstock/report/r-fea45.htm.*

12. Baker in Woodstock Colloquium *Forgiveness in Conflict Resolution: Reality and Utility — The Northern Ireland Experience* (Washington, DC: Woodstock Theological Center, 1997), 66.

13. Lennon in Woodstock Colloquium *Forgiveness in Conflict Resolution: Reality and Utility* (Washington, DC: Woodstock Theological Center, 1996), 56.

14. Leslie Evans points to a need for international criminal tribunals in connection with the 1999 massacre in East Timor. See "Forgiveness in East Timor, but Where Is the Justice?" UCLA Center for Southeast Asian Studies, posted May 28, 2004 (*www.isop.ucla.edu/cseas/article.asp?parentid=11589*).

15. Shriver, *An Ethic for Enemies,* 9.

16. William Bole, Drew Christiansen, SJ, and Robert T. Hennemeyer, *Forgiveness in International Politics: An Alternative Road to Peace* (Washington, DC: U.S. Conference of Catholic Bishops, 2004). Highlights of the commission process are culled mostly from chap. 5, esp. 90–93.

17. Quoted by Donald W. Shriver Jr., in Woodstock Colloquium *Forgiveness in Conflict Resolution: Reality and Utility — The Experiences of the Truth Commissions* (Washington, DC: Woodstock Theological Center, 1998), 100.

18. William Bole, "The Pope and the Politics of Forgiveness," *Living City* (October 2004): 10.

19. Barton Gellman, "Hussein, on His Knees, Begs Forgiveness for Massacre," *Washington Post*, March 17, 1997, A1.

20. Shriver in Woodstock Colloquium *Forgiveness in Conflict Resolution: Reality and Utility — The Experiences of the Truth Commissions*, 100.

21. See Bole, Christiansen and Hennemeyer, *Forgiveness in International Politics*, 69–75.

22. Daly in Woodstock Colloquium *Forgiveness in Conflict Resolution*, 12.

23. Steele, "Practical Approaches to Inter-Religious Dialogue and the Empowerment of Religious Communities as Agents of Reconciliation," in *Inter-Religious Dialogue as a Way of Reconciliation in South Eastern Europe*, ed. Milan Vukomanović and Marinko Vucinić (Beograd: Izdavac, 2001), 100.

24. Steele quotes come from interviews with William Bole, quoted in Bole, Christiansen, and Hennemeyer, *Forgiveness in International Politics*, 156–64.

25. Ibid.

26. See Bole, Christiansen, and Hennemeyer, *Forgiveness in International Politics*, 182–85.

27. Johnston, in Woodstock Colloquium, *Forgiveness in Conflict Resolution*, 36.

28. Pope John Paul II, *No Peace without Justice, No Justice without Forgiveness*, no. 3.

Appendix A / Group Activities and Case Studies

1. PBS Frontline: "The Triumph of Evil: 100 Days of Slaughter," 1999 documentary.

2. Ibid.

3. William Ferroggiaro, "The US and the Genocide in Rwanda 1994: Evidence of Inaction" (National Security Archive, August 20, 2001), 3.

4. Ibid., 3–4.

5. Ibid., 6.

Selected Resources for Further Study and Discussion

THE HISTORY OF WAR

Books, Articles, and Papers

Bausch, William J. *Pilgrim Church: A Popular History of Catholic Christianity*. Notre Dame, IN: Fides/Claretian, 1977.

Cantor, Norman F., and Michael S. Werthman, eds. *The History of Popular Culture to 1815*. New York: Macmillan, 1968.

Dennis, George T., SJ. "Defenders of the Christian People: Holy War in Byzantium," an offprint from *The Crusades from the Perspective of Byzantium and the Muslim World*, ed. Angeliki E. Laiou and Roy Parviz Mottahedeh. Washington, DC: Dumbarton Oaks Publications Office, 2001.

Head, Thomas, and Richard Landes, eds. *The Peace of God: Social Violence and Religious Response in France around the Year 1000*. Ithaca: Cornell University Press, 1992.

Keegan, John. *A History of Warfare*. New York: Alfred A. Knopf, 1993.

———. *The Book of War: 25 Centuries of Great War Writing*. New York: Viking Penguin, 1999.

Kohn, George C. *Dictionary of Wars*. New York: Anchor Press/Doubleday, 1986.

O'Gara, James. *The Church and War*. Washington, DC: National Council of Catholic Men, 1967.

CURRENT THINKING ON WAR AND PEACE

Books, Articles, and Papers

Bourke, Joanna. *An Intimate History of Killing: Face-to-Face Killing in Twentieth-Century Warfare*. New York: Basic Books, 1999.

Dallaire, Romeo. *Shake Hands with the Devil: The Failure of Humanity in Rwanda*. New York: Carroll & Graf, 2004.

Flynn, Stephen E. *America the Vulnerable: How the U.S. Has Failed to Secure the Homeland and Protect Its People from Terrorism*. New York: HarperCollins, 2004.

Grossman, Lt. Col. Dave. *On Killing: The Psychological Cost of Learning to Kill in War and Society.* Boston: Little, Brown, 1995.

Hammes, Col. Thomas F. X. *The Sling and the Stone: On War in the 21st Century.* St. Paul, MN: Zenith Press, 2004.

Hedges, Chris. *War Is a Force That Gives Us Meaning.* New York: Anchor Books, 2002.

Hillman, James. *A Terrible Love of War.* New York: Penguin Books, 2004.

Kalder, Mary. *Old and New Wars.* Palo Alto, CA: Stanford University Press, 1999.

Love, Maryann Cusimano. "Globalization, Ethics and the War on Terrorism." *Notre Dame Journal of Law, Ethics, and Public Policy,* "Violence in America" Issue (2002).

———. "Morality Matters: Ethics and Power Politics in the War on Terrorism." *Georgetown Journal of International Affairs,* "Ethics in Conflict" issue (Summer/Fall 2002).

———. *Morality Matters: Ethics and the War on Terrorism.* Ithaca: Cornell University Press, forthcoming.

Love, Maryann Cusimano, and Martha Crenshaw. "Networked Terror." In *Beyond Sovereignty: Issues for a Global Agenda.* 2nd ed. New York: Thomson/ Wadsworth, 2003.

Loyd, Anthony. *My War Gone By, I Miss It So.* New York: Penguin Books, 1999.

The 9/11 Commission. *The 9/11 Commission Report: Final Report of the National Commission on Terrorist Attacks upon the United States.* New York: W. W. Norton, 2004.

Organizations and Web Sites

Amnesty International. In the United States: 5 Penn Plaza, 14th Floor, New York, NY 10001, (212) 807-8400. Amnesty International (AI) is a worldwide movement of people who campaign for internationally recognized human rights. AI's mission is to undertake research and action focused on preventing and ending grave abuses of the rights to physical and mental integrity, freedom of conscience and expression, and freedom from discrimination, within the context of its work to promote all human rights. AI has members and supporters around the world. At the latest count, there were more than 1.8 million members, supporters and subscribers in over 150 countries and territories. *www.amnestyusa.org.*

Human Rights Watch. 350 Fifth Avenue, 34th Floor, New York, NY 10118-3299. Human Rights Watch is the largest human rights organization based in the United States. Its researchers conduct fact-finding investigations into human rights abuses in all regions of the world. Human Rights Watch then publishes those findings in dozens of books and reports every year. It meets with government officials to urge changes in policy and practice. In extreme circumstances, Human Rights Watch presses for the withdrawal of military and economic support from governments that egregiously violate the rights of their people. In moments of crisis, Human Rights Watch provides up-to-the-minute information about conflicts while they are underway. *www.hrw.org.*

Pew Forum on Religion and Public Life. The Pew Forum is a well-respected non-partisan "think-tank" that seeks to promote a deeper understanding of issues at the intersection of religion and public affairs. Its Web site gives a brief overview of the just war theory and includes related news stories and recent articles by just war thinkers. *http://pewforum.org/just-war.*

THEOLOGY OF WAR AND PEACE

Books, Articles, and Papers

Appleby, R. Scott. "Catholic Peacebuilding." *America* 189, no. 6 (September 8, 2003): 12–15.

Aquinas, Thomas. *Summa Theologica.* In *Saint Thomas Aquinas: Philosophical Texts.* Ed. Thomas Gilby. New York: Oxford University Press, 1960.

Augustine, *The City of God.* In *A Select Library of the Nicene and Post-Nicene Fathers of the Christian Church.* Trans. M. Dods. Ed. Philip Schaff. Vol. 2. Grand Rapids: Eerdmans, 1993.

Cahill, Lisa Sowle. "Theological Contexts of Just War Theory and Pacifism: A Response to J. Bryan Hehir." *Journal of Religious Ethics* 20, no. 2 (Fall 1992): 259–65.

Carlson, John D., and Erik C. Owens, eds. *The Sacred and the Sovereign: Religion and International Politics.* Washington, DC: Georgetown University Press, 2003.

The Catechism of the Catholic Church. New York: Catholic Book Publishing Co., 1994.

Christiansen, Drew, SJ " 'Never Again War': The Presumption against the Use of Force in Contemporary Catholic Social Teaching and the Diplomacy of the Holy See." Paper prepared for a conference on the Relevance of Just War Theory in the Modern Age at the Center for Christianity and the Common Good, University of Dallas, April 7–8, 2000.

————. "The Presumption against Force in the Just War Tradition." Debate presentation, U.S. Naval Academy, Annapolis, MD, June 7, 2004.

Cole, Darrell. "Good Wars." *First Things* 116 (October 2001): 9–13

Compendium of the Social Doctrine of the Church. Pontifical Council for Justice and Peace, 2004.

Dear, John. *The God of Peace: Toward a Theology of Nonviolence.* Maryknoll, NY: Orbis Books, 1994.

Hehir, J. Bryan. "Just War Theory in a Post–Cold War World." *Journal of Religious Ethics* 20, no. 2 (Fall 1992): 237–57.

————. "The New National Security Strategy." *America* 188, no. 12 (April 7, 2003): 8–12.

Hollenbach, David, SJ. "War and Peace in American Catholic Thought: A Heritage Abandoned?" *Theological Studies* 48 (1987): 711–26.

Johnson, James Turner. "Just War, As It Was and Is." *First Things* 149 (January 2005): 14–24.

———. "Two Kinds of Pacifism: Opposition to the Political Use of Force in the Renaissance-Reformation Period." *Journal of Religious Ethics* 12, no. 1 (Spring 1984): 39–60.

Langan, John, SJ. "The Elements of St. Augustine's Just War Theory." *Journal of Religious Ethics* 12, no. 1 (Spring 1984): 19–38.

Massaro, Thomas J., SJ, and Thomas A. Shannon. *Catholic Perspectives on Peace and War.* Lanham, MD: Rowman & Littlefield, 2003.

Merton, Thomas. *Faith and Violence.* Notre Dame, IN: University of Notre Dame Press, 1968.

Mossa, Mark, SJ. "Nonviolence or Just War: Two Legitimate Moral Options?" *Blueprint for Social Justice* 56, no. 4 (December 2002): 1–7.

Nouwen, Henri J. M.. *Peacework: Prayer, Resistance, Community.* Maryknoll, NY: Orbis Books, 2005.

Reichberg, Gregory M., Henrik Syse, and Endre Begby. *The Ethics of War: Classic and Contemporary Readings.* Oxford: Blackwell Publishing, 2006.

Suarez, Francisco. *De Legibus ac de Deo Legislatore.* Ed. Luciano Perena. 6 vols. Madrid: Consejo Superior de Investigationes Científicas, 1971.

Walzer, Michael. *Just and Unjust Wars: A Moral Argument with Historical Illustrations.* 3rd ed. New York: Basic Books, 2002.

Weaver, Alain Epp. "Unjust Lies, Just Wars? A Christian Pacifist Conversation with Augustine." *Journal of Religious Ethics* 29, no. 1 (Spring 2001): 51–78.

Weigel, George. "The Just War Case for the War." *America* 31 (March 2003): 7–10.

Williams, Rowan, and George Weigel. "War and Statecraft: An Exchange." *First Things* 141 (March 2004): 14–22.

SELECTED DOCUMENTS FROM THE HOLY SEE AND THE U.S. CONFERENCE OF CATHOLIC BISHOPS

Note: These documents are available on the Web sites of the Holy See and the U.S. Conference of Catholic Bishops. The Internet addresses of those sites are given after the list of documents.

John XXIII. *Pacem in Terris.* April 11, 1963. An encyclical.

Paul VI. *Address to the United Nations General Assembly.* October 4, 1965.

Gaudium et Spes (Pastoral Constitution on the Church in the Modern World). December 7, 1965. A document of the Second Vatican Council.

Paul VI. *Populorum et Progressio.* March 26, 1967. An encyclical.

U.S. Conference of Catholic Bishops. *The Challenge of Peace.* Washington, DC, 1983.

John Paul II. *Centesimus Annus.* May 1, 1991. An encyclical.
United States Conference of Catholic Bishops. *The Harvest of Justice Is Sown in Peace.* Washington, DC, 1993.
John Paul II. *Evangelium Vitae.* March 25, 1995. An encyclical.
United States Conference of Catholic Bishops. *A Pastoral Message: Living with Faith and Hope after September 11.* Washington, DC, November 14, 2001.
John Paul II. *Message for the Celebration of the World Day of Peace.* January 1, 2002.

Organizations and Web Sites

The Holy See. www.vatican.va (Enter "Just War" in the Search box.)
United States Conference of Catholic Bishops. 3211 Fourth Street, NE, Washington, DC 20017-1194. Click on "Departments and Activities" and then on "Social Development and World Peace." This Web site includes statements by the bishops on a variety of U.S. government policy issues, including comments on war. *www.usccb.org*

JUDAISM AND ISLAM

Books, Articles, and Papers

Alavi, Karima Diane. "Turning to the Islamic Faith." *America* 186, no. 7 (March 4, 2002): 18–20.
Armstrong, Karen. A *History of God: The 4,000-Year Quest of Judaism, Christianity and Islam.* New York: Ballantine Books, 1993.
———. *Holy War.* London: Macmillan London, 1988.
Burns, J. Patout, ed. *War and Its Discontents: Pacifism and Quietism in the Abrahamic Traditions.* Washington, DC: Georgetown University Press, 1996.
Esposito, John. *The Islamic Threat: Myth or Reality?* New York: Oxford University Press, 1992.
Firestone, Reuven. "Conceptions of Holy War in Biblical and Qur'anic Tradition." *Journal of Religious Ethics* 24, no. 1 (Spring 1996): 99–123.
Gopin, Marc. *Between Eden and Armageddon: The Future of the World Religions, Violence and Peacemaking.* New York: Oxford University Press, 2000.
Hashmi, Sohail, and Steven Lee, eds. *Ethics and Weapons of Mass Destruction: Religious and Secular Perspectives.* New York: Cambridge University Press, 2004.
Judaism: Power and Interpretation: In the Name of God: Religion and Violence. Report on a September 19, 2002, Carnegie-Georgetown Forum, cosponsored by Georgetown University.
Kaplan, Laura Duhan. "Rabbinic Concepts and Contemporary Conscientious Objection." *Tikkun* 19, no. 6 (November/December 2004): 9–12.
Kelsay, John. "Religion, Morality and the Governance of War: The Case of Classical Islam." *Journal of Religious Ethics* 18, no. 2 (Fall 2003): 123–39.

Kelsay, John, and James Turner Johnson, eds. *Just War and Jihad: Historical and Theoretical Perspectives on War and Peace in Western and Islamic Traditions.* New York: Greenwood Press, 1991.

Nardin, Terry, ed. *The Ethics of War and Peace: Religious and Secular Perspectives.* Princeton, NJ: Princeton University Press, 1996.

Polner, Murray, and Naomi Goodman, eds. *The Challenge of Shalom: The Jewish Tradition of Peace and Justice.* Gabriola, BC: New Society Publishers, 1994.

Safi, Louay M. "Islam's Jihad for Peace: Transcending the Classical Notions of Jihad." Paper presented for a conference at the Joan B. Kroc Institute for International Peace Studies, University of Notre Dame, April 12–13, 2002, titled *In Multiple Voices: Challenges and Opportunities for Islamic Peacebuilding after September 11th.*

Said, Abdul, Nathan Funk, and Ayse Kadayifici, eds. *Peace and Conflict Resolution in Islam.* Washington, DC: University Press of America, 2001.

Smock, David R., ed. *Interfaith Dialogue and Peacebuilding.* Washington, DC: United States Institute of Peace Press, 2002.

———. *Perspectives on Pacifism: Christian, Jewish, and Muslim Views on Nonviolence and International Conflict.* Washington, DC: United States Institute of Peace Press, 1995.

———. *Religious Perspectives on War: Christian, Muslim and Jewish Attitudes to Force after the Gulf War.* Washington, DC: United States Institute of Peace Press, 1992.

Walzer, Michael. "The Idea of Holy War in Ancient Israel." *Journal of Religious Ethics* 20, no. 2 (Fall 1992): 215–28.

Organizations and Web Sites

Jewish Peace Fellowship. Box 271, Nyack, NY 10960, (845) 358-4601. This is a Jewish voice in the peace community, and a peace voice in the Jewish community; a nondenominational Jewish organization committed to active nonviolent resolution of conflict. *www.jewishpeacefellowship.org.*

Muslim Peace Fellowship. Box 271, Nyack, NY, 10960, (845) 358-4601. This is a gathering of peace-and-justice-oriented Muslims of all backgrounds, dedicated to making the beauty of Islam evident in the world. *www.mpfweb.org.*

THE HISTORIC PEACE CHURCHES/ PEACEBUILDING

Books, Articles, and Papers

Ackerman, Peter, and Christopher Kruegler. *Strategic Nonviolent Conflict: The Dynamics of People Power in the Twentieth Century.* Westport, CT: Praeger Publishers, 1994.

Bacon, Margaret H. *The Quiet Rebels: The Story of the Quakers in America*. New York: Basic Books, 1969.

Christiansen, Drew. "An Exchange of Gifts," *America* 188, no. 7 (March 3, 2003).

———. "What Is a Peace Church? A Roman Catholic Perspective." A paper prepared for the International Mennonite–Roman Catholic Dialogue; Thomashof, Karlsruhe, Germany. November 23–30, 2000.

Hamm, Thomas D. *The Quakers in America*. New York: Columbia University Press, 2003.

Kelly, Thomas R. *A Testament of Devotion*. San Francisco: HarperSanFrancisco, 1996.

Kraybill, Donald B., and Carl F. Bowman. *On the Backroad to Heaven: Old Order Hutterites, Mennonites, Amish, and Brethren*. Baltimore: Johns Hopkins University Press, 2001.

Sampson, Cynthia, and John Paul Lederach, eds. *From the Ground Up: Mennonite Contributions to International Peacebuilding*. New York: Oxford University Press, 2000.

Schlabach, Gerald W. "Meeting in Exile: Historic Peace Churches and the Emerging Peace Church Catholic." A lecture for the Presentation Sisters' Peace Studies Forum, January 23, 2004, Fargo, North Dakota.

Organizations and Web Sites

The American Friends Service Committee, 1501 Cherry Street, Philadelphia, PA 19102 Formed by the Quakers in 1917, the committee works with people of all backgrounds and faiths to confront, nonviolently, powerful institutions of violence, evil, oppression, and injustice. As well as doing relief work around the world, it supports immigration law reform, lobbies against the death penalty, supports Israeli conscientious objectors, and works for peace in many other ways. *www.afsc.org*.

Carnegie Endowment for International Peace, 1779 Massachusetts Avenue NW, Washington, DC 20036-2103. The Endowment is a private, nonprofit organization dedicated to advancing cooperation between nations and promoting active international engagement by the United States. Its work is nonpartisan and dedicated to achieving practical results. This Web site offers current analysis, commentary, and resources on pressing international issues, and includes a special section on nuclear nonproliferation. It also includes *Foreign Policy*, a leading magazine of international politics and economics published by the Endowment. *www.carnegieendowment.org*.

Catholic Peace Fellowship, Box 4232, South Bend, IN 46634. The Catholic Peace Fellowship supports Catholic conscientious objectors through education, counseling, and advocacy. This Web site includes a variety of educational resources for the classroom, as well as articles from newspapers around the country relevant to the Fellowship's work. The site also includes *The Sign of Peace*, a journal that examines matters of war and peace through a theological lens. *www.catholicpeacefellowship.org*.

Christian Peacemaker Teams, Box 6508, Chicago, IL 60680-6508. This is a program of Brethren, Quaker, and Mennonite Churches (USA and Canada) that offers an organized, nonviolent alternative to war and other forms of lethal inter-group conflict. It provides organizational support to persons committed to faith-based nonviolent alternatives in situations where lethal conflict is an immediate reality or is supported by public policy. Some of the places Christian Peacemaker Teams are present are Colombia, Hebron (Palestine), Iraq, Canada, the United States, and the United Kingdom. *www.cpt.org.*

The International Crisis Group. Washington, DC office: 1629 K Street NW, Suite 450, Washington, DC 20006. The International Crisis Group is an independent, nonprofit, nongovernmental organization with staff on five continents, working through field-based analysis and high-level advocacy to prevent and resolve deadly conflict. This Web site includes superb briefings, analyses, and reports on the world's major conflicts. *www.crisisgroup.org.*

The Mennonite Central Committee, 21 South 12th Street, Box 500, Akron, PA 17501. This is the relief, service, and peace agency of the North American Mennonite and Brethren in Christ churches. The MCC mission statement reflects the biblical call to care for the hungry and the thirsty, the stranger and the naked, the sick, and those in prison. Among other things, it does relief work, helps with the AIDS epidemic, provides peace resources, and has established peace projects in various countries. *www.mcc.org.*

Pax Christi International. Pax Christi USA, 532 W. 8th Street, Erie, PA 16502 (814) 453-4955. This is a nonprofit, nongovernmental Catholic peace movement working on a global scale on a wide variety of issues in the fields of human rights, security and disarmament, economic justice and ecology. It is made up of autonomous national sections, local groups, and affiliated organizations spread over thirty countries and five continents, with over sixty thousand members worldwide. *www.paxchristiusa.org.*

Peace Brigades International. U.S. office: 428 8th Street SE, 2nd floor, Washington, DC 20003. Peace Brigades International is a nongovernmental organization that protects human rights and promotes nonviolent transformation of conflicts. Upon invitation, it sends teams of volunteers into areas of repression and conflict to accompany human rights defenders, their organizations, and others threatened by political violence. Their presence, in turn, creates space for local activists to work for social justice and human rights. Peace Brigades has volunteers protecting human rights activists in Colombia, Indonesia, Mexico, and Guatemala. *www.peacebrigades.org.*

ReliefWeb, New York office: Office for the Coordination of Humanitarian Affairs, United Nations, New York, NY 10014. ReliefWeb is the world's leading online gateway to information (documents and maps) on humanitarian emergencies and disasters. It provides timely, reliable, and relevant information from a variety of sources as events unfold, while also emphasizing the coverage of "forgotten emergencies." It is administered by the UN Office for the Coordination of Humanitarian Affairs (OCHA). This Web site was designed for use by humanitarian aid organizations and is the global hub of timely and detailed information on emergencies. *www.reliefweb.int.*

Sojourners. 2401 15th Street NW, Washington, DC 20009. Sojourners is a Christian ministry whose mission is to proclaim and practice the biblical call to integrate spiritual renewal and social justice. The magazine offers a vision for faith in public life; it addresses issues of faith, politics, and culture from a biblical perspective. *www.sojo.net*

United States Institute for Peace. This is an independent, nonpartisan federal institution created by Congress to promote the prevention, management, and peaceful resolution of international conflicts. Established in 1984, the Institute meets its mandate through an array of programs, including research grants, fellowships, professional training, education programs from high school through graduate school, conferences and workshops, library services, and publications. Among other things, it maintains information on the various truth commissions established to examine human rights abuses around the world. *www.usip.org/aboutus/index.html.*

Witness for Peace, 707 8th Street, SE, Suite 100, Washington, DC 20003. Witness for Peace is a politically independent, grassroots organization committed to nonviolence and led by faith and conscience. It works to support peace, justice, and sustainable economies in the Americas by changing U.S. policies and corporate practices that contribute to poverty and oppression in Latin America and the Caribbean. Witness for Peace coordinates educational trips to Cuba, Nicaragua, Mexico, and Colombia. *www.witnessforpeace.org.*

FORGIVENESS

Books, Articles, and Papers

Appleby, R. Scott. *The Ambivalence of the Sacred: Religion, Violence, and Reconciliation.* Lanham, MD: Rowman & Littlefield, 2000.

Bole, William, Drew Christiansen, SJ, and Robert T. Hennemeyer. *Forgiveness in International Politics: An Alternative Road to Peace.* Washington, DC: U.S. Conference of Catholic Bishops, 2004.

Helmick, Raymond J., SJ, and Rodney L. Petersen, eds. *Forgiveness and Reconciliation: Religion, Public Policy, and Conflict Transformation.* Philadelphia: Templeton Foundation Press, 2001.

O'Brien, David J., and Thomas A. Shannon, eds. *Catholic Social Thought: The Documentary Heritage.* Maryknoll, NY: Orbis Books, 1992.

Shriver, Donald W. *An Ethic for Enemies: Forgiveness in Politics.* New York: Oxford University Press, 1995.

Tutu, Desmond Mpilo. *No Future without Forgiveness.* New York: Doubleday, 1999.

ORGANIZATIONS, JOURNALS, AND ACADEMIC PROGRAMS

Organizations

Center for Ethics and Public Policy. *www.eppc.org.*
Center for Human Rights and Conflict Resolution, Tufts University.
    www.chrcr.org.
Center for Human Rights and Humanitarian Law, American University.
    www.wcl.american.edu/humright/center
Institute for Multi-Track Diplomacy. *www.imtd.org.*
International Center for Religion and Diplomacy. *www.icrd.org.*
International Peace Academy. *www.ipacademy.org.*
United Nations High Commissioner for Human Rights: *www.un.org/rights.*
Woodrow Wilson International Center for Scholars, Conflict Prevention Project.
    http://wwics.si.edu.

Journals

Journal of Humanitarian Assistance. www.jha.ac.
Journal of Peace, Conflict, and Development. www.peacestudiesjournal.org.uk/.

Academic Programs in Peace and Conflict Studies

Conflict Transformation Program, Eastern Mennonite University.
    www.emu.edu/ctp.
Fletcher School of Law and Diplomacy, Tufts University. *http://fletcher.tufts.edu.*
Institute for Conflict Analysis and Resolution, George Mason University.
    www.gmu.edu/departments/icar.
Joan B. Kroc Institute for International Peace Studies, University of Notre Dame.
    www.nd.edu/ krocinst.
School of Advanced and International Studies, Johns Hopkins University.
    www.sais-jhu.edu.
University of Bradford, Peace Studies. *www.brad.ac.uk/acad/peace.*

Participants in the Forum on Catholic Traditions on Peace and War

November 6, 2003

Note: Some participants had leadership roles at the forum. Those roles are indicated in parentheses.

Paul Baumann, editor of *Commonweal* (small group facilitator).

Michael Baxter, theology faculty at the University of Notre Dame (panelist).

Captain Wayne Bley, chaplain with the Office of the Chairman of the Joint Chiefs of Staff.

William Bole, nonresident fellow at the Woodstock Theological Center, Georgetown University (observer/analyst).

Timothy Brown, SJ, provincial of the Maryland Province, Society of Jesus.

Stephen Callahan, principal partner of Orbis Management International; formerly provincial assistant for social and international ministries for the Maryland Province of the Society of Jesus; formerly chief of the National Jesuit Commission on Social and International Ministries.

Joan Chittister, OSB, executive director of Benetvision; co-chair of the Global Peace Initiative of Women Religious and Spiritual Leaders; author and lecturer (panelist).

Drew Christiansen, SJ, editor-in-chief of *America* and formerly director of International Justice and Peace at the United States Conference of Catholic Bishops (panelist).

Rear Admiral Thomas Connelly (ret.), formerly vice chancellor for the Archdiocese of the Military Services.

Marie Dennis, director of the Maryknoll Office for Global Concerns and member of the Executive Committee of Pax Christi International.

Frank Frost, television and film producer (small group facilitator).

Rev. J. Bryan Hehir, director of Catholic Charities, Archdiocese of Boston; faculty, Kennedy School of Government, Harvard University; formerly president of Catholic Charities USA (opening address and observer/analyst).

Monika Hellwig, late resident fellow, Woodstock Theological Center; formerly director of the Association of Catholic Colleges and Universities.

Ivan Kauffman, author and journalist; participant in Mennonite-Catholic dialogues.

John Kleiderer, policy analyst for the Office of Social and International Ministries, U.S. Jesuit Conference; formerly with the Jesuit Refugee Service in Tanzania, East Africa (former organizer).

John Langan, SJ, Joseph Cardinal Bernardin Chair of Catholic Social Thought at Georgetown University.

Dolores R. Leckey, resident fellow at Woodstock Theological Center; formerly executive director of the Secretariat for Laity, Family, Women, and Youth at the United States Conference of Catholic Bishops (forum organizer).

Elizabeth Linehan, RSM, philosophy faculty, St. Joseph's University in Philadelphia.

Gasper F. Lo Biondo, SJ, director of the Woodstock Theological Center and co-coordinator of Woodstock's Global Economy and Cultures Project.

George Lopez, senior fellow, Joan B. Kroc Institute for International Peace Studies, University of Notre Dame (panelist).

Maryann Cusimano Love, political science faculty, Catholic University of America (panelist).

Marie Lucey, OSF, associate director for social mission, Leadership Conference of Women Religious.

Hon. Thomas Melady, formerly U.S. ambassador to Burundi, Uganda, and the Vatican.

Paula Minaert, freelance writer and editor.

Mark Mossa, SJ, student at Weston Jesuit School of Theology in Cambridge, Massachusetts; formerly taught philosophy at Loyola University, New Orleans.

Betsy Perabo, specialist in the moral evaluation of soldiering and military institutions; formerly research associate at the Center for Nonproliferation Studies, Monterey, California.

Albert C. Pierce, director of the Center for the Study of Professional Military Ethics, U.S. Naval Academy (policy responder).

Gerard Powers, director of policy studies at the Joan B. Kroc Institute for International Peace Studies, University of Notre Dame; formerly director of the Office of International Justice and Peace, Department of Social Development and World Peace, at the U.S. Conference of Catholic Bishops.

Hon. Anthony Quainton, formerly U.S. ambassador to the Central African Empire, Nicaragua, Kuwait, and Peru; Assistant Secretary of State for diplomatic security, 1992–95.

Pamela Quanrud, economist with the U.S. Department of State, specializing in Russia; formerly director of European and Eurasian Affairs at the National Security Council (policy responder).

Gregory Reichberg, senior researcher at the International Peace Research Institute in Oslo, Norway (panelist).

British Robinson, former national director of Social and International Ministries, U.S. Jesuit Conference.

Robert Royal, president of the Faith & Reason Institute in Washington, DC (panelist).

Richard Ryscavage, SJ, director, Center for Faith and Public Policy, Fairfield University; formerly national secretary for Social and International Ministries, U.S. Jesuit Conference; formerly national director of the Jesuit Refugee Service USA (forum facilitator).

Gerald Schlabach, theology faculty, University of St. Thomas in Minnesota; member of the Bridgefolk movement for grassroots dialogue and unity between Mennonites and Catholics.

Col. Daniel Smith (ret.), senior fellow for military and peaceful prevention policy at the Friends Committee on National Legislation.

Karen Sue Smith, editor of *Church* magazine, published by the National Pastoral Life Center; formerly associate editor of *Commonweal* (small group facilitator).

Amira Sonbol, faculty at the Center for Muslim-Christian Understanding, Georgetown University (presenter: Islamic perspective).

Margaret O'Brien Steinfels, co-director of the Fordham Center on Religion and Culture; formerly editor of *Commonweal* magazine (observer/analyst).

Peter Steinfels, co-director of the Fordham Center on Religion and Culture; religion columnist for the *New York Times* (small group facilitator).

Jean Stokan, policy director for Pax Christi USA.

James Stormes, SJ, national secretary for Social and International Ministries, U.S. Jesuit Conference.

Francis Sullivan, independent consultant; formerly staff director for the U.S. Senate Committee on Appropriations; formerly staff director for the U.S. Senate Armed Services Committee (policy responder).

Most Rev. Walter Sullivan, DD, retired bishop of Richmond; past bishop-president of Pax Christi USA.

Rev. Jim Wallis, publisher of *Sojourners* magazine; convener of Call to Renewal; author (panelist).

Rabbi Harold White, senior Jewish chaplain and lecturer in the theology department at Georgetown University (presenter: Jewish perspective).

Dennis Wholey, producer and host of the PBS program *This Is America with Dennis Wholey* (small group facilitator).

Francis Winters, faculty, School of Foreign Service, Georgetown University.

Index